The United States
and the Struggle
for Southeast Asia

THE UNITED STATES AND THE STRUGGLE FOR SOUTHEAST ASIA

1945–1975

Alan J. Levine

Westport, Connecticut
London

Library of Congress Cataloging-in-Publication Data

Levine, Alan J.
    The United States and the struggle for Southeast Asia, 1945–1975 /
Alan J. Levine.
        p.   cm.
    Includes bibliographical references and index.
    ISBN 0–275–95124–3 (alk. paper)
    1. Asia, Southeastern—Politics and government—1945–   2. United
States—Foreign relations—Asia, Southeastern.   3. Asia,
Southeastern—Foreign relations—United States.   4. United States—
Foreign relations—1945–   I. Title.
    DS526.7.L48   1995
    327.73059—dc20   95–6928

British Library Cataloguing in Publication Data is available.

Library of Congress Catalog Card Number: 95–6928
ISBN: 0–275–95124–3

First published in 1995

Praeger Publishers, 88 Post Road West, Westport, CT 06881
An imprint of Greenwood Publishing Group, Inc.

Printed in the United States of America

The paper used in this book complies with the
Permanent Paper Standard issued by the National
Information Standards Organization (Z39.48–1984).

10 9 8 7 6 5 4 3 2 1

Contents

1.	Southeast Asia and the Cold War	1
2.	The First Indochina War 1945–1954	17
3.	The Southeast Asian Revolts of 1948	39
4.	The Struggle for Indonesia, II	65
5.	The United States and the Beginning of the Second Indochina War 1954–1960	79
6.	The Kennedy Administration, Vietnam and Laos	89
7.	Crisis and Massive American Intervention	99
8.	Buildup and Decision 1965–1968	111
9.	American Withdrawal	135
10.	The End of the Second Indochina War	145
	Notes	155
	Bibliography	173
	Index	183

The United States and the Struggle for Southeast Asia

1

Southeast Asia
and the Cold War

Southeast Asia was a major, if secondary, theater of the Cold War, and the scene of some of its bloodiest episodes. The region was drawn into the struggle partly through the independent initiative of the Vietnamese Communists, but mostly by deliberate Soviet action. The USSR could not bring its power to bear in Southeast Asia, except for its control or influence over the local Communists. Nevertheless, in 1948 and after, the USSR had a powerful impact on events; China would join it as an ally, then later became a rival.

The first phase of the struggle for Southeast Asia was a complicated, three-cornered fight between non-Communist nationalists, the local Communists and the European imperial powers. The Dutch and French learned, the hard way, that the critical conflict was not between them and the local peoples, but among the local contenders for the succession to the European empires. The Americans entered the struggle in an effort to extend the line of containment, already drawn against the Soviets in Europe and the Middle East, to Asia, in reaction to the imminent victory of the Chinese Communists. The need to defend the far southern flank of Allied developed countries and ensure their access to resources that were vital to them (not to the U.S.) helped draw the United States into Southeast Asia, as it had in the Middle East. And, in both cases, the United States was pushed or pulled by its Western European allies, especially Britain, which fought the Soviets and/or the local Communists before the United States did. Thanks to the revolt against colonial rule, the impact of Japanese occupation, long-standing social discontent, and terrain favorable for guerrilla warfare, Southeast

Asia was a battlefield favorable to the Communist side in the Cold War. There, in contrast to many other sectors of the Cold War, the West and its allies confronted communism as an effective revolutionary movement. Some architects of Cold War policies recognized these things at an early date. Frank Roberts, who acted as Britain's counterpart of George F. Kennan, in alerting his government to Soviet designs and methods, warned London in August 1946 that Southeast Asia offered the enemy excellent opportunities for disruptive actions that could seriously harm Western Europe. The counter to this danger was to promote self-government and economic development.[1] But this wise advice was not always heeded.

SOUTHEAST ASIA AND THE WEST TO 1945

Next to the immensity of the rest of Asia, Southeast Asia might seem small, but by any other standards, it was big and diverse, consisting of a mainland— really a giant peninsula (Indochina, Thailand and Burma)—barely connected to a lesser peninsula (Malaya), and a vast archipelago (Indonesia and the Philippines). Indonesia alone sprawled over a sea area the size of the continental United States. Much of the region was covered with dense jungles, mountains and swamps and well suited to guerrilla warfare.

The Southeast Asian mainland was separated from India and China by rugged mountains; much of its population had originated in China, often fleeing before the advance of the Chinese empire. But the cultures of most of its peoples were more influenced by India. The area was itself split by mountain ranges. The principal nationalities, Vietnamese, Thais and Burmese, and the weaker Cambodians, lived mostly in the great river valleys between the ranges and on the coasts. The areas between the major peoples were mostly occupied by smaller, usually more primitive groups, generally at odds with the civilized lowlanders. The major nations fought each other and expanded at the expense of the Cambodians and the hill peoples. But the great distances and rugged terrain between the major civilized centers in the river valleys, and perhaps the fact that they produced much the same sort of things, prevented the development of a closely interacting system of states and close cultural relations comparable to that enjoyed by Europeans. The Vietnamese differed greatly from the other Southeast Asian peoples. Heavily influenced by China, which had once ruled them, they represented an East Asian intrusion in a region otherwise dominated by cultural influences that had entered from the Indian Ocean.

The overwhelmingly Buddhist mainlanders had little in common with the Moslem and Christian peoples of the island world, to which Malaya also belonged. There was one common element in the population of both the mainland and the islands—large and influential Chinese minorities. The Chinese were actually a majority of the people of Singapore and formed some 40 percent of the population of Malaya. Like the Jews of medieval Western and modern Eastern Europe, the Chinese in Southeast Asia formed a disproportionate part of the city populations and middle class, and were widely disliked. Chinese immigration had long existed, but was fostered by the other common element in the region—Western rule.

The Vietnamese, Burmese, Thais and Cambodians had developed something approximating European-type states and national consciousness before Westerners reached Southeast Asia. The Thais, alone of the peoples of the region, kept their independence by using their buffer position between the French and British empires. They cannily played Britain and France off against each other, usually staying on better terms with Britain. The Burmese and Vietnamese were never reconciled to Western rule; they never accepted it as immutable or internalized notions of white superiority, as may have occurred in other colonies. Cambodians tended to view the French as protectors against the neighbors who had swallowed much of their country and had better relations with their rulers.

National consciousness in the islands was largely a product of Western rule, which began much earlier in Indonesia and the Philippines than on the mainland, although the Dutch and Americans did not finish bringing the area under Western control until the early twentieth century. The Indonesians, the second most numerous people under Western rule, may have had a vague feeling of cultural unity for many centuries, but they only became a nation under, and in reaction to, Dutch rule. Serious differences existed among the Indonesians; the Javanese did not get along well with the Sundanese who lived on the west end of Java or the peoples of the outer islands, which had most of Indonesia's wealth. Java, unlike the outer islands and most of Southeast Asia, was already dangerously crowded.

The Philippines were a Western creation, an intrusion of Western culture much as the Vietnamese represented an intrusion of East Asian culture. The Christian majority of the Filipinos represented the unique success of missionary work in Asia, and later of American attempts at mass education; they were at least semi-Westernized, and their views of the world and social structure resembled those of Latin Americans and (perhaps more superficially) North Americans rather than those of their neighbors. But they and the Moslems of the southern Philippines ("Moros") had been bitter enemies up to the peace enforced by the American conquest—one of many divisions in Southeast Asia that would reopen when the Western rulers left.

The impact of the West may have been less in the rest of Southeast Asia than in the Philippines, but, for good or ill, it had been great. Its greatest cities—Singapore, Manila, Djakarta (Batavia), Rangoon and Saigon—had been no more than fishing villages when the Europeans came. The region, Thailand included, had been brought into close relations, commercial and otherwise, with the West, albeit with the usual problems of economies oriented to the export of a few primary products. By World War II, it was the most developed part of the colonial world next to India. Malaya and Singapore, the richest colonies in the world, were on the verge of an industrial revolution. The region as a whole was of considerable, even if far from central, strategic and economic importance. It was a valuable source of rice imports for China and India. Malaya and Indonesia, in particular, were sources of valuable raw materials and some other products, notably tin, rubber, oil and quinine. Before World War II, Indonesia and Burma were among the world's major oil producers. (Indonesia, many decades later, would recover this position.) Seizing Indonesian oil, and getting it to Japan, would be a central problem for Japanese strategy during World War II. Stopping that traffic and other supplies from Southeast Asia was the decisive blow to the Japanese empire.

On the eve of World War II the Southeast Asian peoples had very different relations with the West. The Vietnamese, Burmese and Indonesians were ready to turn on their Western rulers. The Burmese, although far advanced toward self-government, hated both the British and the Indian minority in Burma (which played a role similar to that the Chinese played in other Southeast Asian countries). The French and Dutch had suppressed nationalism in their colonies, arousing growing bitterness. In both Burma and Indonesia, the Japanese allied themselves with the nationalists and ruled largely through them (although they secretly planned to annex Indonesia as a colony.) The Vietnamese had to wait to act, for up to 1945, the Japanese deemed it more efficient to rule through Vichy French collaborationists than put Indochina under direct control or native puppets. The Thais readily allied themselves with the apparently overwhelming power of Japan. Nationalist sentiment had not developed strongly in Cambodia or Malaya; the Malay and Chinese communities got along fairly well with the British, however much they disliked each other. The Philippines, as usual, differed considerably from the rest of the region. The Americans had readily conceded national independence, which was scheduled for July 1946.

Only the Filipinos, the Chinese and some small nationalities like the Kachins and Karens of Burma strongly opposed Japan from the start. The other peoples of the region, however, were soon disillusioned with their new rulers. The Japanese were utterly ruthless toward the Chinese and Filipinos, and were not very nice even to their nominal allies, often seizing men for forced labor. Southeast Asia's normal economic ties were disrupted; the Japanese extracted natural resources but could not deliver substitutes for Western machinery and consumer goods. Areas dependent on imported food went hungry. When the war ended, northern Vietnam suffered famine, and Malaya, British Borneo and Sumatra were near famine.

The war inflicted great turmoil and suffering on Southeast Asia, but the Communists and non-Communist nationalists of the area used it effectively to further their aims. The Communist parties of the area, mostly founded as by-products of the first Soviet drive to take over China in the 1920s, had usually been small and ineffective until 1941. The war changed this drastically. As in the Balkans during World War II, the anti-Axis resistance was an important route to power. In the Philippines, Malaya and Vietnam, they led the principal resistance movements to the Japanese occupation (although they did not necessarily do much fighting) or became important elements in the resistance. In Indonesia and Burma, the Communists, although few and weak when the war ended, used its aftermath to become major factors in local politics.[2]

WARTIME PLANNING

Just how drastically things had changed was not understood in the West during the war. Except in the Philippines, Western intelligence knew little of what had gone on under the Japanese occupation. The extent of political activation underway was not recognized, although it might have been expected. The situation in Eastern Europe during World War I, and what had happened after the collapse of the Russian, German, Austro-Hungarian and Turkish empires should have suggested what might happen in Southeast Asia. Events in the Balkans during World War II might also have been suggestive. The visible hostility of the Burmese and Indonesians in 1942, and the fact that attempts to land agents in Indonesia usually failed did not register. Although President Franklin Roosevelt and some others feared that eventually there would be trouble if nationalist demands were not satisfied, Westerners—even those strongly opposed to imperial rule—seem to have assumed that the colonial peoples would essentially be passive spectators of a Western return after Japan was beaten. Americans assumed that the issue was whether to persuade or force the Western Europeans to "grant" the first steps toward an orderly, gradual attainment of independence, or (even sillier) that American noninterference would enable the Europeans to maintain their empires, which would be a desirable element of strength. That view was not popular with the public, but many Western European specialists in the State Department obstinately clung to it for years after its absurdity should have been clear.

Within this framework there were further mistaken assumptions. Many Americans wrongly expected that the British would be the biggest obstacle to decolonization. The Americans were cleverly manipulated by the Dutch, who led Roosevelt and most officials to think that Dutch colonial policies were more liberal than they really were.

With more reason, Roosevelt was particularly suspicious of French colonial policies, and he focused his attention on Indochina. He wanted to force the French to turn that colony over to an international trusteeship. Finally, however, he retreated to allowing France to regain Indochina, if it promised eventual independence to Indochina. Even this intention lapsed with Roosevelt's death. American policy in 1945–1946 was to neither question nor aid the restoration of colonial rule, while urging the Western Europeans to prepare the colonial peoples for self-rule. The Americans refused to sell arms and ammunition to the French and Dutch—both of whom had received plenty of American lend-lease equipment during the war—or move their troops and supplies on U.S. ships.[3]

With an inertia and unimaginativeness characteristic of James Byrnes' tenure as secretary of state, this policy, or nonpolicy, lasted long after it should have been recognized as inadequate. To be sure, American policy makers had much else to worry about right after World War II. But, considering that Japan's move into Southeast Asia had triggered the Pacific war, and that the war made the U.S. the dominant power in the Pacific, the United States took remarkably little interest in the region for several years. Alterations to the boundaries between the Allied theaters, made late in the war to free U.S. forces for operations to the north, had left most of Southeast Asia within Admiral Louis Mountbatten's overburdened Southeast Asia Command—a nominally inter-Allied, but actually British, headquarters on Ceylon. In 1945–1946, the West's relations with most of the Southeast Asian peoples were largely conducted by Mountbatten's command; and he made many of the critical decisions affecting the future of the area.

SOUTHEAST ASIA, WESTERN RECOVERY AND THE SOVIETS

Although Southeast Asia was not economically vital to the West, which had gotten along without access to it during World War II, the Soviets seem to have been sure that Western Europe's recovery would be crippled without access to the area (and even some Westerners still thought this was true). This warped assessment, based on a classical Leninist obsession with the economic aspects of imperialism, was the key to Soviet policy in the late 1940s, and had bloody repercussions in Southeast Asia. During 1948, the Soviets encouraged the Communists in Indonesia, Malaya, the Philippines and Burma to take power, joining the Communists in Indochina, who had already been forced to take up arms against French reconquest in 1946. This was to be an indirect but critical blow to the recovery of Western Europe.

In 1947, Stalin reacted to the American announcement of a policy of containment, aid to Greece and Turkey, and the Marshall Plan, by a major revision of policy. It had become clear that his hopes that Communists would take power in France and Italy, and perhaps elsewhere, by political maneuvers, had misfired; the French and Italian Communists had been ejected from the ruling coalitions in their countries. A front was concealing in much of the world against the policy of creeping advance Stalin had followed since the latter part of World War II. Up to this point, while the Soviets and their followers had profited from the postwar economic troubles, they had not deliberately promoted them. Stalin now resolved to smash through the hardening Western front and destroy the Marshall Plan, and Europe's recovery, with every weapon short of war.

But his new policy, if recognizing the reality of Western opposition, was based on a heavy dose of wishful thinking. It was now decreed that there would soon be a catastrophic economic collapse in the West—not just a transient postwar depression, as more pessimistic Communist economists had predicted. Much publicity was given to economic analysts who argued that the creation of the "people's democracies" in Eastern Europe had *already* decisively damaged the world capitalist system, and even implied that the coming downturn could be the long-awaited "final crisis" of capitalism—although Stalin himself was too cautious to stake his reputation on the new line, and he did not actually purge the more pessimistic school. The terrible economic effects of the disastrous winter of 1946–1947, which seemed to have virtually stopped Western Europe's halting reconstruction efforts (and had been the immediate trigger for the Truman Doctrine and the Marshall Plan) might have seemed, for a short time, to suggest that the prediction of an economic catastrophe was justified.

The new policy within Europe to hasten and exploit the predicted crisis by arousing labor unrest and attacking democratic socialism. Pressure would be brought to bear on Western outposts behind Soviet lines (Berlin and Vienna) and Soviet control over the satellites would be completed; Tito would be replaced as ruler of Yugoslavia by a Soviet puppet. Stalin told the Czech leaders that he intended to get the United States out of Europe and Asia; he aimed to destroy American power, but his actions would not have any military character and would be calculated not to alarm the American public or let the U.S. government take military countermeasures. Documents the Americans stole from a satellite diplomat indicated that the Soviets hoped that the local Communists would disrupt the French, Belgian and Italian economies, and that at least in the case of Italy, this would lead to a Communist seizure of power.[4]

The new line—or those aspects of it suitable for public consumption—was expounded in September 1947 by Andrei Zhdanov, then Stalin's heir apparent, at the founding meeting of the Cominform, a new international organization of several European Communist parties. Zhdanov explained that World War II had been a major defeat for capitalism. The "people's democracies" had been subtracted from the capitalist system; the United States and Britain were the last imperialist powers left, and Britain now depended on the United States. The colonial system was in crisis. "This has placed the rear of the capitalist system in jeopardy. The peoples of the colonies no longer wish to live in the old way. The ruling class of the metropolitan countries can no longer govern the colonies along the old lines." Attempts to crush the national liberation movement had led to protracted colonial wars between the Dutch and Indonesians and French and Vietnamese. The world was now split into two camps: "the imperialist and antidemocratic camp" led by the United States and the "anti-imperialist and democratic camp" led by the Soviets. The United States—bluntly likened to the Nazis—planned an alliance with a restored Germany and war, and the Marshall Plan was a scheme to subjugate Europe and avert an American economic crisis. But war was not quite imminent; and the "imperialists" could be restrained. Communists must stress "peace" slogans. The "democratic" camp did not consist solely of Communist countries. Vietnam and Indonesia were "associated" with it, and Egypt, Syria and India allegedly sympathized with it. Zhdanov did not explicitly call for further revolts in the colonies. But his analysis of the situation in the colonial world, which deliberately recalled Lenin's classic definition of a revolutionary situation, and his description of Vietnam and Indonesia as Soviet allies, and support for their struggles against the French and Dutch, at least implied a green light for further revolts in the colonial countries. The tone of the speech was optimistic. The chief immediate task of Communists was to smash the Marshall Plan; Zhdanov's speech implied that if that was accomplished, large-scale victories could be expected.[5]

Up to late 1947, the Soviet policy in the colonial world had been to favor Communist participation in nationalist coalitions and a relatively moderate stance in negotiations with the European authorities. The Soviets had strongly supported the Indonesian nationalists against the Dutch, but had soft-pedaled support for the Vietnamese. The Dutch Communists were unimportant, but the Soviets had no wish to anger French opinion and injure the French Communists. The Zhdanov line of head-on confrontation rendered these considerations unimportant; exploiting local revolutionary situations was now desirable. The Soviets pushed the Communists in Indonesia, Malaya, the Philippines and Burma into revolting against the local governments and colonial authorities. Despite great differences in conditions between these countries, genuine revolutionary situations seemed to exist in all of them. British rule in Malaya, and the newly independent Burmese and Filipino governments were weak and shaky, while the Indonesian nationalists were at war with the Dutch. The Malayan and Filipino Communists had played an important part in the anti-Japanese resistance and had never been properly disarmed. The Burmese and Indonesian Communists, insignificant in 1945, had grown strong while participating in the nationalist political coalitions. There were reasonable prospects for Communist seizures of power, and even if they misfired, they should cut off exports to Western Europe and hamper its recovery. The new line was transmitted to the Southeast Asian Communists at the combined congresses of the Indian Communist Party and the "Conference of Southeast Asian Youth" held in Calcutta in February 1948. More specific directives went to the Malayan, Burmese, and Indonesian Parties, at least; and they and the Filipino Communists launched rebellions during 1948. (The reader should be warned that the Soviet role in sparking these revolts is controversial and has been denied by some historians.)[6]

Although, like everything else in the anti-Marshall Plan campaign, the Communist uprisings of 1948 misfired, they did cause endless trouble for the West (not to mention the local peoples). The hope of what observers of the USSR called the "Zhdanov" period in foreign policy—that Western Europe was near collapse and a head-on attack, short of war, would finish it off proved laughably wrong. After Zhdanov's death, his associates and the economist Voznesensky (the leading optimist about a Western collapse) were purged. But some other elements—the "two camps" analysis and the stress on peace slogans, remained valid until Stalin's death and even later. Although admitting that there had been an "artificial temporary stabilization of capitalism" and expecting a long struggle, the Soviets remained optimistic. In November 1949, Malenkov, the new crown prince, stressed the continuation of an uncompromising policy and the importance of the colonial revolution.

The Soviets were now being joined in overt, major involvement in Southeast Asia by the Chinese, whose ideas had already strongly influenced the Vietnamese and Malayan Communists. In November 1949 Liu Shaoqi, a major lieutenant of Mao Zedong, stressed that China's revolution would be a model for others. He described the basic "Maoist" political formula of a "united front" of all anti-imperialist groups, which included elements of the bourgeoisie," but led by the Communist party throughout, waging guerrilla war from prepared bases. "Armed struggle is the main form of struggle for the national liberation struggles of many colonies and semi-colonies." The "way of Mao" "may also be the basic way for winning emancipation by the people of other colonial and semicolonial countries where similar conditions prevail."[7] The Soviets seemed to approve this speech, which potentially implied acceptance of China's supremacy in the underdeveloped countries; later, in 1951–1952, they would partially retract this for a time. The Chinese approach galvanized the American role in the area.

THE AMERICANS AND SOUTHEAST ASIA

The United States, absorbed in enormous problems and commitments elsewhere, had responded to the wars in Indochina and Indonesia with little more than hand-wringing, although it had finally been angered into halting the Dutch effort to reconquer the East Indies. During 1949 the U.S. government became increasingly perturbed about the Communist threat in Southeast Asia, especially in Indochina and the Philippines. It was now aware of how badly things had gone in the former American colony.

Some Americans, including Undersecretary of State Robert Lovett, had believed that Indonesia might be vital as a source of supplies for the Marshall Plan. That was not so, but the Americans gradually recognized, in 1948–1949, that Southeast Asia might be economically critical for Japan, even if it was not vital for the West. And, over the long term, the acquisition of the area by the Soviet-Chinese alliance would put major resources under Communist control. It would drive a wedge between India and Japan, politically isolate Japan, even if it could survive economically, and threaten Australia. Its loss might mean the recreation of the "Greater East Asia Co-Prosperity Sphere" under Chinese rather than Japanese control.

But the tendency to greater involvement coexisted uneasily with American military strategy, which ruled out military commitments beyond the offshore island chain running from Japan through the Philippines. And the State Department was still torn by quarrels between its European and Far Eastern divisions. The former feared a clash with the French and the Dutch; the Asian specialists rightly pointed out the disastrous nature of French and Dutch policies. (British policies were clearly unexceptionable.) The British, unhappy about the lack of an active American policy in Asia outside of Japan, urged the Americans to become more involved in Southeast Asia. The British favored encouraging a regional association of the Southeast Asian countries, an idea finally realized, many years later, in the Association of Southeast Asian Nations (ASEAN). The cogency of the arguments of the State Department's Asian specialists finally sank in and was recognized in policy planning papers in March 1949, which called for pressure on the French and Dutch and modest aid to friendly countries in the area.

In December 1949 National Security Council paper 48/2 elaborated American policy in Asia. It stressed that the Soviets were not responsible for all revolutionary activity and rated the "current conflict between colonialism and native independence" as the "most important political factor in Southeast Asia." Although unenthusiastic about the quality of nationalist leadership, it emphasized that "The question of whether a colonial country is fit to govern itself, however, is not always relevant in practical politics. The real issue would seem to be whether the colonial country is able and determined to make continued foreign rule an overall losing proposition for the metropolitan power. If it is, independence for the colonial country is the only practical solution, even though misgovernment eventuates. A solution of the consequent problem of instability, if it arises, must be sought on a nonimperialist plane. In any event, colonial-nationalist conflict provides a fertile field for subversive activities, and it is now clear that Southeast Asia is a target for a coordinated offensive directed by the Kremlin."[8]

No one opposed blocking a Communist offensive in the region, but how to do so, especially in Indochina, was a difficult question. The Americans knew perfectly well that France could not simply beat the Vietnamese back into colonial submission; but they assumed—or at least hoped—that the belated, hesitant changes in French policy during 1949 were a step toward developing a nationalist counter to the Vietnamese Communists. As events (described in the next chapter) showed, that was a slim hope indeed. But the effort seemed a necessary one, for the Americans were persuaded that a great deal depended on what happened in that one particular piece of Southeast Asia.

DOMINO THEORY

In February 1950 the National Security Council concluded that Thailand and Burma would go Communist if Indochina did, and directed the State and Defense Departments to prepare a program for Indochina.

This was the first appearance in American appreciations of the nucleus of what later became the "domino theory," the notion that if one country in Southeast Asia fell under Communist rule, in whatever manner, the rest would do so, like a row of dominos being knocked over. The idea was shared by the British, who may have originated it. The British authorities in Southeast Asia, and the Chiefs of Staff in London were sure that Indochina was the key to Southeast Asia, and the whole of the region would probably fall to Communist rule if Indochina did.[9] By early 1950, so much attention was focused on Southeast Asia that American intelligence analysts believed that a Communist move in Korea would not occur until after the Communist programs for Southeast Asia were finished or defeated.[10]

It should be noted that American policy makers extended to Southeast Asia a sort of reasoning that many had found convincing in evaluating situations in Europe and the Middle East. They had generally assumed, in making the 1947 decision to aid Greece and Turkey, that should those countries succumb to Soviet pressure, much of the Middle East and perhaps part of North Africa would quickly follow. Secretary of State Marshall, after the Communist coup in Czechoslovakia in 1948, thought it might stimulate similar action in Western Europe.[11]

The belief that a Communist victory in Indochina would have disastrous consequences tended to grow stronger. In the early 1950s, the domino theory, or protodomino theory, occurred in several variants; predictions about what would happen varied widely even within the same agencies. The idea that all of mainland Southeast Asia, much less the islands as well, must fall under Communist control if Vietnam or one of the other principal mainland countries did was occasionally questioned by some military men. (This was in contrast to the situation in the late 1960s, when the military were generally the most ardent supporters of the domino theory.) In late 1951, General J. Lawton Collins, the U.S. Army Chief of Staff, argued that while Thailand and Burma would probably go Communist if the Communists won in Indochina, the British would be able to hold Malaya. In April 1952 the Joint Chiefs of Staff suggested that it was by no means certain that any country but Thailand would fall under Communist control if Indochina was lost.[12]

But it was generally thought, then and later, that the results would be worse than that. Generally, American officials expected Thailand and Burma to fall into the Soviet-Chinese orbit if Indochina did. But quite a few estimates qualified even that point, suggesting that would happen only in the absence of effective Western assistance. Some suggested that a Thai "accommodation" with the Soviet bloc might be averted if the United States gave Thailand security guarantees or took some other timely counteraction.[13] Other officials, however, maintained that the whole mainland would inevitably follow Indochina.[14] Some official observers felt that Malaya must inevitably fall to the Communist rebels if Thailand did.[15] Others felt that the islands *might* be held even if the whole mainland was lost.[16] Some argued explicitly that the islands too must inevitably fall if the mainland did.[17]

Virtually no one differed with the thesis that Southeast Asia as a whole was a vital area. Even a sober and cautious observer like Charles Bohlen feared that if Southeast Asia fell, the Cold War would be lost.[18] It was widely expected that Japan would make an "accommodation" with the Communist powers if the latter gained control of Southeast Asia.[19]

Ultimately, no other Southeast Asian country went Communist after the Indochina states did. The domino theory proved erroneous for several reasons. One was that, by the 1970s, the whole world political picture had changed. The Soviet-Chinese conflict and the collapse of a more or less united Communist movement destroyed one basis of the domino theory; the Soviets and the Vietnamese Communists were at odds with the Chinese, and also the Cambodian Communists. There was no one orbit for anyone to fall into. Another point, less often noted, was that by the end of the struggle for Indochina, Communist attempts to take power in most other Southeast Asian countries had already been made, only to fail. The internal component of the threat had already been smashed. The Communist parties, in most of these countries, were burnt-out cases.

But there were other problems with the domino theory that might have been suspected even when it was propounded. Western observers probably misunderstood the probable reactions of Thailand. Thailand was generally believed to be the most delicately balanced domino, the one that would tip first if Indochina or Burma fell under Communist control; either the local Communists would seize power or the existing ruling group would accommodate to what was perceived as an inevitable "wave of the future," much as the Thais had joined up with Japan during World War II. This view, however, was probably mistaken. As their position as the only people in Southeast Asia to escape Western conquest suggested, the Thais—both rulers and peoples—wanted to remain independent. The Thai oligarchy had sided with Japan, an outside power, thinking that they could at least keep their internal autonomy. The oligarchy can have had few illusions that they would retain their position if the Communist powers won in Southeast Asia, much less the world. And the nearest Communist nations, China and Vietnam, unlike relatively remote Japan, were traditional enemies of Thailand. The identification of communism with traditional enemies also hurt the chances of revolution in Thailand—all the more so when all Communists had to choose between those enemies. Thailand had not undergone actual occupation, and the control of the oligarchy survived World War II unbroken. The most discontented part of the country, the northeast, was relatively flat, open and unsuited to guerrilla warfare. Thailand was thus much less vulnerable to either "accommodation" or revolution than was generally supposed.

The domino theory also did not fully take into account the fact that the center of gravity in Southeast Asia lay in the islands, not on the mainland. Indonesia, Malaysia and the Philippines held more people and wealth than the mainland, and militarily would still be dominated by American airpower and seapower whatever happened on the mainland. That might not enable the Americans to prevent those countries from going Communist by more or less internal processes; but the Americans could certainly prevent other Communist powers from bringing critical pressures to bear, if they wanted to. And the islanders normally took little interest in what happened on the mainland, to peoples with whom they had little in common. Even the mainland states did not form a cohesive, closely connected whole whose peoples would be strongly and immediately affected by what happened in a neighboring country.

That the Americans, apart from the specific dilemma involved in getting entangled in Indochina, would be in deep water in Southeast Asia, and other underdeveloped areas, was seen by some at the time, especially William Schaub, an official of the Bureau of the Budget. In a critique of National Security Council (NSC) paper 68, the blueprint for extended containment and a military buildup proposed in early 1950 and put into operation during the Korean War, Schaub noted that it failed to deal with the "war for men's minds" and, like much (not all) early commentary on the Cold War, oversimplified the issues dividing the world.

"NSC 68 deals with this problem as being one involving the 'free world' and the 'slave world.' While it is true that the USSR and its satellites constitute something properly called a slave world, it is not true that the U.S. and its friends constitute a free world. Are the Indo-Chinese free? Can the peoples of the Philippines be said to be free under the corrupt Quirino government? Moreover, what of the vast number of peoples who are in neither the U.S. nor the USSR camp, and for whom we are contesting? By and large, by our standards, they are not free. This free world vs. slave world treatment obscures one of the most difficult problems we face—the fact that many peoples are attracted to Communism because their governments are despotic or corrupt or both. And they are not going to become the friends of a major power simply because of that power's military strength. Rather, their friendship is to be had at the price of support of moves which will improve, or failing that replace their present governments." "The neat dichotomy between 'freedom' and 'slavery' is not a realistic description either of the situation today or of the alternatives as they appear to present themselves to large areas of the world." He noted that "An upsurge of unadulterated nationalism might for the time being lessen or remove the military threat of Russia, but it would over time tend to accentuate the subtle undermining of our own system and guarantee the eventual loss of the cold war through the proliferation and subsidization of unstable little tyrants."

Schaub argued that "The gravest error of NSC 68 is that it vastly underplays the role of economic and social change as a factor in the 'underlying conflict.' " He cited, as an example, the importance of land reform in many areas and noted that "A revealing commentary on NSC 68 is that it does not basically clarify or utilize the Chinese experience in the discussion of issues and risks, nor does it point toward a course of action which can effectively deal with probable repetitions of that experience in the future. There is no follow-through on the social and economic schisms which today provide the basic groundswell for disorder and weakness, which make our task so difficult, and for which we have not developed guidelines and techniques adequate to cope with the vicious ideological pretensions and methods of the Communists."

Schaub carried this line of argument too far when he belittled Soviet power, but he rightly pointed out that in a prolonged Cold War military strength would not be enough.[20]

Schaub evidently did not consider the likelihood that the continuing process of decolonization, must, all by itself, produce "unstable little tyrants" over much of Asia and Africa. But he had pointed out what would be the most difficult dilemma—not the most dangerous, to be sure, but the most intricate—of the Cold War. And, if only because the world was lucky enough (and it may have been just luck) to avoid nuclear war, it was the one that would lead to the most anguish for the West.

2

The First Indochina War
1945–1954

The wars for Indochina were by far the longest and bloodiest of the Southeast Asian struggles. Ironically, the role of the Soviets and the Chinese Communists was initially far less than in the other Communist efforts in the area. The Vietnamese Communists acted more or less independently of, although not necessarily in conscious opposition to, Soviet directives. The results left the Soviets little to complain about. The Vietnamese Communists built the most formidable Communist party and army in Southeast Asia and their own little empire, and they did the Western powers far more damage than many seemingly more formidable foes. The stupid policies of the French and the Japanese, the impact of World War II, and brilliant Communist leadership all contributed to this result.

Contrary to widespread belief, French rule in Indochina before World War II was not especially oppressive in social and economic terms. The problems of the peasants, the overwhelming majority of the Vietnamese people, did not differ much from those of the peasants in the East Asian nations. Largely tenants exploited by absentee landlords, they farmed inadequate dwarfholdings. But until the end of the First Indochina War, the Vietnamese Communists' appeal was based mainly on nationalist sentiments, not on social conflicts. It was not the economic policies of the French, but their failure to permit political development and their largely successful attempt to crush non-Communist nationalism that promoted the rise of communism, along with their tendency to give even minor administrative jobs, which in other colonies would have gone to natives, to Frenchmen. During the 1930s, the Communists, whose organization was more resistant to police attack, were already beginning to supplant the non-Communist nationalists, whose groups were repeatedly smashed. They had the benefit of the leadership of Ho Chi Minh (Nguyen Ai Quoc) one of the ablest of all Communist leaders. An early member of the French Communist Party, Ho returned home as a Comintern agent. Staunchly pro-Soviet through almost all of his career, Ho was very much the sort of man the Soviet rulers would have liked Mao Zedong to be. Stalin's successors, at least, genuinely admired him as an able and popular tactician with no annoying pretensions to doctrinal originality and properly deferential to the USSR. Vietnamese Communism was very much his personal creation.[1] A peculiarity of Ho's methods, not often noted, which appeared several times in his career, and which he shared with Stalin, was a preference for right-wing instruments and allies. Stalin, as Franz Borkenau once noted, deeply believed that it paid more to cheat the right than the left. And so did Ho. But Ho was nothing if not eclectic; he also borrowed techniques from the Chinese.

After the Vichy French authorities submitted to Japanese occupation in 1940–1941, their grip on Indochina began to slip. In 1941, which in exile in China, Ho formed an effective anti-Japanese and anti-French united front, the Vietminh, under Communist leadership. The Vietminh had a classic "minimum program" of national independence and social reforms; it seemed to be a "bourgeois" nationalist movement.

Helped by the Nationalist Chinese and the American Office of Strategic Services (OSS), the Vietminh slipped agents into northern Vietnam, and established a base area under its control in the Viet Bac area of Tonkin. In 1944 the Vietminh formed a guerrilla army under Vo Nguyen Giap, a Chinese Communist-trained soldier. The Vietminh rescued Allied pilots but its activities were mainly directed toward securing postwar political power. It planned to operate on a large scale if there was an Allied invasion, but its few attacks were aimed at the Vichy French. Only one accidental clash took place with the Japanese.

The Japanese made a Communist victory possible by eliminating the French. They knew that the French were in contact with de Gaulle and wrongly expected that the Americans would land in Indochina. On March 9, 1945, the Japanese attacked and crushed the French forces. They installed a weak, conservative Vietnamese government nominally loyal to Bao Dai, the Vietnamese emperor, who had previously been a pliable French puppet. The Vietnamese, Cambodian and Laotian governments declared their "independence" of France. But the Japanese never allowed the Vietnamese government any real authority and kept Cochin China (the extreme south) under their direct control. Their plunder of the rice crop and the breakdown of the transportation system under Allied attack led to famine. The Communists regarded the famine as a decisive factor in their success. The Vietminh rapidly made converts among workers and peasants. Other classes did not support them but did not oppose them either.

THE COMMUNIST SEIZURE OF POWER

During August, rumors of Japan's approaching surrender led the Vietminh to move its troops—it probably had no more than 5,000 armed men—near Hanoi. The day after the Japanese themselves surrendered to the Allies, they gave up their authority to the Vietnamese government. The latter, however, no longer functioned. The Japanese turned a blind eye when the Vietminh moved into the vacuum. On August 17 an uprising took over Hanoi and the major cities. Bao Dai was forced to abdicate. The Vietminh took over the weapons the Japanese had taken from the French. Despite the guerrilla preparations, the Vietnamese Communists' "seizure of power" resembled the Bolshevik Revolution more than anything else. On September 2, 1945, Ho Chi Minh proclaimed the independence of the "Democratic Republic of Vietnam."[2] He posed as a moderate democratic nationalist and was widely accepted as such; the gullible American OSS officers Ho dealt with were impressed by the fact that he had borrowed phrases from the American Declaration of Independence. In fact, as events soon showed, Ho was preoccupied with destroying rival Vietnamese political groups—Trotskyites and religious sects in the south, pro-Chinese nationalists in the north—and that had priority over the struggle against the French.

THE VIETMINH AND THE ALLIES

Ho Chi Minh soon had to deal with the Allies. At the Potsdam Conference in July, the Western powers had decided that if Japan surrendered, Indochina south of the sixteenth parallel would be occupied by Southeast Asia Command (SEAC) while Chinese forces disarmed the Japanese north of that line. (SEAC was nominally an inter-Allied command, but the Americans ceased to participate in it in October 1945.) The decision to allow Chinese participation proved unfortunate.

No Allied power openly contested French sovereignty over Indochina. China did not want to see France regain it; but the Chinese had other and higher priorities. The French basically planned to restore a reformed version of the prewar regime in their colonies. They vaguely promised representative assemblies and various reforms, but permanently excluded self-government and independence. They were determined to return, by force if need be, but did not expect anything like the resistance they encountered.

Mountbatten's mission was just to disarm and remove the Japanese. Since Saigon was the Japanese headquarters in Southeast Asia, it was high on the list of areas to be occupied. But only a small force was sent; the French were expected to take over governmental responsibility.

At Saigon, the British found an unexpected and confusing situation. Allied intelligence on the political situation there, as in the rest of Southeast Asia, was poor; the rise of nationalism was a surprise. As in Indonesia, they were caught between pledges to respect the sovereignty of their European allies and their own inclination to come to terms with local nationalists and disengage. Rightly or wrongly, the legalities of the situation were a real factor in the French and Dutch colonies. In Syria, a few months earlier, even Churchill had felt compelled to enter an ugly confrontation to force the French to honor their pledge to make Syria (a League of Nations mandate, not a true colony) independent; but no such pledge had been made in Indochina. Because France was a more important ally than the Netherlands, and the British Cabinet knew of the Communist leadership of the Vietminh, the British ultimately went further to support the French than the Dutch.

The Communists were much weaker in Cochin China than in northern Vietnam. The Vietminh formed a loose united front with other groups, who were less inclined to negotiate with the French than Ho, and readier to provoke violence. A Trotskyite party openly opposed the Stalinist Communists, while the Cao Dai and Hoa Hao religious sects had set up their own little states. General Douglas Gracey, the British commander, forbade the carrying of weapons and all public meetings in an attempt to "restore order." He reinstalled the French authorities in control and rearmed the French troops who had been imprisoned by the Japanese. The French soon provoked trouble with the Vietnamese, who massacred hundreds of French and Eurasian civilians. Mountbatten thought Gracey had exceeded his orders, but nevertheless backed him, while pressing the French to negotiate with the Japanese. The British Cabinet ordered Mountbatten to give the French limited help, and approved sending a full British-Indian division to Saigon. A cease-fire was negotiated, but soon broke down. The British had to use Japanese troops as well as their own to cover the arrival of French reinforcements. In October a first round of French-Vietminh talks failed, when the French refused to discuss the issue of sovereignty. The British disengaged their forces as soon as possible, leaving in early 1946. They had played a critical role, making a swift French reoccupation of vital areas in southern

Indochina possible. The Vietminh lost control of the cities but continued guerrilla warfare in the countryside.[3]

In his stronghold in the north, Ho had only the Chinese to deal with. A large Chinese force—much larger than the other Allies had expected—had arrived in mid-September, looting as it advanced. The Chinese did not let the French troops who had fled to China return; and the French captured by the Japanese in the north remained prisoners. The Chinese readily dealt with Ho, although they also aided the anti-Communist nationalist groups, the VNQDD and the Dong Minh Hoi. When they disarmed the Japanese, they let the Vietminh get most of the Japanese weapons and sold the Vietnamese some of their own. By late 1945, the Vietminh regular army in the north was well armed and was being trained with the help of some Chinese and Japanese instructors. Ho reluctantly made some concessions to the pro-Chinese nationalist groups.

He continued to try to cultivate the Americans and unsuccessfully tried to appeal to the American government. He still camouflaged the Communist nature of his regime, going farther than any effort of this sort undertaken by Communists elsewhere. In November 1945, Ho "dissolved" the Indochina Communist Party. It continued to exist in secret and, when necessary, was referred to as the "organization" or as a "Marxist Study Group." In 1946 the Vietminh was submerged in a broader front, the Lien Viet, although the older name stuck to the regime. In January 1946 the government held elections of doubtful validity, which the Vietminh front won. In fact, the Vietminh and the non-Communist parties had arranged a deal; the latter were guaranteed a number of seats in the national assembly in return for not contesting the elections.

Ho's friendly contacts with the OSS and efforts to gain American support have sometimes been cited as evidence that he was a "potential Tito" and only the American government's reluctance to follow up these gestures prevented a friendly relationship. There seems to be little evidence for this idea, which is in any case anachronistic; even Tito was not yet a "Titoist" in 1945. The Vietnamese Communist approaches were in line with Soviet policy at the time and nothing in Ho's career suggests that he was ever willing to break the front of Communist solidarity. Ho was, if anything, particularly hostile to Tito. When the Soviet-Chinese conflict erupted, Ho did his best to reconcile his quarreling patrons.

The Vietminh's seizure of power in August 1945 probably took place without Soviet foreknowledge. It did not fit well with Stalin's general policies at that time; he was after bigger game than a Communist Indochina. But both Ho and the Soviets tried to keep their policies in line from

September 1945 on, Ho by camouflaging the Communist nature of his regime, the Soviets by praising the Vietminh as they would non-Communist nationalists. Soviet diplomats and publications treated events in Indochina as like those in Indonesia; they gave the latter country more attention. They bitterly attacked the actions of the British and French.

A complicated Franco-Vietnamese-Chinese triangle developed in 1946. Ho reopened talks with the French, while the latter negotiated with the Chinese. Ho's readiness to make a deal allowing French forces to enter the north seems strange at first. But his main aim was to play for time and get rid of the Chinese and the groups they backed. Ho shared the hopes of the Soviets and the French Communists that the latter would take over France, or at least become the leading element in a coalition regime. He did not want a fight that might prejudice the French party's chances.

Quite apart from any deference to Stalin and his French comrades, Ho's actions were very much in his own interests. The victory of the French Communists would probably give him all Indochina without a shot. And if there was a war with the French, it was desirable to delay it as long as possible to get the army ready and prepare a base area in the interior.

Ho now wished to get rid of the Chinese. A limited French return seemed a lesser evil than the Chinese remaining. Their usefulness to the Communists had been exhausted; now they were dangerous. They had mercilessly plundered the Vietnamese, and held a protecting hand over Ho's rivals, who controlled some important areas. The Chinese might decide to crush his regime out of anti-Communism or ambition. It must be remembered that in 1946 even Mao Zedong did not expect to conquer China as soon as he did, and there seemed a good chance that China might be permanently divided between the Communists and the Nationalists. The latter might seek compensation for losses in the north in Indochina. Ho's Soviet mentors were doing something similar at that very moment, trying to turn their occupation of northern Iran and Manchuria into permanent control. It was not yet clear that the Western powers would stop them; and even if they did, Ho must have wondered if the West would rescue *him* from the Chinese.

Alternatively, the Chinese might sell the Vietminh out to the French. The Chinese government, in fact, had chosen the latter course; on February 28, 1946, it reached an agreement with France, which gave up its privileges in China, and gave the Chinese considerable concessions in Indochina in return for a Chinese promise to depart. On March 6, with a French landing force already heading for Haiphong, Ho reached an agreement with the French. They recognized the Democratic Republic of Vietnam as a "free state" within the French Union. A maximum of 25,000 French troops were to enter the north, and most were to leave in ten months. The French came ashore after a clash with the Chinese, who left slowly and reluctantly. The Vietminh and the French later joined forces to smash the VNQDD and the Dong Minh Hoi, who opposed the French-Vietnamese agreement. Subsequent negotiations, however, went badly. Fighting had never ended in the south, while the French created a puppet Cochin Chinese separatist movement to keep that area, the richest part of Vietnam, from Ho's control. The French would not concede real sovereignty to Ho's government, and the French behaved in a way that would enrage even the most moderate anti-Communist nationalist.

THE WAR BEGINS

During the fall, it became clear that negotiations had failed, and the French enlarged their foothold in the north, provoking fighting. The French elections of November 1946 showed Ho, if not Stalin, that a Communist victory in France could not be counted on in the near future. There was no point in displaying more patience. The Vietminh initiated outright war with a surprise attack on the French garrison in Hanoi. As the Communists expected, the attack was repulsed. The Vietminh forces, numbering about 60,000 men, retreated to the long-prepared base area in the Viet Bac. One of Ho's great political feats had been winning over most of the tribesmen who formed most of the population of the Viet Bac, and who traditionally hated Vietnamese. A lengthy guerrilla campaign began in the mountains and jungle, replete with atrocities by both sides.[4] For some years the Viet Minh was thrown almost entirely on its own resources; the arms acquired in 1945–1946 were supplemented only by a trickle of material smuggled in from Thailand and the Philippines.

The Vietnamese modeled their strategy on that followed by the Chinese Communists since the 1930s; their own exposition of their strategic policy borrowed and quoted extensively from Mao's "On Protracted War."

Mao's pattern of taking power departed, albeit marginally, from previous orthodoxy in two ways. Mao (or the writings attributed to him—many of his ideas were actually originated by other Chinese leaders) stressed that the "national bourgeoisie"—a vague Communist term covering native big businessmen in backward countries not too closely connected to the imperialists—could join the revolutionary coalition and continue to operate for a considerable time after the Communists took power. Second, the Communists must dominate any "united front" of parties and classes from the start. Mao rejected, as Lenin and Stalin had not, the possibility that the

Communists might play second fiddle to other groups in the early stages of an anti-imperialist struggle. "Maoism," or as the Chinese put it, "the thought of Mao Zedong" was thus both narrower and more tolerant than the older Soviet-style orthodoxy. Mao did not, however, (as is often said) invent the idea of basing revolutions in backward countries mainly on the peasants. Lenin and Stalin never envisaged anything else.

Reduced to a rough formula, Mao envisaged forming a rural-based political and military organization waging prolonged guerrilla, and then conventional, warfare from remote, "inaccessible" base areas; the struggle would develop in several distinct stages. Mao did not enumerate them, but Western analysts of his writings usually identified three.

In a first phase, the Communists would reach out to the peasants, after some political preparations, with "armed propaganda" by small guerrilla units that would initially avoid fighting the authorities. The population would be organized (not necessarily starting with the peasants right off), in "associations" of farmers, women, artisans, and so on. Ultimately, a whole underground government would be developed, what the French expressively called "parallel hierarchies." Guerrilla units would be built up.

In a second phase, the guerrillas would start offensive operations, mainly hit-and-run raids and ambushes, while a regular force with heavy weapons was built up in the base areas, which, if possible, would be defended if attacked. Mao despised "pure" guerrilla warfare by small lightly armed units with a constantly shifting locale and wanted to get away from it as soon as possible. Ultimately, when the enemy was sufficiently worn down and the Communist strength had grown, mobile warfare would be started with the regular force; finally the enemy would be crushed in conventional operations. Judging when to shift between forms of war, incidentally, was a tricky business, and proved particularly so in both Indochina Wars. And a shift to conventional war, although possible only when the Communists had become very formidable, was particularly dangerous. If the enemy regular forces retained their cohesion and morale, they might yet defeat the Communists in conventional battles. That had happened to the Greek Communists in 1944 when they attempted to seize Athens from the Anglo-Greek expeditionary force; they had never recovered from that defeat.

There were certain ambiguities and gaps in Mao's views. There was obviously a big difference between engaging in civil war against native authorities like the Chinese Nationalists, as Mao had done up to 1936, and after World War II, and fighting a foreign enemy, like Japan (or France— although there was also a difference between fighting a simple invader like the Japanese and a returning but once well-established colonial power). What these differences meant was not always fully spelled out by Mao or other theorists. Later in life, Mao argued, or pretended to, that his method was "the" formula for Communist victory practically everywhere in the underdeveloped countries; and indeed the main path to world revolution. (As we shall see in Chapter 4, however, his policies toward Indonesia cast doubt about whether he believed this literally.) But even his followers did not pretend that in the late 1940s. The applicability of the doctrine, for example, in a small country where no base areas might be found or where the Communists could not obtain heavy weapons for the final stage of conventional operations was doubtful. The whole problem of "base areas" was a relative one. In China and Vietnam during the First Indochina War, it was possible to establish bases practically inaccessible to the Nationalists, Japanese and French (although the Vietminh located much of its base within China), but what was effectively immune to attacks by them might be accessible to more technologically advanced enemies. And, while the doctrine was relevant to the situation in Vietnam, it was so only in a complex way. In 1945 the Communists had leaped from the first preparatory phase to a seizure of power in Bolshevik style. Now they were forced back to sometime early in the second "guerrilla" phase.[5]

The French had a tiger by the tail. In the fall of 1947 they launched their only major offensive. Paratroops and deep armored thrusts into the Viet Bac were to capture the Communists' leadership and their main supply depots, and then wipe out their main forces. The French narrowly missed capturing Ho, and the Communist force evaded destruction. After that the French held a tenuous bridgehead in Tonkin (northern Vietnam), and some exposed outposts strung along the Chinese border. Their forces numbered about 115,000 men. They could not even police the Red River delta, nominally "behind" their lines, where most of the people of Tonkin lived. Vietnamese could regularly travel between the delta and the Viet Bac. Nor could the French reinforce their troops significantly. French law forbade sending draftees to Asia, so the war was fought by French professional soldiers, Foreign Legionnaires and African and Indochinese troops.

Had the French mobilized and sent a large force to Indochina and presented a rational political program, they might conceivably have crushed the Vietminh while the enemy was still isolated from major outside help. But this was not a real possibility in the actual circumstances of the late 1940s. With an economy damaged by World War II and under Soviet threat, it was unlikely that any French government would send a really large army eastward for any purpose. Those most willing to fight the Vietminh were the least willing to make concessions to Vietnamese non-Communist nationalists. The French leaders regarded the war as a minor, old-fashioned colonial conflict, or pretended that it was. An admission that it was a large-scale war and an attempt to mobilize, and send French draftees east would probably have caused general rebellion against the war effort.

Politically the French were in a blind alley. They could not deal even with the areas they controlled, even though the Vietminh lost some ground. During 1947 and 1948 the large Catholic minority, which had originally backed the Vietminh on patriotic grounds, swung over to the French side. So did some of the surviving VNQDD and Dong Minh Hoi nationalists, who were bitter at the Communists. The brutality and arrogance of Ho's delegates in the south in 1945–1946 had alienated many nationalists there, and drove the Cao Dai and Hoa Hao into alliance with the French. The Communists in the south remained weaker and much more poorly armed than those in Tonkin.

The French realized that this jumble of ill-assorted groups was not enough of a base of support. They finally formed a quasi-puppet regime for all of Vietnam, dropping plans for a separate Cochin China. They sought an arrangement with Emperor Bao Dai, who had been in exile since 1945. There was little evidence that he would be of value or that Vietnamese respected him. France really needed to come to terms with the non-Communist nationalists, not a corrupt figurehead. (Bao Dai's character may be judged from the fact that in 1954, after receiving a suitable bribe, he made a representative of organized crime head of the Saigon police.) Sluggish negotiations led to the "Elysée Agreements" of March 1949, which were not ratified until January 1950. The agreements made Vietnam an "associated state," "independent within the French Union." Foreign policy and military affairs remained under French control. Vietnam was to have both limited diplomatic relations with a few countries and its own army, under French command. French nationals retained a special status in Vietnam. Similar arrangements were made with Laos and Cambodia, where the French had easily defeated the weak nationalist military forces; but they did not satisfy many Vietnamese, no matter how anti-Communist.[6] But the Elysée Agreements enabled France to gain American support. This made it possible to fight on for several more years, although another event had already made victory strategically impossible. The Chinese Communist armies had reached the Vietnamese border.

CHINA AND VIETNAM

The Vietnamese Communists, like most of the other Communist parties in Southeast Asia, were still primarily oriented toward the Soviets. Since 1946, however, they had formed ties with the Chinese Communists, as well as applying the Maoist military formula. The latter were interested in Vietnam even before their conquest of China. They had organized a network of agents in the country to get money from the wealthy Chinese minority. Their agents in Thailand helped smuggle weapons to Vietnam. The small Communist guerrilla forces operating in south China sometimes took refuge across the Vietnamese border.

With south China secured, Mao began a major effort to help the Vietminh. The Soviets seem to have deemed Indochina a Chinese sphere of influence, even when, in 1951 and 1952, they showed some reservations about the general validity of the Chinese strategy for "colonial and semicolonial" countries. In December 1949 the Chinese and Vietminh exchanged military missions, and may have already concluded a modest agreement for the Vietnamese purchase of military equipment. A major aid agreement was arranged in April 1950. When the Chinese Communists took Hainan island, it became a base for smuggling equipment to Indochina by junk. The Vietminh sent 20,000 soldiers to China for training and formed them into cadres for five regular infantry divisions; the Chinese later trained two more divisions and a Soviet-style artillery division.

The French forts along the ridge forming the Chinese-Vietnamese border still interfered with the transport of heavy equipment; so the Vietminh moved to eliminate them. Although some officers had urged evacuating the border ridge in 1949, the French had remained astonishingly complacent. In October 1950 they suffered a terrific defeat; the border ridge fell. Most of the defending force was destroyed. The Chinese set to work improving communications across the now-open border; their influence on the Vietminh increased.

The Vietminh army was reorganized on Chinese lines; Chinese Communist writings were translated into Vietnamese and Maoist terminology and practices were adopted. In consequence many in the West wrongly came to think that the Vietminh regime was simply a Chinese satellite, as Czechoslovakia was a satellite of the USSR. But Ho and the dominant element in his party took a different view.

During 1951 and 1952 small Chinese forces occasionally raided Tonkin in support of the Vietminh. In December 1950 the Chinese may have briefly considered open intervention in Indochina. But if they did, they was probably a reaction to their first great success in Korea, and they soon dropped the idea.[7]

THE AMERICANS ENTER THE PICTURE

Between 1945 and 1949 the United States had hardly had a serious policy toward Indochina; it was distracted by far more important issues elsewhere. It had not seriously opposed, but had refused to assist, the French return to Indochina. Contrary to what is sometimes claimed, the State Department definitely disapproved of France's attempt to restore its prewar position by force. But it was unwilling to have a major quarrel with France over the issue. Undersecretary of State Acheson pointedly advised the French in December 1946 that trying to retake Indochina by force would be unwise. During 1947 and 1948 the Americans lamely assured the French that they had no desire to see the French supplanted by the Communists, but warned them that colonial empires were becoming a thing of the past and that they ought to be more generous toward the Vietnamese.

The possibility that Ho Chi Minh was primarily a nationalist or a "potential Tito" was explored in 1948 and 1949, but research offered little comfort on this point, and the Americans were increasingly concerned about Southeast Asia. In May 1949 the State Department decided to accept the "Bao Dai solution" embodied in the Elysée Agreements as at least a starting point for a non-Communist settlement, although Acheson and most observers doubted that this would actually prove an effective counter to the Vietminh. Charles Reed, the chief of the State Department's Southeast Asia Division, warned that the situation in Indochina was hopeless. He urged writing the area off and making Thailand the main focus of any effort to stop a Communist advance in Southeast Asia.

The Western world would have very good reason to wish that this advice had been heeded.

In February 1950 the British and Americans recognized the "Associated States."

The Americans sent a survey mission to Southeast Asia. In May Truman approved an aid program of $60 million. The survey mission had stressed the need for a forceful approach with the French if American policy was to succeed. But this advice was ignored. The aid decision was the first step toward the disastrous American intervention in the Second Indochina War. By 1954 the Americans would be paying 80 percent of the cost of the French war effort in Indochina, but they secured no commensurate influence over French policy and strategy. The French paid little attention to American views and minimized direct contact between the Americans and the Vietnamese government and army.

There was a fundamental difference in outlook between the French and Americans. For the Americans, the Elysée Agreements were but a starting point for Vietnam's transition to independence and an effective anti-Communist policy in the area. For the French, they were, at best, the last straw, and many French leaders had grave mental reservations about actually carrying them out. In 1950 and after, the Americans, and the British, regarded Indochina as a front in the Cold War, even if they suspected French motives. Except for some soldiers, like General Jean de Lattre de Tassigny, few Frenchmen, except when talking for American consumption, really shared this perspective. Their objective in Indochina was to save French influence, which at least verged on effective control there. The idea of smashing the Vietminh to create independent non-Communist states in Indochina, or sacrificing French interests there in order to beat the Communists made no sense to them. Generally speaking, the French either wished to keep Indochina a French colony or semicolony or get out.

The Truman administration perceived what was going on, but believed that it was in a poor position to pressure the French. They were too likely to react by pulling out of Indochina or by becoming refractory on issues such as European integration or German rearmament. And, after the Korean War began, military considerations were too pressing. Especially after China intervened in Korea, Korea and Indochina were regarded as two separate fronts in the same struggle. Some American officials, however, remained pessimistic. George Kennan warned Secretary of State Acheson in August 1950 that the United States and France were in a struggle that they could not win.[8]

Although in terms of local politics the struggles in Indochina and Korea may have been fundamentally different, the world's Communists also insisted that the two conflicts were alike. Shortly after the victory on the border ridge, the Chinese defeated the United Nations' (UN) forces in North Korea. World-wide Communist propaganda gleefully predicted that Seoul, Hanoi and Manila would all be "liberated" in 1951. Ho no longer cared much about camouflaging his aims; in February 1951 the Communist party reappeared as the Lao Dong or "workers' party." Although nominally it was only a Vietnamese party, documents captured by the French in 1952 showed that Ho continued to plan to take over Laos and Cambodia as well.

General Giap hoped to crush the French forces in Tonkin in conventional battles before large amounts of American aid reached Indochina, and the French feared he would succeed. They and the Americans also feared in late

1950, and much of 1951 that the Chinese Communists might invade Tonkin with their own forces, a preoccupation much underestimated by later historians. It was generally agreed that if the Chinese attacked, the French would be lucky to evacuate Tonkin without heavy losses. The small French air force, all propeller-driven, was concentrated on three vulnerable airfields and might easily be smashed on the ground or shot down by Chinese jets. The airfields were never bombed, but during the struggle for Dien Bien Phu daring Communist commando raids destroyed many planes.

But Giap's new opposite number, General de Lattre, who had ably commanded the French forces under Eisenhower in 1944–1945, was the one really able French commander in Indochina. General de Lattre shook up his command, mobilized French civilians to release troops from guard duty, and ordered ships sent to evacuate French women and children to return empty, commenting, "Now the men won't dare let go!" Between January and June 1951 three Vietminh offensives against the Red River delta area were repulsed, albeit narrowly, with heavy losses. General de Lattre had averted imminent and widely expected defeat.

The Communists returned to guerrilla warfare, conserving their regular forces. De Lattre built fortified posts around the Red River delta to free troops for mobile operations (this "de Lattre line" was perhaps originally intended to stop a Chinese invasion) and expanded imaginative operations by French commandos (*Groups de Commando Mixte Aeroporte*) in support of pro-French Tai tribesmen behind the Vietminh "lines." At times there were up to 15,000 of these "counterguerrillas" in the Communist rear. They failed to cut the Vietminh supply route to China, but Giap sometimes had to deploy a large part of his regular troops against them. They might have accomplished more if they had received more support.

In the fall of 1951 de Lattre tried to gain the initiative by capturing Hoa Binh, an enemy supply center, but the French finally had to evacuate the town. An approximate stalemate seemed to develop, but in fact the French position was eroding. Bao Dai's "National" government and army were not very effective; the government fell under the domination of the Dai Viets, a far-rightist secret society, which was to play a disastrous role in the Second Indochina War.

General de Lattre died in 1952; his successors were far less dynamic. Occasional French spoiling attacks on what seemed to be, but usually were not, vulnerable Communist forces were interspersed with small Communist attacks on French positions. The Chinese gradually improved the supply routes to the Vietminh, as the latter chipped away at the Red River delta. By the spring of 1953 it was estimated that the Vietminh's underground administration effectively controlled 5,000 of the 7,000 villages there. French efforts at "pacification" copied methods used long before under totally different conditions in colonial North Africa and never got off the ground. Because Ho's regime was more obviously Communist, and economic conditions in the "liberated" zones were deteriorating, positive political support for the Vietminh probably waned after 1950. But the French had little to say that was intelligible to the Vietnamese peasants and could not protect them from terror and intimidation. Although some disgusted nationalists defected from the Vietminh to the Bao Dai regime, disillusionment with the Communists could not be translated into real gains for the anti-Communist side. The Vietminh held almost all Tonkin beyond the de Lattre line, and much of southern and central Vietnam. The sects, not the French, held off the Communists in the far south. In 1953 the Communists had perhaps 300,000 men (half guerrillas) facing 190,000 men of the "French Union forces" (a third of whom were Indochinese) and 100,000 Vietnamese in the "National" army. And with the end of the Korean War, the Chinese were free to concentrate on supplying the Vietminh, whose firepower was approaching that of the French ground units. The French position was practically hopeless; indeed many feared that even if the war turned in their favor that would merely provoke Chinese intervention. They were trying to control an area four times the size of the area held by the Americans and the South Vietnamese in the Second Indochina War, with far fewer men and far less support in airpower and supplies—but rather less self-pity. Although opposition to the war was more violent in France in the early 1950s than it ever was in America in the Second Indochina War—40 percent of the equipment arriving from France was sabotaged—the French forces retained their cohesion and struggled on gallantly. The French commanders dreamed of drawing the Reds into a set-piece battle that would enable them to smash the enemy's main force; there were even hopes that the Vietminh might be gradually worn down, for economic conditions in the Viet Bac were dreadful. But many knew these hopes were slim. Others hoped that a worldwide settlement of the Cold War would free France of the Indochina albatross. But the men fighting in Indochina would be retired long before that day dawned.[9]

Although the American government sometimes uttered optimistic predictions about the future to bolster French morale, it was well aware that things were not going well. Intelligence estimates described the situation as a "stalemate," and implied that things would probably get worse. But the Truman administration hoped that the aid program would improve the French position, and that eventually the development of the Vietnamese

"National" government and army would turn things around. Even the most pro-French observers admitted that drastic political and economic reforms were needed for the National government to succeed. And by 1952 it was clear that the French will to carry on was declining. Apart from continuing aid to the French and trying to delicately persuade them to show more sense, nothing could be done. Should the French withdraw, the Vietminh would inevitably win. Neither a French departure nor an American intervention could be considered. Given the Korean War and the threat of World War III, the United States had no forces to spare for Southeast Asia. It was unwilling to promise France more than air and naval support even against an outright Chinese attack.[10]

Eisenhower's secretary of state, John Foster Dulles, had less patience with the French than his predecessor. In July 1953 he finally made them promise complete independence to the Indochina states. The Americans were now more enthusiastic about continuing the war than the French. They strongly backed the new "Navarre plan" formulated by General Henri Navarre, the new French commander in Indochina. Navarre professed to aim for complete victory, but privately hoped for a "draw" to allow negotiations to begin on a satisfactory basis. Navarre envisaged building his strength to 250,000 French Union troops and 300,000 Indochinese troops in order to form a large mobile force and reach a decision by the end of 1955. Navarre hoped to secure the Red River delta, clear the coastal plain of central Vietnam, and then turn his forces north to destroy the Vietminh regular force. The French government gave him some reinforcements, although less than promised. Even in 1954, the Americans estimated that the French forces were equal in effective fighting power to just five U.S. divisions.

THE FINAL CRISIS

The Vietminh, and Navarre himself, disrupted these plans. The Vietminh had mounted a major invasion of Laos in April 1953. The French were embarrassed when they could not stop the Communists from temporarily overrunning most of the country.

In mid-1953 General René Cogny, the French commander in Tonkin, proposed sending a small force to Dien Bien Phu, a valley in western Tonkin, to supply and encourage the Tai guerrillas. Over Cogny's opposition, Navarre expanded this operation to build a major "air-land base" to block the best invasion route into Laos. Dien Bien Phu was seized by a paratroop drop in November 1953. It soon became apparent that the French force there would not block the Vietminh's movements, and that the Communists would attack Dien Bien Phu, which was overlooked by surrounding hills. In December, instead of evacuating Dien Bien Phu, Navarre chose to accept a major battle there. He reinforced the garrison to the equivalent of a division, nine infantry battalions supported by ten light tanks and some fighter-bombers based at Dien Bien Phu itself. The French gravely underestimated the weight of attack that the Communists could mount. French intelligence officers did not think that the Vietminh could transport much artillery or ammunition to the Dien Bien Phu area. Although they correctly estimated that the enemy could bring to bear a probable infantry strength equivalent to three divisions, Navarre gambled that only two Communist divisions could be supplied at Dien Bien Phu for any length of time.

Apparently Giap's supply officers did doubt that the supply problems could be overcome, but the Chinese were ready to give all necessary help. They aimed at a negotiated settlement of the war, but were ready to ignore strong American warnings against action in Indochina and intervene there in a limited but decisive way. The Chinese not only sent more personnel and supplies to the Vietminh, but decided to join in the fighting at Dien Bien Phu. A whole Chinese antiaircraft regiment with 37 mm guns played a major role at Dien Bien Phu, as did Chinese artillerymen; a Chinese adviser, Li Cheng Hu, may have devised the battle plan.

The French assumed that the Vietminh would have little artillery and discounted the fact that Dien Bien Phu was overlooked by high ground. They did not bother to camouflage their positions, and, because there was little wood for construction, were only lightly dug in. On March 10, 1954, they were stunned when artillery opened fire from the forward slopes of the surrounding hills. The Communists had stealthily built protected firing positions. The Communists soon knocked out the French planes based at Dien Bien Phu. Infantry attacked the French positions. Accurate antiaircraft fire, another surprise, stopped planes from landing and made supply by airdrop costly. Some Tai units deserted. The garrison was in a desperate position, although the French continued to send in reinforcements long after it should have been clear that they were throwing men away. The Communists gradually compressed the French position and choked off air supply. As the Communists drove trenches toward the French lines, the weight of artillery and antiaircraft fire increased.[11]

The desperate French begged for help. Much against American advice, the French had arranged for the upcoming Geneva Conference, originally intended to discuss a political settlement for Korea, to discuss Indochina.

The Americans were sure that under the circumstances any political settlement, whether a coalition government, partition, or early national elections, must end disastrously for the anti-Communist side. It was obvious that without American action Dien Bien Phu would fall and leave France in a bad position at the negotiations.

The United States government had not decided what to do if the French in Indochina were about to collapse *without* overt Chinese military intervention. President Eisenhower had been markedly unenthusiastic about intervening in Indochina earlier; on January 8 he remarked that he could not see putting U.S. ground forces anywhere in Southeast Asia but Malaya. And he was well aware that the French were sick of the war.[12]

The siege of Dien Bien Phu made the question critical. General Paul Ely, the chairman of the French Chiefs of Staff, visited Washington in late March. He could not even get a clear-cut American promise to intervene even to counter Chinese air attacks. But the chairman of the Joint Chiefs of Staff, Admiral Arthur Radford, a hard-liner, was sympathetic. He and Ely discussed a possible operation, "*Vautour*" (Vulture), to relieve Dien Bien Phu by a massive American air attack. "Vulture" went through several variants; most envisaged attacks by B-29 bombers and carrier-based planes with conventional weapons, although using tactical atomic weapons was discussed. Bernard Fall, the leading authority on the battle of Dien Bien Phu, maintained that "Vulture" could have saved the garrison.

Secretary of State Dulles drafted the text of a joint congressional resolution to authorize an intervention in Indochina. But the American leaders were not interested in just rescuing the Dien Bien Phu garrison and strengthening the Western bargaining position at Geneva, which was all that the French really wanted. If the United States intervened at all, in their view, the objective must be the total defeat of the Vietminh. Eisenhower opposed involving American forces in an "indecisive" action. He insisted that an intervention must be approved by Congress and supported by other nations.

The military was bitterly divided. The Army Chief of Staff, the highly respected Matthew Ridgway, was an especially strong opponent of intervention. Only Radford strongly favored intervening in Indochina; only the air force gave a qualified, unenthusiastic assent, while the army and the marines definitely opposed intervention. They rejected estimates by Radford's supporters that the French could win the war with only American air and naval support and tactical atomic weapons. The army believed that, even with the use of tactical atomic weapons, far larger air and naval forces, and at least seven American divisions, would be needed, and that it was necessary to assume that the Chinese would intervene.

Further obstacles to intervention emerged on April 3 when Dulles and Radford met the leaders of Congress, who were unenthusiastic. Dulles suggested that the loss of Indochina would lead, although perhaps not inevitably, to that of all Southeast Asia. The congressional leaders insisted that the United States should not move without European and Asian allies, and especially the British, and a French promise to accelerate full independence for Indochina, and maintain their forces there until the enemy was beaten. This made a congressional authorization in time to rescue Dien Bien Phu practically impossible, although American forces prepared for it and carried out reconnaissance flights over Dien Bien Phu and even southern China. Eisenhower would not act without Congress, although he publicly stressed the importance of Indochina. On April 7, he invented a famous phrase, comparing the effects of the fall of Indochina to that of the fall of the first of a "row of dominoes." He had implied, in a letter to Churchill on April 4, that the fall of Indochina must lead to the loss of all of Southeast Asia and ultimately of Japan. Yet he never endorsed the "domino theory" unconditionally, and indeed publicly repudiated it a month later. Indeed, at a National Security Council meeting on April 6, he had expressed hostility to the idea that all Southeast Asia would go Communist if Indochina did.

Dulles worked to form a coalition to assure "united action" in Indochina, but it is likely that his real aim was to provide pressure on the Communists at Geneva and pave the way for a future alliance arrangement in Southeast Asia. Australia, New Zealand, Thailand and the Philippines were willing to join any action, but the British refused, maintaining that military action or even the formation of a coalition for such action would damage the chances for a settlement. They had little faith in "Vulture's" effectiveness, but professed to be more optimistic about the basic situation in Indochina. Foreign Secretary Anthony Eden told the American ambassador that the French could not lose the war before the coming of the rainy season, however badly they conducted it. That was, at least, an overestimate of the French will to fight. By opposing the "united action" stipulated by Congress, and accepted by Eisenhower and Dulles as an irreducible requirement for American action, the British seemed to block American intervention—or more likely, gave the Eisenhower administration an excuse not to act. Sherman Adams, then Eisenhower's closest associate, doubted that the president was serious about intervening. The administration's efforts to impress the public with the importance of Indochina failed. Polls showed overwhelming public reluctance to intervene there. And Eisenhower was increasingly impressed by the army's high estimate of the costs of intervention. American policy was not exactly coherent; it rejected partition, which the British were reluctantly accepting as a solution, but refused to intervene. The Americans wanted the French to fight on without direct support, which the French were obviously unwilling to do.[13]

The failure of the French to obtain aid from their allies started a major rift in the Western alliance. The French could not be expected to admire British stolidity in the face of their misfortune, and they did not. But they also knew that the lack of British cooperation was just an excuse for American inaction; Britain, after all, had little to contribute to "united action." Having been pushed to fight on in Indochina long after they had become fed up with the war, the French had been unable even to get a limited operation to rescue their men at Dien Bien Phu. The Indochina crisis was one of several events demonstrating the Western powers' failure to formulate clear-cut policies to deal with the Soviets and their allies in the former colonial world.

Dien Bien Phu fell on May 7, 1954. Eisenhower and Dulles now hastily repudiated the "domino theory" which had hardly played the decisive role in *their* thinking later widely attributed to it. On May 11 Dulles remarked that Cambodia and Laos were not very important. Both men stressed that even if all Indochina fell Southeast Asia would not necessarily be lost; Eisenhower declared that the domino effect would be offset once a system of collective defenses was set up.

Although only a small part of the French forces in Indochina had been lost, the French will to fight had snapped. Navarre had irresponsibly tried to clear the coast of south-central Vietnam during the siege of Dien Bien Phu. That move failed. The Vietnamese "National" army was collapsing, and the Vietminh main force had rapidly regrouped after Dien Bien Phu, although it is not certain whether the force was in a condition to attack the Red River delta, for it had suffered heavy losses. Guerrillas made it hard even to keep the road between Hanoi and the sea open. Navarre prepared to evacuate the area south and west of the Red River; abandoning all of Tonkin was contemplated.

The new French prime minister, Pierre Mendes-France, pledged himself to seek a cease-fire by July 20, but this apparently damaging promise was offset by his threat to finally send draftees to Indochina if no cease-fire was arranged, Eden's diplomatic skill, and the threat that the United States might intervene after all. The USSR and China were reluctant to take further risks. They helped restrain the Vietminh and made possible an armistice agreement dividing Vietnam into two zones at the seventeenth parallel.[14] The French and the Associated States had suffered over 170,000 casualties; Communist and civilian losses may have numbered several times that. And the end had not yet come. Within a few months, France would be at war again, in Algeria, whose revolt was probably triggered by the demonstration of French weakness in the east. Desperate French officers, influenced by thinking about counterinsurgency techniques and experience of brainwashing in Communist prison camps, would attempt to copy Communist methods during the Algerian War; they would bring France within sight of civil war.

The key to the Communist success in Vietnam had been the ability, using the Vietminh front, to focus nationalist sentiment and seize power at the end of the war. It must not be forgotten, although many Western commentators later did, that the decisive seizure of power occurred in 1945. The Communists, between 1946 and 1954, did not lead a revolt, but a war of resistance against French reconquest. Guerrilla warfare was not the key to the seizure of power. It followed, rather than preceded, the Vietminh's becoming the national government. And, although the Vietnamese Communists learned much from Mao, their ideas diverged from those of the Chinese. Rather than fighting relatively backward foes in a civil war, they fought a heavily armed expeditionary force of a major Western power. They were more dependent on outside support than the Chinese, and their strategy was more psychologically oriented. They put more emphasis on influencing the outcome by propaganda, and seeking a decisive battle, not necessarily to crush the enemy outright, but to demoralize him. The West's simplistic picture of Vietnamese Communist doctrine as "Maoist" led to disastrous surprises in the Second Indochina War. So did the American refusal to learn from the bitter experience of the French, even in matters of military tactics.

The French, to be sure, had much to answer for. Their actions, at least after 1945 did not cause the Communist domination of the independence effort, but their failure to come to terms with Vietnamese nationalism made beating the Vietminh all but impossible. The French effort was weakly supported at home. Except for de Lattre, none of the French commanders were distinguished. Underestimating the enemy and lacking adequate intelligence, they vacillated between defensive-mindedness and recklessness. But the French could later take a sour satisfaction as their half-hearted American allies showed that incompetence and stupidity were not a French monopoly. And, though France's rule in Indochina had not been an admirable one, even at its worst, it was not as remotely atrocious as that of its totalitarian native successors.

3

The Southeast Asian Revolts
of 1948

In 1946 and 1947, while war raged in Indochina, the other Southeast Asian countries seemed relatively quiescent, as far as the Cold War was concerned. Until 1947 the Soviets had—except in Greece (classified as a special case of fighting "monarchofascism")—generally rejected armed insurrections by Communists beyond the range of support by the Soviet army or satellite forces. In colonial countries, Communists had sought to join nationalist coalitions and had some success in this. In Burma and Indonesia, newly formed Communist parties grew greatly in strength. In confrontations with the colonial powers, the Communists generally soft-pedalled violence and tended to side with the more moderate nationalist elements.

The Chinese Communists as yet had only minor links to most Communists in the region, although they did powerfully influence the largely Chinese Malayan Communist Party, which sought their advice and interpreted Soviet directives in the light of Maoist ideas.

Right after World War II the Soviets remained the dominant influence on the Communists of the region. The change of the Soviet line in 1947 had a drastic impact. As we have noted earlier, Zhdanov's speech of September 1947 implied a green light for insurrections. The new line was broadcast to Southeast Asian Communists at the Southeast Asian Youth Conference and the Second Congress of the Indian Communist Party, both of which were held in Calcutta in February 1948 at the same time as the coup in Czechoslovakia. More explicit instructions were delivered by private routes. The Indian Communists helped to push their Burmese comrades toward rebellion; the Australian Communists played a similar role for the Malayan

Communists. Musso, the senior Indonesian Communist leader, was sent home from Moscow to lead his comrades to final victory. During 1948, the Indonesian, Malayan, Philippine and Burmese Communists all tried to seize power.[1]

THE STRUGGLE FOR INDONESIA, I

Indonesia was by far the biggest country, and was strategically the center of Southeast Asia. The Soviets, throughout the Cold War, were always conscious of this fact, something Western commentators lost sight of because of their obsession with Indochina. The Communist attempt to seize power came in the midst of a war for independence against the Dutch that had already gone on for three years.

The Japanese had been welcomed as liberators in Indonesia and gave the Indonesian nationalists considerable authority. In August 1945, as the war neared its end, the Japanese told Sukarno and Hatta, the leading nationalists, that they would grant Indonesia independence on September 7. But younger nationalists, arguing that independence from a beaten Japan would be worthless, forced Sukarno and Hatta to jump the gun. On August 17 they declared Indonesia's independence. The Japanese army had been directed to maintain order until the Allies arrived. Unlike the Japanese naval command, it at first seemed to oppose the revolution. But the generals soon changed their minds and came to terms with the Indonesians. The Japanese Navy in particular, which had backed the nationalists from the start, helped arm the Indonesians, who were well-armed, much more so than the Vietminh. They built a force of 150,000 to 200,000 men, supported by 3,000 to 4,000 renegade Japanese, who helped man tanks and antiaircraft guns.[2]

None of the Allies had solid information about the situation in Indonesia, and none realized the great political transformation that had occurred under Japanese rule. The newly proclaimed Indonesian Republic was widely thought to be a Japanese puppet group without much support. Even some U.S. officials hostile to Dutch rule believed this for a time. Lord Mountbatten was ordered to reoccupy key areas of Indonesia, disarm and evacuate the Japanese and free Allied prisoners and internees, and establish peaceful conditions. The British were obligated to the Dutch to maintain a minimum of order, if not to suppress the revolution. They instructed the Japanese to "maintain order," but the Japanese ignored this until the British arrived.

When the British reached Java in late September, they found a genuine Indonesian government and armed forces with popular support. Mountbatten, backed by London, followed the same policy of coming to terms with nationalists that he had already launched in Burma. He pressed the resentful Dutch to negotiate with the Indonesians, but the small Dutch units the British had brought with them provoked armed clashes, while the Indonesian government failed to prevent extremists from attacking Allied prisoners, Eurasians and other minority groups. Mountbatten had to send reinforcements to Java. Further armed clashes led to a full-scale battle at the city of Surabaya in November when Indonesian forces, supported by renegade Japanese, refused British demands to disarm. Mountbatten, shocked, warned London that should outright war develop he would need six divisions and many months to secure the country and give the Dutch a good chance to take over. He feared for the morale of his men, most of whom were Indians. He was unable to disarm the Japanese forces and, in fact, had to use them against the Indonesians. The British, supported by the Americans, pressed the Dutch harder to come to terms.

The Dutch did not return to Java in force until March 1946, after they recognized the Indonesian Republic as the de facto authority there outside the Allied-held areas. Their policy was paternalistically liberal. Unlike the French, they did not seek to restore their rule permanently. Deeming Indonesia unready for self-rule, they aimed to restore a colonial administration as a starting point for the gradual transfer of power to a responsible Indonesian government. Although forced to recognize that the Indonesian Republic was not just a Japanese trick, they still saw its leaders as traitors. Underestimating the depth of nationalist sentiment, they thought that much of the Republic's support was superficial, and that if they and the British acted forcefully many moderates would come to terms.

As later events showed, the Dutch contempt for the Indonesian government was far from unfounded. But their policy was a classic case of the pursuit of the impossible. Reconquering Indonesia, if possible at all, would be a long and bloody affair, one that must cause so much Indonesian resentment that the goal of creating a sound basis for independence at a later date would be defeated. But the Dutch stubbornly pursued this aim for over three years, until outsiders finally stopped them. Unable to simply crush the nationalists, the Dutch set out to do so obliquely. They wanted to arrange a situation in which the Indonesian Republic would be the inferior partner in a condominium arrangement. Dutch-Indonesian negotiations, punctuated by fighting, strongly affected the internal struggle among the Indonesians.[3]

INDONESIAN POLITICS AND DUTCH ATTACKS

The Indonesians quarrelled bitterly over negotiations with the Dutch, and were split between those who had worked with the Japanese, like Sukarno and Hatta (the dominant element in the government), and those who had not. The latter faction was led by Sutan Sjahrir, a Westernized Sumatran whose views were close to those of Western Social Democrats. This faction favored a more moderate stance in negotiations, and broadly speaking, formed the "left wing" of the nationalist coalition. The advantage of having a "pro-Allied" figure as leader of the Indonesian government led to Sjahrir's becoming prime minister in November 1945.

The Communists loyal to Moscow belonged to the "left wing." But a peculiarity of Indonesian politics was the existence of a long-standing "national Communist" tendency led by Tan Malaka, the former Comintern agent for all of Southeast Asia. These national Communists had collaborated with the Japanese (some of whom, however, had also backed people known to be Stalinists toward the end of the war) and bitterly opposed negotiations with the Dutch. They were also violently hostile to the Stalinists. Paradoxically, the Indonesian Communist Party was refounded by national Communists, only to be taken over by "Moscow" Communists returning from the Netherlands in early 1946. Many Stalinists, however, had secretly joined other left-wing parties, especially the Socialist and Labor parties, during 1945. Whether this was a deliberate long-range plan to infiltrate the other groups or was dictated by the fact that no formal Communist organization had existed when the revolution broke out is unclear. But the new Stalinist Communist Party grew rapidly, especially when an attempted coup by Tan Malaka was defeated in June 1946. The Communists took over the labor movement.

The Dutch and the Indonesians reached the Linggadjati agreement in November 1946. The Dutch recognized the Republic as the de facto authority in all of Java and Sumatra, including the areas they occupied. The two sides agreed to form a democratic federal state, the "United States of Indonesia" (USI) no later than January 1, 1949, and for a Dutch-Indonesian union under the Dutch crown. The USI would comprise the Republic and two states under Dutch control—Borneo and the "Great Eastern State." But many clauses of the Linggadjati agreement were ambiguous. The Dutch maintained that it meant that the Republic accepted their leadership, an interpretation rejected by the Indonesian nationalists, who maintained that they should be superior to the other two states, which they regarded, with reason, as Dutch puppets. The Dutch went further, demanding effective control of the USI's economic affairs and a role in maintaining law and order on Java and Sumatra. All Indonesians rejected this. Relations worsened as the Dutch continued to blockade Republican ports and the Indonesians broke the cease-fire. In June 1947 the Sjahrir government fell when it tried to make more concessions to the Dutch. Another Socialist, Amir Sjarifuddin, who had been minister of defense since 1945, replaced Sjahrir. Sjarifuddin was probably, although not certainly, a long-standing Communist and the most important of those who had infiltrated other parties in 1945. He offered even more concessions than Sjahrir, but the Dutch decided to attack.

They quickly seized Java's major cities and the richest parts of Sumatra. But the Indonesian forces evaded destruction and fought on. The British and Americans opposed the Dutch attack, but not very effectively, while the Soviets firmly backed the Indonesians, supporting demands that the Dutch return to their original lines. That favorably impressed the Indonesians. They were less pleased by a feeble American offer of "good offices," although the Americans and the British imposed an arms embargo on the Dutch. The Indonesians believed that the Americans could easily force the Dutch into line if they wished. Privately, the Americans did put pressure on the Dutch. In September 1947 Secretary of State Marshall warned them against trying to wipe out what was left of the Republic.

Once the Dutch reached their territorial objectives, they accepted a cease-fire and negotiations under UN auspices. In January 1948 an agreement was reached aboard the USS *Renville*. The Dutch continued to hold the areas taken in 1947, but promised to hold plebiscites under UN supervision to determine whether those areas would be part of the Indonesian Republic or another component of the USI. Indonesians hated the agreement; their government accepted it reluctantly and perhaps only because the military command felt unready to renew fighting. The Sjarifuddin government was forced to resign within a week, and the left-wing—"Sajap Kiri"— went into opposition as the Sukarno-Hatta group took over. The "Renville" agreement was a failure. The Dutch continued forming new puppet states and an interim federal government, and violated the agreement by suppressing freedom of speech and assembly in the occupied areas, and holding unsupervised plebiscites.[4]

Although increasingly annoyed at the Dutch, the Americans took no effective action. The Indonesians became increasingly pro-Soviet. The Dutch had taken the richest food-producing areas and their blockade of the remaining Republican areas was effective. Food and supplies of all sorts were scarce; the population was increasingly discontented. Despite their exclusion from the government, the Communists' position was strong. The Socialist party split; Sjahrir left to found a new Socialist group that backed the Hatta government.

INDONESIA AND THE ZHDANOV LINE

After the Calcutta conference, the Communists abruptly changed their line. The "Sajap Kiri," under increasing Communist domination, was reorganized in late February as the "People's Democratic Front." In line with the doctrine of the two camps, the Front now opposed the "Renville" agreement, and demanded breaking off the talks with the Dutch. The Communists hoped to gain control of the government by political maneuvers and persisted in this for several months. By July, however, it became apparent that this could not be achieved. Sjarifuddin's actions as minister of defense had aroused suspicion; he had put Communist supporters in high positions in the army, brought much of the irregular forces under Communist influence, and set up secret arms dumps known only to his supporters. It was estimated the Communists controlled about a third of the armed forces.

The Hatta government began a "rationalization" program to reduce the swollen army, which was too big for the available arms and supplies, from 450,000 to 160,000 men. Aimed at Communist-influenced units, it roused great resentment; most men did not want to be demobilized. The Communists decided to start an armed revolt if their next set of maneuvers did not force Hatta out. The government learned of this and took counteraction, trying to remove commanders loyal to the People's Democratic Front.

The Soviets now intervened more directly. Stalin perhaps felt that the Communist leaders on the spot, who had failed to keep their position in the government and then responded sluggishly to the change in line, needed supervision by someone "close" to him. On August 3, Musso, an old-line leader of the Indonesian Communists who had been in exile since 1935, returned from the USSR and took over as party secretary. In late August and early September, Sjarifuddin and other leaders of the Socialist and Labor parties announced that they had been Communists all along. (Some observers doubted that this claim was true in Sjarifuddin's case, maintaining that he decided to join the Communists because of disappointment with American passivity in the face of Dutch actions.) Many Communist leaders seem to have been unenthusiastic about the new line, which was a product of Moscow's influence. The People's Democratic Front was reorganized along tighter lines; but as it was now obviously under Communist control many members of the constituent parties left. In parts of the country the Socialist party simply broke away.

Musso spoke of having a "Gottwald plan" to seize power, a reference to the recent seizure of power in Czechoslovakia by the Communists led by Klement Gottwald. But his attempts to secure a new cabinet with Front ministers in key points failed. The government began releasing the national Communists, jailed since 1946, to create a counterweight to the Stalinists. The latter planned an armed revolt, but expected to take some time to get ready—perhaps until November or later. The fusion of the parties in the People's Democratic Front was not yet complete, and the Communists hoped that the Dutch would attack, leaving the Communists the last bastion of resistance, with sole access to Sjarifuddin's secret arms dumps. Musso embarked on a political tour, strongly appealing to troops being demobilized and to the peasants. The government proceeded with demobilization and the removal of Communist officers; some were arrested.

On September 18, when Musso was near the city of Madiun, pro-Communist military groups fearing government action seized control of the city. The local Communist organization joined in. Musso, his hand forced, decided to act prematurely; the result was a disaster. The government could not spare forces from the front, but the number of troops joining the rebels was relatively small. Madiun was retaken on September 30. Fighting elsewhere lasted into October, but the Communists were crushed. They had seriously overestimated their popular support; peasants supported the government and the small working class was apathetic.

Had the Communists waited, things might have been different. Talks with the Dutch collapsed over the question of the Dutch role in an interim government, and the Dutch attacked on December 19. They captured Sukarno, Hatta, and the other Indonesian leaders. But the Dutch could not police the areas they nominally occupied; guerrilla resistance continued. Had the Communists still been intact when the Dutch struck, the situation might have been ideal for them. The Indonesian Communists' inability to control their followers may have cost them a real chance to take power.

The Dutch precipitated the end of the war, but not in the way they had hoped. The American government, fed up, ended the foolish dithering that had let the conflict drag on. It suspended Marshall Plan aid to the Netherlands; it was clear that the Senate would end it permanently if the Dutch did not come around. The Dutch quickly caved in and agreed on terms with the Indonesians.

The Communist party rapidly recovered from the defeat of 1948. It was taken over by leaders who had not taken part in the Madiun rebellion, but remained hostile to the Indonesian government. During the Korean War it launched an effective political strike and a campaign of terror against European enterprises on Java and Sumatra to support the Communist war effort in Korea.

During 1951, the Soviets showed greater recognition of the fact that Burma, India, Ceylon and Indonesia were neutral in the Cold War, and let Communist parties in South and Southeast Asia follow a more flexible policy toward their governments. While armed struggles continued in some countries, the Indonesian Communist Party was free to work with the major parties backing the Indonesian government. In January 1952 the Communists proposed an alliance with what they called the party of the "national bourgeoisie," the PNI, which was actually the party of the government bureaucracy and was closely associated with President Sukarno. This was the first step toward a strategy of a peaceful takeover in alliance with Sukarno. It would bring the Communists close to power in the 1960s before going awry and leading to disaster.[5]

MALAYA: RESISTANCE TO REBELLION

The war that began in Malaya in 1948 became the most publicized of the Southeast Asian revolts. Although in some ways far from typical, it strongly influenced Western ideas about how to fight Communist guerrillas.

Strategically and economically, Malaya was a major target. Among the world's largest producers of tin and rubber, it was the richest country in the colonial world and one of the few to successfully industrialize. Nearby Singapore, although politically separate, was one of the world's great ports. Though a small country, four-fifths of Malaya was covered by rain forest; it was far more of a "jungle" country than Vietnam or Burma and it had plenty of cover for guerrillas. World War II had let the local Communists build a strong position in a complex society that had not jelled into a nation.

Malaya's five million people consisted largely of Malays and Chinese. The Malays, the natives of the country, had good relations with the British; there was little nationalist sentiment before World War II. But they disliked the Chinese, who were recent immigrants to the country, and who were the economically dynamic element of the population. The Chinese were mostly workers in mines, on plantations and in industry, or were businessmen; the Malays, farmers, fishermen and aristocrats. The Chinese as yet had few real roots in the country, and had little interest in Malaya's independence, or indeed in Malaya at all. Instead they strongly identified with China. Although generally better off than most Malays, the Chinese formed the overwhelming bulk of supporters of the Malayan Communist Party, which was the strongest organization in the Chinese community.

The British took a deep interest in the Communists. A British agent, a Vietnamese named Loi Tak, infiltrated them and became the Communist party's secretary-general in 1939. (He temporarily shifted his "loyalty" to the Japanese during the occupation, but reverted to British control after Japan surrendered.) But this feat had less impact than might be expected; it did not prevent the Communists from becoming a serious menace and showed the limitations of such infiltration. In deference to his employers, Loi Tak may have steered the party from violence at some points, but he nevertheless increased its strength.

While Malays reacted apathetically to the Japanese invasion, Chinese were firmly anti-Japanese. The British released Communists from prison and trained some of them in sabotage and guerrilla warfare. During the defense of Singapore they armed a large Chinese force that included Communists. The graduates of the British training course became the nucleus of a guerrilla force, the "Malayan People's Anti-Japanese Army (MPAJA)," formed in March 1942. It was supported by an auxiliary organization, the "People's Anti-Japanese Federation." The MPAJA armed itself with British weapons collected from battlefields the Japanese had failed to police. It got advice and further training from some British officers who had fled to the jungle rather than surrender. The Communists kept them virtually prisoner. The MPAJA based itself on the support of hundreds of thousands of Chinese squatters who had fled the Great Depression, and then the Japanese, to set up small farms on the edge of the jungle. The MPAJA established an elaborate system of camps and trails in the jungle, and contacted the primitive aborigines who lived deep in the interior. The Japanese treated the Chinese with the usual brutality and played the Malays off against the Chinese with some effect.

In 1943 the Southeast Asia Command established contact with the MPAJA. The British do not seem to have realized the extent of Communist control over the MPAJA, or perhaps still counted too much on their relations with Loi Tak. Mountbatten, who seems to have been poorly advised, decided to back it as the main resistance force in Malaya, although it fought little against the Japanese. (In fact, it did most of its fighting against a small Guomindang resistance force.) In 1944–1945 the British launched an elaborate effort to supply the MPAJA, airdropping arms and liaison personnel in preparation for an invasion of Malaya.

Japan's surrender took the Communists by surprise. Violating British orders, they disarmed some Japanese and "Indian National Army" troops.

Building their strength to 6800 armed men, they took effective control of part of Malaya through Communist-controlled "People's Committees" and attacked Malay and Guomindang (Chinese Nationalist Party) guerrilla groups and terrorized non-Communists. A faction favored seizing power and resisting a British return by force—this may have been party policy earlier in the war—but Loi Tak overruled them. Ironically, he may have been the decisive element in keeping the Malayan Communists in line with Soviet policy. It has sometimes been claimed that the Communists thus missed a great opportunity, but this is unlikely. Events in Greece had shown that the British, who landed no less than three divisions in Malaya, would deal harshly with a Communist attempt to seize power; they were unlikely to be more indulgent in one of their colonies. (Had the British not returned to Malaya, however, nothing would have stopped the Communists from taking over.) Under considerable pressure, the MPAJA formally disbanded and gave up some of its weapons. It actually handed in more weapons than it had received from the British detachments in Malaya—but it hid those it recovered from airdrops that had gone astray or had taken from the Japanese.[6]

In conformity with the prevailing Soviet line, the Communists turned to a "legal"—or pseudolegal—struggle, although documents show that at least after January 1946 the leaders ultimately expected to return to some sort of armed struggle. In contrast to the prewar period, the British allowed full freedom of speech, press, assembly and labor organization. Concentrating their efforts in urban areas, the Communists, using violence and threats, had considerable success in taking over the labor movement. They tried to develop a "united national front" with left-wing Malays. The war, and a British proposal to form a centralized Malayan Union in preparation for eventual independence, had activated the Malays politically. Most objected to the Union scheme as too favorable to the Chinese, and the British finally dropped it. The Communists penetrated the left-wing Malay Democratic Union and allied themselves with the pro-Indonesian Malay Nationalist Party against the British. But these alliances proved unstable; ethnic enmities were strong.

THE UPRISING

In March 1947, Loi Tak was finally exposed; he vanished with the Communist party's funds. Chin Peng, a long-standing hard-liner, replaced him. Although not a great strategist, he was one of the toughest and most indomitable of Communist leaders. By 1948, the party's position in the unions, and its power in general, seemed to be declining. Workers were less discontented than they had been as conditions improved, and the British were preparing new laws to curb the party's position in the unions. Chin Peng and many others were unhappy with the current line—perhaps wrongly, since some authorities hold that if continued it might yet have made Malaya ungovernable and ensured a Communist victory after the colony received independence. Unlike some other Communist parties, the Malayan Party welcomed the line broadcast by the Calcutta Conference.

Chin Peng had already consulted the Chinese Communists; in late 1947 Chou Enlai had endorsed armed struggle, but would not say whether the time was ripe for it in Malaya. In March 1948, influenced by Laurence Sharkey, the head of the Australian Communist Party, the Communists formally decided to prepare for a "people's revolutionary war," although their planning was confused. (There are indications that hard-liners had started reforming the guerrilla force shortly before this.) A British plan to restrict the party's labor activities apparently led to a decision to act in June, although the "Malayan People's Anti-British Army" had not yet completed mobilizing. The Soviets greeted the revolt with great enthusiasm; they gave it more attention and publicity than any other of the 1948 series.[7]

British intelligence in Malaya had not recovered from the war. Perhaps overconfident because of Loi Tak, it had concentrated on keeping track of Malay nationalist activities. The revolt was a surprise; and British forces were weak and poorly trained. The Communist strategy was to launch a series of strikes, and then, while avoiding British troops, drive the police and Europeans engaged in essential economic activities out of small towns and villages and from isolated places, forming "liberated areas." They hoped to eventually expand into the more thickly settled rural areas and build up their strength for full-scale battles with the British.

But the strikes, and the first wave of terrorism, misfired. The Europeans stayed put and the economy was not disrupted. The British declared a state of emergency and banned the Communist party. A special constabulary, mostly Malay, and a special jungle-trained unit, "Ferret Force," were hastily formed to harry the Communists and keep them off balance. The Communists were shaken by their initial failures; some observers hold that had the British brought in reinforcements sooner they might have crushed the revolt quickly. But the crisis for the Communists, if there was one, passed. Renaming their force the "Malayan Races Liberation Army," they prepared for a long struggle, reorganizing their supporting organization, the Min Yuen, along more efficient lines. The guerrillas concentrated on ambushing road traffic, and sometimes attacked trains. By conviction or coercion, they clearly dominated the Chinese community; they replaced their losses easily and could have put more men in the field had they had more weapons. During 1949 the Communists recruited some Malay guerrillas, who dominated a few villages. In 1950, the British were clearly losing the war. The Communists could not drive them into the sea, but if the British left the Communists would win.

VICTORY IN MALAYA

Early in 1950 the British decided to send more troops; they eventually had 40,000 soldiers and 45,000 police in Malaya. In March 1950 they created a new post, director of operations, to guide the war effort. The director, General Harold Briggs, decided on a bold new policy to cut the link between the Communists and the supporting population, give the people security against intimidation, and gradually win them over. It was a classic example of what was later called a "population security" strategy. The main element of his plan was to resettle the squatters in defended "New Villages" with clear titles to agricultural land and modern amenities. The rulers of the Malayan states had to be persuaded to allot land for this. Briggs streamlined the war effort and especially the mechanisms for coordinating the civil authorities, police and the military. The government encouraged the recently organized Malayan Chinese Association as a counterpole to the Communists in the Chinese community. It introduced a military draft and indefinite detention for suspects. In June 1951 it launched "Operation Starvation" to control the distribution of food and prevent any from reaching the guerrillas. The British went so far as to close all restaurants in contested areas and insist that rice be distributed only after it was already cooked.

By February 1952 some 400 New Villages were finished, and 400,000 people resettled. The New Villages were the scene of a decisive struggle. Each village was run by a Chinese-speaking British officer and some Chinese assistants, who were eventually to replace him. The special constabulary was to provide local defense until—and if—they could be replaced by "Home Guards" from the village itself. At first the New Villages were not under secure control. It has been estimated that only 10 percent of the Chinese in the New Villages were actively pro-Communist—but only 10 percent strongly opposed them; the struggle was for the allegiance of the remaining 80 percent. The guerrillas, their supplies threatened, had to attack the New Villages to disrupt the program and assert their domination over the population. But this led to battles on ground chosen by the British, and the Communists were repulsed; given the Reds' lack of heavy weapons it is hard to see how they could have succeeded. British intelligence improved.

Using captured Min Yuen members, the British introduced agents into the Communist organization, and their propaganda efforts (directed by Chinese) began to improve. In 1952 the Communists saw the heaviest losses of the war.

In 1952 Briggs was replaced by General Gerald Templer, who also became civilian High Commissioner. Templer's contribution to victory in Malaya was mainly in the civil and political area. Independence for the "Federation of Malaya" was promised. During 1952 elected village councils were introduced, and everyone born in Malaya received citizenship. The Rural and Industrial Development Authority was formed to promote the development of Malaya in general, for Malays were becoming jealous of the "rewards" being given the Chinese. It was vital for the British to avoid an outright communal conflict. That would defeat their aim of a viable free Malaya as much as an outright Communist victory—if it did not make the latter possible. A national education system and civil service, and a mixed-race "Federation Regiment," were formed. Shortly before Templer arrived, an alliance between the Malayan Chinese Association and the principal Malay group was created.

The Communists did not sit still. They had known for some time that their policies had been inadequate. In line with a change of policy decreed for all Asian Communist Parties, they had issued a new directive in October 1951, although it was not implemented for months. It repudiated terrorism as a mistake, and resolved to expand the Communists' mass base to win over the "medium bourgeoisie." Attacks on New Villages, economic targets, and civilians were stopped. The Communists had been operating in company-sized units; they now split up into platoons. They decided to form "fall back" positions in the deep interior and the Thai border area, and began building base camps in the unpoliced area of southern Thailand. The Communists had some support from local Chinese, and were able to smuggle some weapons into Malaya. They won over the Sum-Sums, a mixed Malay-Thai group living just inside Malaya, and renewed ties with the aborigines in the deep jungle. The aborigines had been totally ignored by everyone else; the Communists were the first civilized men to befriend them. The guerrillas started jungle gardens to supply their own food.

The British, fearing the development of a permanent enemy base in the mountain spine of Malaya, pursued them. Attempts to relocate the aborigines near the coast, like the Chinese squatters, failed disastrously; used to relatively cool mountain areas, they sickened and died in the hot lowlands. In 1953 the British built air-supplied jungle forts with clinics to win over the aborigines, and began spraying the guerrilla's farm plots with poison.

The Thais agreed to allow pursuit operations across the border. During 1953 the British began eating away at the guerrilla organization. Some Communists who had surrendered were formed into a special force and used to hunt their ex-comrades. In 1955 the number of armed Communists, which had peaked at 8,000 in 1951, fell to 3,000 men. An attempt by the Malayan prime minister to negotiate peace failed.

Malaya became independent in 1957. The war went on, well enough so that in July 1960 the "emergency," declared twelve years earlier was ended. Chin Peng hung on with a few hundred men in the Thai border area, launching an occasional raid and hoping for a catastrophe that would let him intervene.[8]

The British success in Malaya greatly influenced the development of "counterinsurgency" techniques elsewhere, although some of their ideas had been independently paralleled in the Philippines. A distinct British pattern for counterinsurgency developed, which had a major but uneven impact on American thinking. The British emphasized the need of civil-military coordination during an insurrection, with the civil government maintaining domination and the rule of law. This did not mean interpretations of civil liberties that would suit contemporary American sensibilities; in fact far-reaching powers of preventive detention were necessary, along with extreme measures of gun control. At least in theory, in Malaya, the mere unauthorized possession of *ammunition* was a capital crime! But the legal system continued to function. Torture—which the French had sometimes used in Indochina and were to employ freely in Algeria—was ruled out. Prisoners were not usually killed, despite strong provocation, for the enemy invariably killed captured British and Gurkha soldiers.

The true target, the British stressed, was not the guerrilla armed force but its supporters in the population and their links with the guerrillas. The British put great emphasis on intelligence, and much less on purely military techniques and firepower. Artillery and air strikes were of little use in Malaya. Victory was achieved by concentrating the population under tight control in defended villages, combined with "civic action" and, almost as important, inserting agents into the enemy organization. In the British strategy, some of the enemy (not just the undecided) most be won over; in the ideal final stage of a war they would help hunt the guerrillas.

The British themselves repeated this pattern, almost exactly, against non-Communist rebels in Kenya, and used elements of it, generally speaking with less success, in Cyprus, South Arabia, and Northern Ireland, and, as foreign advisers, in the Dhofar area of Oman. The Americans, without understanding them too well, tried some of the British methods in different circumstances in Vietnam. But their attempt to concentrate the peasants into "strategic hamlets" was a disaster. In truth, the situation in Malaya was in some ways a peculiar one, not readily comparable to any other. The government was an honest and efficient colonial administration, respected by the people it ruled. Nationalist sentiment was weak. The guerrillas had been based on a readily identifiable minority of the population. The squatters were not deeply rooted peasants and were easily transplanted in a rich country with much unused land. Neither land reform nor independence were crucial issues. The Communist appeal was based on a fusion of Chinese nationalism, excited by Japanese aggression, and a belief in the myth that the Soviet Union had modernized itself with fantastic speed and that that feat could be quickly duplicated by other Communist countries. The Communists' supporters cared little about Malaya and had no violent hatred of the West. They disliked Europeans, but liked Malays and Indians even less. Few in number, the Communists lacked heavy weapons; even Thailand was not an "active sanctuary" comparable to that enjoyed by the Communists in the Indochina Wars. The war had never been truly intense; government and civilian losses were under 10,000 in twelve years. The Malayan war did have peculiar difficulties of its own—particularly preventing it from turning into a racial war between Malays and Chinese. But in most ways it was a smaller and more manageable conflict than most of the other revolutionary struggles that developed in the post-World War II era. The truly praiseworthy achievement of the British and their allies in Malaya was not a military one but their success in promoting political development—a success perhaps overlooked because it took place within a colonial framework and did not fit too well with contemporary neurotic obsessions about the evils of imperialism. Curiously, many "anti-imperialist" Americans, despite many years in which to assimilate British, and other, experiences, failed to grasp a point the British understood almost instinctively—that communism in a revolutionary situation had to be countered not just by military force but by developing institutions and programs to handle the problems which it fed on.[9]

THE PHILIPPINES

In the Philippines, wartime resistance and a long heritage of peasant unrest made for a formidable Communist threat in 1948, a threat never fully defeated.

Filipino peasants, especially on the main island of Luzon, were largely tenants who had long suffered from an oppressive relationship with their landlords. Although the country had a formally democratic government, political parties were personal cliques or factions of the upper class. They either sided with the landlords or had little interest in rural matters. For many years the Communists had little interest in the countryside either; they were a city party and concentrated, unsuccessfully, on gaining control of the unions. The Communist route to the countryside was a peculiar one. Their Socialist competitors were far more interested in peasant problems, and had some success in organizing the culturally peculiar Pampanga-speakers of central Luzon, who, although not worse off economically than their fellows elsewhere, had been more touched by modern developments and were unusually discontented. In the late 1930s, the Communists persuaded the Socialists to fuse with them. Ex-Socialist leaders, notably Luis Taruc, remained prominent in the united party and formed its right wing, and its link to the peasants.

In 1941–1942 the Communists began resistance to the Japanese. Equipping themselves with weapons abandoned on the retreat to Bataan, or salvaged from the battlefields there, and helped by some Chinese Communist veterans, they created the "Hukbalahap," the "People's Anti-Japanese Army," and a support organization, the Barrio United Defense Corps. The Huks built a strong position in central Luzon, following policies like those of the Chinese Communists at the same time. They redistributed land owned by collaborators or landlords who had fled Huk-held areas, but left "patriotic" landlords alone, while reducing their share of the crop. Rising to an armed strength perhaps as high as 10,000, the Huks, unlike the MPAJA or the Vietminh, fought hard against the Japanese. In expanding they clashed with other American-controlled units in early 1944. The Huks remained only a relatively large segment of the resistance and never dominated it. For a time in 1944 they may have planned to set up their own Philippine government, but they wisely dropped the idea.

MacArthur's command distrusted the Huks and did not give them any of the supplies brought to Luzon by submarine. The returning Americans followed a confused policy toward the Huks. They supported the Philippine government's refusal to accept Huk-appointed government officials, and arrested Taruc and three other Huk leaders for unauthorized killings of alleged collaborators. But the Huk leaders were released after the war ended; and while some Huk units were disarmed, most were not—indeed most Filipino guerrillas were not disarmed, with unfortunate consequences for law and order. The Huks managed to get more weapons from careless Americans.[10] In July 1946 the Philippines became independent; the Huk problem seemed, for a while, to be just another of a sea of domestic Filipino woes. The Islands had been utterly devastated by the war and economic recovery took many years. Many observers felt that psychologically the Filipinos never recovered from World War II; national cohesion and self-discipline were never again what they had been.

REBELLION

After the war ended, the Communists failed to gain control of the labor movement, but organized a Huk veterans association and a National Peasants Union into a front organization, the "Democratic Alliance." They allied themselves with the Nationalist Party in the 1946 presidential election; but the Liberal candidate, Manuel Roxas, won. The Democratic Alliance won several congressional seats in central Luzon, but the government refused to seat them, claiming that they had won through fraud. But the government at least matched the Communists in that vice. Roxas's government was corrupt and he was widely, although probably wrongly, suspected of having been a collaborator during the war. The government harassed ex-Huks and in March 1948 finally outlawed the Huk organization and the National Peasants Union, but not the Communist party. Roxas's death was followed by peace attempts; President Elpidio Quirino offered an amnesty and negotiations.

The party leadership had long been split between moderates and those who favored a militant line. The Zhdanov line gave the latter group their head, and in May 1948 they decided to launch an armed struggle. Few Huks accepted the amnesty; most were bitter at the government's injustices and the lack of land reform. In August 1948 the negotiations ended, and the Huks formally took up arms in their old stronghold in central Luzon.

The Communists' popular appeal was squarely based on the land issue and their resistance record. Most Huks were tenant farmers who paid half their harvest to their landlords and were hopelessly in debt. Few Huks were well-indoctrinated Communists. The Huks were generally not anti-American; and nationalism was not an issue in the Philippines. Like their Malayan counterparts, the Huks lacked an outside sanctuary and ready access to weapons. Their only known help from the outside came from some Chinese agents and smuggled funds, and some American servicemen who stole arms for them. That channel of help was ultimately turned against the Huks when an American spy penetrated one of the Huks' ten regional commands.

The Quirino administration, which won reelection by ballot stuffing in 1949, proved utterly ineffectual. Widely unpopular, it at first did not take the Huks very seriously. The army, poorly equipped and led, expended its strength on futile large-scale sweeps that the Huks easily evaded. The army and police mistreated civilians; looting and worse crimes were common. Many people turned to the Huks when villages were burned or women raped. The Huks developed an excellent intelligence system, penetrating the American Embassy and military advisory group.

MAGSAYSAY AND THE DEFEAT OF THE HUKS

By 1950 the Huks were operating on the outskirts of Manila, but their actions against cities and army camps finally aroused the government. Quirino was jolted into seeing the need for reform, if only in the military effort, while the Americans recognized the disastrous situation in their ex-colony. In July 1950 Quirino appointed the chairman of the Congressional National Defense Committee, Ramon Magsaysay, as secretary of defense. Magsaysay had been a successful guerrilla commander during World War II, and was well aware of the grievances of the peasants. A dynamic, popular leader, he launched an imaginative new effort. He was helped by a close friend, Colonel Edward Lansdale, who was then serving with the Central Intelligence Agency (CIA). (Lansdale was inevitably, but falsely, credited with being the "mastermind" behind Magsaysay.) The Filipinos in fact owed little to American advice. Although they profited from American military aid, they rightly ignored the American Military Advisory Group's advice as worthless save in purely technical matters.

Magsaysay quickly reformed the military. The constabulary was integrated with the army, while the worst soldiers were discharged and the mistreatment of civilians ended. The army was expanded. It had already been reformed into independently operating battalion combat teams; each assigned its own zone of control. Special scout ranger squads of volunteers were attached to each battalion to attack small groups of Huks or guide bigger units when needed. A special army unit, Force X, operated as disguised Huks. The military improved its intelligence system and created a system of rewards for surrendered weapons and captured Huks. It formed a Civil Affairs office to improve relations with civilians. The army established schools and assigned army lawyers to represent peasants in the courts. To encourage Huks to give up, Magsaysay founded an Economic Development Corporation to resettle surrendered Huks on unoccupied land on the southern island of Mindinao. The scheme was so popular that some people pretended to be Huks to take advantage of it.

Shortly after he took office, Magsaysay brought off a major coup. Curiously, while indulging in all sorts of petty persecution of pro-Huk individuals and innocent people, the government did not outlaw the Communist party until late 1950. Magsaysay's contacts with a disaffected Politburo member provided a lead to the Politburo's whereabouts. It was captured on October 18, 1950, along with many valuable documents, which among other things revealed ambitious plans for rapid expansion and victory by May 1952. Taruc termed this a "crushing blow." Plans for an uprising in Manila coordinated with an assault from the outside were ruined. The capture of the Politburo and the fighting of 1951 proved the military turning point of the war. Its political turning point was the election of November 1951. Magsaysay and a National Movement for Free Elections, firmly backed by the American Embassy, prevented Quirino from fixing the elections as he had in 1949. Magsaysay used soldiers to protect political meetings from disruption.

By late 1951 the Communists saw that they were no longer winning, and had to concentrate on preserving their existing strength. During 1952, the Huks had to move their base from central Luzon to the distant and thinly populated Sierra Madre mountains. Rapidly losing popular support, they increased the use of terror; but this cost them more popular sympathy. Like the government before Magsaysay arrived, they were reduced to flailing away aimlessly, and their numbers rapidly fell. Their strength, which had peaked at 12,800 armed men in 1950, fell to 4,000 in late 1952. The ex-Socialists in the Communist party were increasingly disaffected. Taruc had long been pessimistic about the Huks' prospects. Even in 1950 he had warned that no real revolutionary situation existed outside central and southern Luzon, and that the plan to win in two years was overoptimistic. He favored seeking a broad united front with the opposition Nationalist party, arguing that only the development of a split in the ruling class would enable the relatively small and weakly armed Huks to triumph. Although these ideas were probably quite compatible with the Soviet line after 1951, the party rejected them, and rivals undercut Taruc's authority. Taruc became increasingly disaffected in 1952–1953 and began trying to negotiate a peace with the government.

There was a last crisis in 1953. The incumbent Liberals planned to rig the November presidential election; but Magsaysay broke with them to become the Nationalist candidate for president. Realizing that if the Liberals' scheme succeeded, all faith in the political system might be destroyed, the Americans pulled out all the stops in both covert and open efforts to secure a fair election. Since Magsaysay was tremendously popular, this guaranteed his victory. The Huk organization soon broke down; Taruc and his supporters gave up in 1954. The war did not end, but trailed off. The Huk remnants, although feuding among themselves, were deeply embedded in part of central Luzon. They ultimately degenerated into a Mafia-like organized crime group. When a Communist guerrilla force was revived many years later, it had to be built from the ground up.[11]

For Magsaysay's victory had not been conclusive. Although he had made major changes, there had been no decisive reform of land tenure or the Filipino political system. The drive for change was aborted by Magsaysay's tragic death in a plane crash in 1957. The land issue, feuding and corruption in the political elite, and extremely rapid population growth simmered on. The situation slowly degenerated, culminating in the disastrous kleptocratic tyranny of Ferdinand Marcos. The Communist party, which had nearly vanished at one point, revived. In the late 1960s a new guerrilla force took the field, while Moslems on Mindanao revolted. The anti-Communist war had to be fought all over again, this time in a new and bloodier form. Only the belated revolution of 1986 saved the Philippines from ruin.

BURMA

Strategically, Burma was the least important of the Southeast Asian countries wracked by rebellion in 1948. The Soviets showed less enthusiasm for the Burmese revolt than the others. Yet the Burmese Communists came far closer to winning than their comrades in Indonesia, Malaya and the Philippines—so close that it was a fluke that Burma did not go Communist.

Burma suffered greatly during World War II. Most active Burmese nationalists, although strongly leftist, had welcomed the Japanese invasion and participated in the government and army formed under Japanese auspices. The nucleus of the Burmese Communist Party, which may not have been formally organized until July 1945, was one of the few Burmese groups to back the Allies. In 1944–1945, the groups that had backed Japan, disillusioned with their new masters and aware that the Allies were winning, joined an underground organization, the "Anti-Fascist People's Freedom League" (AFPFL), that included the Communists. When the British broke into central Burma, General Aung San took his Burmese National Army over to the British. An uneasy truce between the nationalists and the British lasted until the war ended.

The British government, ignoring Admiral Mountbatten's advice, at first intended to maintain a modified form of the prewar administration for a prolonged period before granting Burma its independence. But in January 1947, after much argument, and facing threats of rebellion by the AFPFL, which had maintained an army called the People's Volunteer Organization (PVO), Britain agreed to early independence under an AFPFL government.

Although Burma recovered quickly from the war and was prosperous for an underdeveloped country—it was fertile and not densely populated—the new government faced formidable challenges. The Burmese proper formed only 70 percent of the population. Their relations with the numerous minority nationalities, of whom the Karens were the most important, had never been good and had become worse during the war. Pro-Japanese Burmese troops had fought, and sometimes massacred the minorities, who had remained loyal to Britain. The Burmese peasants had been in thrall to Indian moneylenders and absentee landlords before the war; although most of the Indians had fled from the Japanese, the peasants feared their return, and the legal status of their land tenure was unsettled. The government lacked Burmese personnel with administrative and technical experience; British civil servants did not want to stay and the Burmese did not want them. There was a public atmosphere of utopianism and unreality. The AFPFL was dominated by extreme left-wing socialists committed to a program of nationalization and welfare that would have been hard to execute even in a rich advanced country. And in July 1947 the Burmese nationalist leadership was practically destroyed. The able and popular Aung San and his leading colleagues were murdered in a crazed coup attempt launched by their rightist rival U Saw. Aung San had had relatively good relations with the minority nationalities and had kept the potentially mutinous PVO in line.[12] When Burma became independent on January 4, 1948, the government faced a formidable threat of rebellion.

In the turmoil of the postwar period the Communist party had gained great strength working within the AFPFL coalition. For a time the Communist leader, Than Tun, was the secretary of the AFPFL and the All-Burma Peasant Union. But personal rivalries among the Communist leaders split the party. A small leftist minority broke off, forming a "national Communist" group, the Communist Party of Burma, nicknamed the "Red Flags." (The orthodox Soviet-line Burma Communist Party was called the "White Flags." Henceforth references to the Burmese Communists refer to these Stalinists unless otherwise specified.) The "Red Flags" began a revolt in the Irrawaddy Delta area in July 1946, using guerrilla tactics. Although the government could not destroy them, the "Red Flags" seemed only a nuisance. Aung San defeated a formidable bid by Than Tun for the leadership of the whole AFPFL; the "White Flags" were shoved out of the AFPFL in October 1946. Although badly beaten in the elections of 1947, the Communists continued to seek power through political maneuver. They tried to come to terms with the AFPFL after Aung San's murder, persisting in this policy until October 1947.

UPRISING AND DISINTEGRATION

As in Indonesia, the Zhdanov line, transmitted primarily through the Indian Communist Party and the Indian-Burmese Communist leader Goshal, had a particularly dramatic impact. The party suddenly reversed its position, denouncing the government for concluding a treaty with Britain. In December 1947 Goshal expounded the Zhdanov line, denouncing the Communists' earlier "opportunist" and "reformist" line and their membership of the AFPFL. He called for preparation for a seizure of power, attacking the arrangements for Burmese independence as phony. The Communists rejected the AFPFL's appeals for a revived coalition and launched a revolt at the end of March 1948.[13]

They did not plan a guerrilla war; they hoped for a quick victory through a general uprising. The government got advance warning of their plans from Thein Pe, a dissident moderate Communist, and the intended seizure of Rangoon misfired. The government seemed about to crush the revolt. But then more rebellions broke out. Part of the PVO, grumbling about the government's terms for disbanding the organization, revolted, and was joined by part of the army. The PVO rebels were close to the Communists ideologically and often worked closely with them. The Karens, who occupied strategic positions fairly close to Rangoon, also revolted, provoked by atrocities committed by government troops. A situation of indescribable confusion developed; by 1949 at least five separate groups were in revolt. But the Burmese people, undergoing a Buddhist revival, supported the AFPFL government. The Communists tried to win over peasants in the areas they held, by redistributing land and farm equipment and abrogating debts, but they struck no real roots in the countryside. The government had an equally radical reform program. Prime Minister U Nu struck many Westerners as a woolly minded character, but he was very popular and a real leader. His views were far to the left, although unlike most Burmese socialists, he was not a Marxist. But he was firmly devoted to liberty, the Buddhist religion and Burma's independence. He was not personally to blame for the mistreatment of the minorities. Despite the rhetoric of his frequent appeals to the rebels, he had no use for the idea that there were "no enemies to the left," and saw the Communists as foreign puppets. Burma, which got little help from the outside, was saved by his steely nerved determination to prevail.

The war for Burma was fought by small forces. The rebel factions in all mustered perhaps 20,000 men; the 7,000 Karens were the strongest force in the field, both Communist groups together mustering only 5,000 men.

For a time the government may have had no more than a thousand reliable troops, although its tiny air force enabled it to track enemy movements and strafing attacks made rebel concentrations costly. It survived, barely, because of the divisions of its enemies. Some PVO men hated the Karens so much that the latter's rebellion caused them to defect to the government. Than Tun was no Ho Chi Minh and failed to form a stable united front among the rebels; in any case many Karen leaders were Christians and distrusted the Communists even more than they distrusted other Burmese. The Communists had never recruited much among the non-Burmese. The "Red Flags" only came to terms with the orthodox Communists in 1952, when the tide had turned.

In February 1949 the government hit bottom. With the Karens attacking Rangoon, most of the cabinet favored surrendering to the Communists, presumably because they were at least fellow Burmese. U Nu overruled them, and by a narrow margin the Karens were defeated. The government then took the offensive. It retook Mandalay, the second biggest city, and the oil fields, gaining in strength. In February 1950 the Communists and the PVO formed a "People's Democratic Front" government at Prome. But some of the PVO, resenting Communist domination, defected to the Rangoon government. In May the government retook Prome; more PVO men gave up. Only in 1950 did the Communists turn fully to orthodox guerrilla tactics. Some cadres went to China for training, and the Communists tried to shift their base to the area along the Chinese border. (Their earlier center of strength in central and southern Burma had been too far from the frontier to get Chinese help, although the new Chinese Embassy in Rangoon had secretly aided them.) The Communists presumably hoped to duplicate the Vietminh's base area in Tonkin. But the minorities in the frontier region would not cooperate and the government's pursuit was relentless. In 1951 the government broke the back of the rebellions, although some Karens fought on until 1964 and the Communists carried on, on a small scale, for decades. In the mid-1960s, having taken the Chinese side in the Soviet-Chinese conflict, they tried again to form a base near the frontier with Chinese help. But they were smashed. Than Tun was killed by one of his own men.[14]

In its later operations the Burmese government was hampered by one of the stupidest covert actions carried out by the U.S. government during the Cold War. In 1949–1950 some 2,500 Chinese Nationalist troops had fled into Burma, where they refused to disarm. During the Korean War they were reinforced by more refugees from China and troops airlifted from Taiwan; ultimately they reached a strength of 12,000 men. Aided and nominally supervised by the CIA, they reportedly invaded the Chinese province of

Yunnan in 1951 and again in 1952. Both attacks were repulsed—indeed there is some doubt about whether they were ever carried out! The effort did not divert Chinese forces from Korea. The Nationalists then settled down as a sort of warlord enclave and took up the more profitable business of raising opium. The Burmese—who still considered themselves "neutral" in the Cold War—were furious at the Nationalists' activities and terrified that the Chinese Communists would use them as an excuse to attack Burma or annex the frontier area, which was the subject of a long-standing territorial dispute. They diverted major forces to deal with the Nationalists, without success. The affair embittered Burmese-American relations. The Burmese only slowly and painfully obtained the departure of the Chinese in the 1950s, and 1960s; some never left.[15]

Burma was a spectacular demonstration of the fragility of many postcolonial states. It was an early example of a colony gaining its independence relatively peacefully, only to collapse into chaos. The Communists came very close to victory. Had the AFPFL government been toppled, even by a non-Communist group, the "Moscow" Communists' central position, tighter organization and Burmese composition would have enabled them to come out on top in the scramble for power. The split in the Communist party, Than Tun's inability to form a stable united front, the courage of U Nu and the government's narrow success in holding Rangoon, which was not only the capital but the only real link to the outside world, saved Burma from Communist rule. But the country never really recovered from—or even put down—the rebellions of 1948. Even in the 1970s the government effectively controlled only 60 percent of Burma. The rebellions and the AFPFL government's unrealistic economic policies damaged the economy and the government degenerated into a military dictatorship. Burma never became a Soviet or Chinese satellite, but the Communist powers could take some satisfaction from the results. For very little expense or effort they had helped wreck a potentially prosperous non-Communist country.

By 1954 the first phase of the struggle for Southeast Asia seemed to have ended in a draw. In retrospect, the turning point in the fight for the region came in 1950 or 1951; the policies or trends that led to victory or defeat in each country (except Indonesia) were firmly fixed in those years. At first sight, the struggle seemed to have ended, by mid-1954, in a clear dividing line cutting across Southeast Asia such as already existed in Europe and Northeast Asia. But in fact the result was far from stable. The greatest opportunities for the Indonesian Communists, and the bloodiest war for Indochina, still lay ahead.

Still, the specter of "Maoist" guerrilla warfare should have been dispelled by the events of 1948–1954. It is a curious fact that when the guerrilla struggles were most intense, in the late 1940s and early 1950s, they attracted little attention. Then the Western world had bigger troubles to deal with; and the initial Communist aspirations in the area were largely foiled with only a comparatively small American involvement save in Indochina. Even after 1949, Southeast Asia was a secondary theater for the Americans in the Cold War. Experts such as General Samuel B. Griffith aroused only modest public and official interest in guerrilla war in the early 1950s. The peak of excitement about such matters came in the 1960s, long after the specter of the invincibility of the revolutionary guerrilla should have disappeared. In a further "paradox" a tendency to exaggerate the threat of revolutionary guerrilla warfare in a strategic sense was accompanied by a tendency to underestimate the tactical difficulties of fighting guerrillas in an unfavorable political situation. Thinking about the subject was conditioned by the well-publicized campaigns in Malaya, the Philippines and the Greek Civil War. Yet none of these examples was really typical. By the rather dismal standards of most of the world, even the Greek and Philippine governments of the late 1940s were relatively efficient and responsible. In none of these cases were the Communists the generally accepted representatives of nationalism; only the Greek Communists had the advantage of an active sanctuary like that enjoyed by the Vietminh. They faced able leaders, and in the case of the Philippines, a great national hero. The experiences of those countries were of uncertain value for understanding other struggles.[16]

4

The Struggle for Indonesia, II

During the 1960s, any appearance of approximate stability in Southeast Asia disappeared, to be replaced by fears that indirect Chinese aggression, taking the form of Maoist-type guerrilla warfare, was about to submerge the area, and by the belief that the most important target was Vietnam. Defeating guerrilla-style "wars of national liberation" was seen as the key to foiling what was perceived as a *Chinese* threat; for the Soviets, in this period, were widely regarded as "moderates" compared to the "Stalinist" Chinese leaders. (The stupidity of Western, and especially American, leaders in this era is shown by the fact that they publicly accepted and repeated the Communists' own propagandistic designation of their efforts.) The traumatic experience of the Second Indochina War led Americans, in particular (whatever their views on the war), to become fixated on the idea that Vietnam was the main theater of the struggle for Southeast Asia. They eventually realized that North Vietnam was not, as many first supposed, just a Chinese satellite. But it was less often recognized that these other concepts, too, were scarcely even half-truths. The Soviets remained a major factor in Southeast Asia. They too backed "wars of national liberation," even while China was semiparalyzed by the loss of Soviet aid and its internal conflicts. The islands, not the mainland, remained the most important area of Southeast Asia. In the key struggle for Indonesia, Maoist-type guerrilla war was irrelevant. Instead, Soviet-style policies of alliances with radical, anti-Western nationalist fanatics came close to winning an enormous victory, only to fail at the last minute and by a tiny margin. The increasingly acute conflict between the USSR and China, and their general policies toward the world, impinged critically on the struggle for Southeast Asia, and Indonesia in particular.

SOVIET AND CHINESE POLICIES AND CONFLICTS

Contrary to what is often said, Stalin never considered all the "neutralist" ex-colonial countries merely Western puppets; nevertheless, he had generally not considered them useful, or indeed all that important in his scheme of things. Nikita Khrushchev followed a more flexible policy which, however, was firmly based on older Communist ideas. While envisaging Communist revolutions in the backward countries, Lenin had also pursued alliances with non-Communist nationalist regimes against the West. Soviet policies toward the backward countries alternated between periods of emphasis on local Communists, and periods when the stress was on alliances with non-Communists against the West; Khrushchev's reign marked the ascendancy of the latter tendency. By the time Khrushchev came to power in the mid-1950s, there did not seem to be many revolutionary opportunities for Communists, in the short run, in any case. The revolutionary situations generated by World War II and the first wave of decolonization had largely spent themselves, and the Western powers were alert and hostile to overt Communist actions.

The Soviets not only devoted some effort, including foreign aid, to influencing the genuine neutralist countries, such as Nehru's India, but pursued active alliances with established regimes whose purported "neutralism" actually disguised violent hostility to the West and those countries friendly to it. This group included many of the Arab countries, notably Egypt and Syria, and later (after the 1958 revolution) Iraq and also Indonesia. The Soviets' relations with many of these countries were complicated and uneasy, for, while they disliked the West, they often distrusted the Soviets too. The Arab governments especially were often at odds with each other, and often persecuted the local Communists, while, at least for brief intervals, there seemed to be chances that the Communists in Syria and Iraq might take power. (In Indonesia, as we shall see, things seemed to be simpler.) It was thus hard for the Soviets to maintain friendly relations with all their potential allies. The Soviets might turn a blind eye to the persecution of Communists, but they still resented it. And Khrushchev never ruled out exploiting opportunities for actual Communist seizures of power.

The Soviets used terms such as "national liberation struggle" and "wars of national liberation" to cover *both* violent efforts by non-Communist elements against the West *and* attempts to create Communist regimes. And the Soviets even envisaged the possibility of quietly drawing some of the more radical anti-Western pseudoneutralist countries fully into the Soviet orbit, and gradually transforming them into orthodox Communist regimes by a process of conversion rather than revolution in the conventional sense. In the late 1950s Soviet theoreticians devised a special transitional form of regime they called "national democracy" to cover this possibility. (This paralleled vague theorizing about a "peaceful road to socialism" for some of the advanced countries.) Castro's Cuba was briefly classified as a "national democracy," but Castro jumped over to the Soviet side too quickly to stay in that category long. There is reason to think that the Soviets had Indonesia foremost in mind when they devised it.[1]

The Chinese never entirely approved of Khrushchev's views in such matters. (It should be emphasized, here, that the author does not wish to suggest that the Soviet-Chinese conflict was due simply to disagreements over strategy and relations with the West, a simplistic view quite common, however, in the 1960s.) In the mid-1950s the Chinese were at least as ready as the Soviets to cultivate Nehru and other neutralists—diplomatically—but they resented the Soviets granting them much aid. After November 1957, the Chinese were far more optimistic about world events moving in favor of the Communist side; it is possible that the elaborate bluff Khrushchev ran about Soviet strength after Sputnik took them in as well as the West. As Soviet-Chinese relations worsened, the Chinese professed greater nonchalance about both local wars and nuclear war than the Soviets. They seemed to consider a Third World War more likely than the Soviets did, and were readier to back "armed struggle" policies in the backward countries—although they were not necessarily more reckless than the Soviets in their day-to-day policies, as many Westerners supposed during the early and mid-1960s. They were quite contemptuous of Soviet talk about "national democracy"—although, as we shall see, they were not averse to exploiting the possibility it categorized.

As the Soviet-Chinese alliance completely collapsed, the Chinese behaved in a way that convinced many Westerners that they, not the Soviets, were the big threat to the rest of the world—although the common supposition of the 1960s that the Chinese were "worse" than the Soviets probably owed as much to wishful thinking about the latter as to Westerners being overimpressed by the Chinese threat. The immediate result of the Soviet-Chinese conflict was not China's coming to terms with the United States—as would have been the case had the traditional logic of the balance of power ruled—but a state of three-cornered Cold War, with China at odds with both "superpowers" at once, which lasted until the early 1970s.

At first, the world Communist movement seemed to have fissioned down the middle; the Chinese seemed to gain the support of almost all of the Asian Communist parties, and some in other parts of the world. It was not yet apparent that the arrogance and ineptitude of the Chinese would soon cost them their position. By 1970 most Asian Communist parties would return to being pro-Soviet or, like the Japanese, become fully independent.

The Chinese did back their talk of armed struggle during the middle and late 1960s. They tried to aid all the Communist revolutionary efforts in Asia and some non-Communist efforts. They energetically interfered in the newly independent African nations, with a particular emphasis on the Congo (Zaire) and several countries neighboring it. They gained some influence in Tanzania and Mozambique, but their clumsy efforts to overthrow other governments merely alienated most Africans. They tried to revive the Communist struggle in Burma, and develop another Vietnam-style conflict in Thailand, but failed there too.

For a time, they seemed to successfully compete with the Soviets for influence in Vietnam itself, and they formed an apparently firm alliance with Indonesia, even as the local Communists there seemed to be about to take power. To President Johnson, as he made the most crucial decisions on American involvement in Indochina, North Vietnam's actions, whoever sponsored them, seemed to combine with those of the Chinese-Indonesian alliance, to put non-Communist Southeast Asia in the grip of closing pincers.[2] Whether or not he was right in seeing what was happening as a large-scale strategic design is unclear, but events in Indonesia were important enough. How Indonesia drifted, first into the Soviet, then into the Chinese orbit, and out again is the subject of the rest of this chapter.

INDONESIA IN THE 1950S

Despite their disastrous failure in 1948, Indonesia's Communists made a startling recovery in the early 1950s. Although richer in resources than most underdeveloped countries, Indonesia was badly divided and poorly run. The Dutch promotion of federalism during their attempt to reconquer Indonesia discredited that concept; an extremely centralized structure was imposed on a country to which it was unsuited. There was tremendous inflation and bitter hostility toward the Dutch and the Chinese, who dominated the economy. Heavily overpopulated Java, which dominated the central government, exploited the increasingly unhappy outer islands, which generated most of the country's exports and revenue. The Javanese were unable or unwilling to move to the thinly peopled outer islands, and

Java was so densely populated that there was no way to give the large landless element land. Indonesia was even more dependent than it had been under the Dutch on the export of a few raw materials, notably tin and rubber, whose prices fluctuated wildly. The government and armed forces were swollen and inefficient, and fanatical Moslem terrorists were only gradually subdued. The non-Communist political parties had a weak popular base, and Indonesia suffered from what might—charitably—be described as poor leadership. President Sukarno was a noisy, charismatic demagogue. Although immensely popular he had little interest in domestic affairs. The Communist approach to power would depend, to a great extent, on Sukarno's character, or lack of it. Behind the facade of "progressive democrat" and charming rogue he often presented, he was a power-hungry chauvinist who hated democracy and the West. In 1960, in a typically verbose self-revelation, he remarked, "I belong to the group of people who are bound in spiritual longing by the romanticism of revolution. I am inspired by it, I am fascinated by it, I am completely absorbed by it, I am crazed, I am obsessed by the romanticism of revolution."[3] The wretched Indonesians had to listen to this sort of thing for twenty years.

The Indonesian Communists had taken full advantage of Stalin's change in line allowing a resumption of united fronts with nationalists to ally themselves with Sukarno. In truth, armed struggle of the kind waged elsewhere was not possible anyway. Maoist-type guerrilla war was irrelevant in Indonesia. The Communists' base of support lay in Java, which had a good transportation network and was firmly under the thumb of the government and army. Guerrilla warfare had been just possible, on Java, against the small Dutch occupying forces; it was not a practical way to overturn an *Indonesian* government.

D. N. Aidit, the dynamic new Communist leader, built a large, legal party emphasizing broad appeals and nationalism, and the support of Sukarno. Sukarno, in turn, saw the Communists as a counterweight to his rivals in the moderate democratic parties, the Socialists and the Masjumi (a moderate, modernist Moslem group), and to the army. The Communists took over the national labor federation and built a strong popular following, especially in eastern and central Java, appealing especially to white-collar workers, intelligentsia and the "abangan"—the element of the Javanese peasantry which was landless and had mixed its belief in Islam with animist and Hindu ideas.[4]

The CIA subsidized the Masjumi, but that and aid to Sukarno's government failed to prevent Indonesia's drifting toward the Soviet bloc. During 1956, Sukarno became friendlier to the Communist side in the Cold War;

in November he decided to introduce what he called "Guided Democracy" into Indonesia. A "national council" would replace the elected parliament as the nominal source of power, and the effective role of the non-Communist parties would be ended. "Guided Democracy" also meant an increase in Javanese domination. Non-Javanese and moderate elements were driven out of the government and toward open rebellion. During 1956, and using Czechoslovakia as a cover, as they had with Nasser's Egypt, the Soviets made an arms deal with Indonesia, which became a major recipient of Soviet weapons and economic aid. Indonesia, not Indochina, was the main focus of Soviet aid and attention in Southeast Asia until the mid-1960s, receiving more Soviet help than any other underdeveloped land except Egypt.

Sukarno then moved against the Dutch, who still controlled West New Guinea. The Indonesians had always insisted that this area—"West Irian"—rightfully belonged to them, although its people were not Indonesians and showed no desire for Indonesian rule. And West New Guinea was likely to be an economic burden to anybody who held it. The demand for West Irian, however, was very popular in Indonesia and the Communist powers strongly backed the Indonesian claim. In late 1956, when the Dutch again refused to give up West New Guinea, Sukarno confiscated all Dutch property in Indonesia and expelled all of the Dutch and most of the Eurasians from the country. The nationalized property was put in the army's care; as in Nasser's Egypt, "socialism" in Indonesia meant inefficient control of the economy by soldiers.

During 1957, rebellion began to sputter in the outer islands. In February 1958 military units there openly revolted and supported attempts by the Socialists and the Masjumi to set up an alternate government. The rebels' objective was not secession, but to force the central government to take a more moderate course, fairer to the outer islands. Although the Americans had not instigated it, the movement had American support.

The Eisenhower administration had long been unhappy with events in Indonesia; it was well aware that "Guided Democracy" was, as Secretary of State Dulles suggested, a nice-sounding name for what would end up as Communist despotism. In December 1957 it had resolved to support a revolt against Sukarno, if one developed. Some in the administration even contemplated open U.S. military intervention.

But it was slow to act when a revolt actually started. The CIA and the British aided the rebels and even provided American-piloted planes to support them—with embarrassing results when an American pilot was shot down and captured. Western aid was too little and too late, and the rebels were badly outnumbered and seem to have lacked the will to fight. The

Soviets, by contrast, backed Sukarno promptly and decisively. Since Indonesian pilots were not yet fully trained, Czech instructors flew the MIG jet fighters sent to equip the Indonesian Air Force. They quickly won air superiority. The main rebel forces were soon beaten, although resistance lasted in some areas until 1961. The United States hastily reversed its policy in May 1958. It tried to mend fences with Sukarno, and let him buy American military equipment. The American ambassador in Djakarta, Howard P. Jones took a surprisingly friendly view of Sukarno, and tried hard for the next seven years to win his friendship.[5] But this policy was a complete failure.

As in its support of a coup attempt in Syria in 1956, the CIA effort had backfired; it had helped Sukarno discredit the remaining moderates. Since some of their members had taken part in the rebellion, the Socialists and the Masjumi were restricted, and then, in 1961, dissolved. Parliament became a puppet organization. The tragicomedy of Indonesian politics was reduced to a triangle composed of Sukarno, the Communists and the army. Sukarno still aimed to maintain his personal dictatorship, and kept the Communists out of decision-making positions. He played the army and the party off against each other. The army had gained power from its acquisition of Dutch property, to which the property of Chinese and Indonesian businessmen were soon added. It did not oppose the end of democracy and was quite docile toward Sukarno.

But Sukarno increasingly favored the Communists. He seems to have followed Aidit's advice, especially in foreign affairs, and may have come under Communist influence from other sources. (His second wife, Hartini, is widely thought to have been an agent of the Soviets, the Chinese, or the Indonesian Communists—or perhaps all three at different times). In 1961 Sukarno announced that he was a "Marxist" (by which he meant "Marxist-Leninist") and the Twenty-Second Soviet Party Congress hailed Indonesia as a "national democracy." Sukarno ignored Indonesia's disastrous economic decline (the economy was kept afloat only by Western aid) and resumed the effort against West New Guinea. (It provided a convenient occasion to arrest some opposition leaders.) This time he meant business. Indonesian raiding parties entered New Guinea and an invasion fleet was assembled. Moreover, he obtained a surprising amount of Soviet support; Khrushchev even sent Soviet personnel to man some of the Soviet-built planes and submarines that had been given to Indonesia. In line with a general policy of appeasing the radical pseudoneutralist states of what was then called the "Casablanca bloc," the Kennedy administration intensified efforts to buy Sukarno's friendship. It dropped the previous policy of neutrality in the New Guinea dispute and backed Indonesia. It continued to supply weapons to Indonesia and forbade Dutch planes from crossing American territory to get to New Guinea. The Americans brought strong pressure to bear on the Dutch. Perhaps welcoming this as an excuse, the Dutch caved in in August 1962. Under a face-saving formula provided by the UN, the Dutch agreed to hand over West Irian in 1963. A plebiscite was to be held in 1969 to determine the real wishes of the inhabitants. Predictably, this crude appeasement of a crude power grab had disastrous results, which are still unfolding; the West Irian population revolted against Indonesian misrule and a guerrilla war is still going on there.[6]

Up to 1963, things in Indonesia had gone well from a Soviet point of view. Khrushchev continued to attach great importance to Indonesia, in terms of aid, arms supplies and active support the Soviets' interest in that country clearly outweighed that in Vietnam.[7] Khrushchev's policy of leaping over the Western alliance system and forming alliances with radical "mini-imperialist" states seemed to be scoring an even greater success than in the Middle East. Unlike the Egyptian leader Gamal Nasser, Sukarno had no annoying anti-Communist tendencies, and there was no conflict between him and closer Soviet allies or agents, such as existed between Nasser and the Syrian and Iraqi leaders, and between the latter and the local Communists. A figure out of a trashy novel by Harold Robbins rather than a serious man, Sukarno seemed easier to handle than the Arabs. Supporting the existing regime and bringing Indonesia's Communists to power seemed to flow together smoothly; the Americans were even paying part of the bill! The Soviets were a bit worried about the policy of the Indonesian Communists. As Khrushchev told Aidit in 1959, it seemed to the Soviets that he had overdone expanding the party's membership, to the point that its quality and discipline had been eroded. With Sukarno as a godfather, or perhaps a Castro, a pro-Soviet Communist Indonesia would develop, it seemed, without much fuss, giving the Soviet bloc a dominant role in Southeast Asia. The mere "peaceful" continuation of existing trends in Indonesia would have had all the consequences the Americans feared would result from a Communist victory in Vietnam. But then the Soviet-Chinese conflict spoiled things.

The Indonesian Communists at first avoided taking sides in it. But Aidit ultimately landed on the Chinese side, although he tried not to openly offend the Soviets. Sukarno seems to have followed Aidit's lead. Aidit's position seems strange, since his party's strategy was in line with Soviet rather than Chinese ideas, and Indonesians generally dislike Chinese. His decision was perhaps influenced by the fact that his party relied on money extorted from the Chinese minority in Indonesia; the Chinese government could apply counterpressures on Aidit's victims. Despite Sukarno and Aidit's pro-Chinese stance, the Soviets did not give up the hope that Aidit's party might come back to their side, and the Soviet and Czech intelligence services continued to conduct operations in support of the Indonesian Communists, and supported Sukarno's aggressions.[8]

Since 1961 the British, bent on liquidating their last colonial commitments, had been working on a plan to form their colonies in Borneo and Singapore into a federation built around Malaya. "Malaysia" proved the sole success of the many British efforts to encourage federations among their ex-colonies; but Sukarno opposed it. He supported a genuine but abortive local revolt in Brunei in December 1962. In 1963, with West Irian securely in his pocket, Sukarno turned decisively against Malaysia, denouncing it as a "neocolonial" plot. Although the Soviets appear to have preferred a move against Portuguese Timor, they and the Chinese backed Sukarno in a limited war against Malaysia. Sukarno, in an effort to hold the fighting at precisely the level most convenient to the Indonesians, ingeniously dubbed it a "confrontation" rather than a war. Indonesian raiding parties attacked Malaysian Borneo, and Sukarno tried, unsuccessfully, to start internal revolts there. But the British kept forces in Malaysia, and firmly supported it, despite an initial American coolness toward their efforts. (Even after the fighting began, the U.S. government continued to supply spare parts for Indonesian planes. The zenith of lunacy was finally reached when it gave Sukarno a small nuclear reactor!)

The war went badly for the Indonesians. Partly believing their own propaganda, they believed that Malaysia was a fragile structure that would collapse under attack. They could not start a real guerrilla war inside Malaysia. The British displayed great skill during 1964, despite the difficulty of defending a long jungle frontier with small forces, and forced the Indonesians to end raids deep into Sarawak in Malaysian Borneo. The British strategy was essentially defensive, although they sometimes slipped into Indonesian Borneo to ambush enemy units going to and from the border. The Indonesians then tried to land raiding parties in Malaya and revive the Communist revolt there, but their commandos were quickly rounded up. Indonesian agents tried to exploit the conflict between Chinese and Malays, but without much success. It looked like the British might become sufficiently exasperated to launch naval attacks against Indonesian bases. That scared Sukarno into reducing pressure on Malaysia. But the war sputtered on; small-scale fighting was interspersed with negotiations. The Malaysians and the British would have been happy to reach a settlement, but the Indonesian terms were remarkably vague. The war seemed to be a stalemate. Inside Indonesia, however, matters were headed for a conclusion.[9]

During 1964 and 1965, Indonesia's economy was in a state of collapse. The peasants were short of fertilizer and pesticides, and hyperinflation set in. President Johnson had less qualms about siding with Malaysia than his predecessor and less patience with Sukarno and similar characters elsewhere. The Americans finally ended all aid except for food.

Sukarno refused to be perturbed by such minor matters. He devoted his attention to forming a close alliance with China and crushing the last opposition to the Communist Party. In August 1965 he announced the formation of a "Peking-Djakarta Axis." Perhaps he was nostalgic for the days when he had worked with the Japanese. The Chinese at first avoided using the term "Axis," but finally swallowed their embarrassment and adopted it too. Sukarno appears to have finally reached a clear understanding with the Communists; their leader would succeed him as ruler of Indonesia. As a gesture to them he abolished the Murba party, a small but influential national-Communist group that loyally supported him but was hostile to China. Possibly at the suggestion of the Chinese, Sukarno decided to arm a civilian militia, a "fifth force," in addition to the regular armed forces and the police. China offered 100,000 weapons for the new force, which was to grow up under the wing of the pro-Communist air force. Even without the fifth force, there seemed to be little to stop Indonesia's coming under Communist rule.

The army, or its high command, was the last potential center of opposition. Although junior officers and enlisted men still admired Sukarno, and some units were already under Communist control, many army leaders were known to dislike the party. Yet they had not offered real resistance to it or Sukarno. But in 1965, for some reason, Aidit, or Sukarno or both chose to gamble on rushing things. (The fifth force was just being formed.) The Communists may have feared that Sukarno, who suffered from a kidney ailment, would not live much longer, and it would be the lesser risk to tackle the high command while the dictator was still alive. A coup was hastily and poorly prepared to decapitate the army. Sukarno almost certainly knew and approved of the plan, if he did not propose it himself. The Chinese may have egged on Sukarno and Aidit for reasons of their own. On the night of the coup they indicated to foreign visitors that they had expected and supported it.

The coup was timed, probably at the last minute, to take advantage of the fact that several pro-Communist army units were in Djakarta for an Armed Forces Day parade. It was to be carried out by two Communist-controlled paratroop battalions, Sukarno's personal guard, a unit of tanks and armored cars and 2000 men drawn from the Communist Youth Front, who were being trained, as part of the new fifth force, at the main Indonesian air base at Halim near the capital.

On September 30, 1965, troops surrounded Sukarno's palace, and seized key points in the capital such as Radio Djakarta and the telephone exchange. But the armored force did not arrive. Units from Halim went to the houses of seven leading army generals to seize them. Some resisted and were killed on the spot; others were taken to Halim and killed there. But General Nasution, the minister of war escaped, although he was injured. On learning of this, Sukarno left his palace and joined Aidit at Halim. But he took no overt action. Colonel Untung, a confidante of Sukarno and an officer in his guard, announced over Radio Djakarta that loyal forces of the "September 30 Movement" had acted to foil a coup against Sukarno by a "council of generals." (There had been rumors of a military coup for months, but there is no real evidence that one was actually planned. It is conceivable, however, that Sukarno and the Communists acted out of fear of one.) Untung declared that a revolutionary council would be formed in Djakarta and local councils would be established in the rest of the country. Counterrevolutionary elements would be purged. A list of the members of the main council was given; it did not include Sukarno or Aidit, but named followers of both. The Communists announced their support of the "September 30 Movement." Yet Aidit too stayed in the background, and the party made no other overt move.

Nasution's escape proved decisive. He quickly contacted General Suharto, who was outside the inner circle of the General Staff, but commanded the army's strategic reserve. Suharto had not been on the list of generals who were to be seized, perhaps because he was not deemed sufficiently important or because he was believed to be out of action because of a family tragedy. While the plotters acted as though paralyzed, Suharto moved boldly. He went to his headquarters, and took command of the army. Ignoring Sukarno's order that the armed forces should stand still, he rallied reliable army and police units. The coup forces had failed to deal with the army's own communications system. Suharto moved against the two battalions guarding Sukarno's palace and retook Radio Djakarta. He then attacked the Halim air force base; it fell with few casualties. Sukarno and Aidit had fled, after trying at the last minute to draw back. Aidit was caught later and killed. The coup quickly collapsed, except in the Communist stronghold of central Java, where a pro-Communist army division made a stand against Suharto's forces. But the area was overrun during October.

The defeat of the coup was the signal for a horrible massacre of the Communists, partly by the army and partly by local civilian enemies of the

Communists. It went far beyond anything necessary to pull the party's teeth. Nor were Communists the only victims; there were pogroms directed against the Chinese minority, and many people were murdered in private feuds. In central Java the Communists managed to massacre many of their enemies before they were crushed. The wave of murder did not run its course until perhaps 300,000 people had been killed.

Sukarno's feeble attempts to stay in power and protect the Communists merely ruined him. It became clear that he was at least an accomplice in the coup, although the new army-dominated regime never fully exposed his role out of deference to his past as a national hero. It finally made Sukarno relinquish his authority to Suharto; Sukarno remained under house arrest until his death in 1970. Suharto established a military dictatorship, albeit one more liberal and more efficient than the dictatorship it had replaced; this regime has lasted to the present. It quickly made peace with Malaysia and became friendly to the West. The Indonesian Communists were reduced to an underground remnant, now loyal to the Soviets rather than the Chinese.[10]

The Western powers and the Indonesians had narrowly escaped disaster, for a Communist victory in Indonesia would have been a far more serious defeat than the loss of Indochina. Had he not stumbled into the bungled coup, Aidit would probably have become ruler of Indonesia. The need for the coup was questionable. The army had offered no principled opposition to either Sukarno or the Communists; only the attack on its leaders forced it into action. Any worries over Sukarno's health were clearly exaggerated. The coup was poorly planned and executed. The plotters had underrated Suharto and failed to take over the army's telecommunications system. There was no contingency plan to cover failures, and the Communists, evidently depending too much on the front afforded by the "September 30th Movement," did not mobilize the mass of party members to act to support the coup. Perhaps the Communist leaders suspected that Khrushchev had been right, and their members were not reliable enough to call to the barricades. Some military officers involved, and even some Politburo members, appear to have been poorly briefed, perhaps because it was feared that the party had been penetrated by army agents. Yet the coup nearly succeeded; had Nasution not escaped the army might not have been rallied. The armored force's failure to appear made Suharto's counterattacks much easier.

Later it was often claimed by those justifying the decision to fight in Vietnam that that action had encouraged resistance to the Communists in Indonesia, and even made a decisive difference there. There may be some truth in this. Had the United States abandoned the Southeast Asian mainland, the Indonesian military might have concluded that communism was the "wave of the future," and submitted, rendering a coup unnecessary. But in a larger view this argument is muddled, self-justifying claptrap, disguising the fact that the basic American policy of appeasing a radical-nationalist dictatorship allied to the Communist powers had failed disastrously. (Similar policies had failed in the Middle East.) If any Western power could claim credit for salvaging the situation, it was Britain, which had blocked Indonesian ambitions in Malaysia, at first with only slight and grudging American support. Had the British not defended Malaysia, it would have been swallowed up, and the Sukarno-Communist combination would have been unbeatable. Dictatorships that succeed at aggression are rarely overturned at home. As in the Middle East in the 1960s, the position of the democracies was saved by the mistakes of their enemies and by local opposition supported by the minor Western powers, and not by the United States.

5

The United States and the Beginning of the Second Indochina War 1954–1960

The Second Indochina War was little more than a sideshow in the larger dimensions of the Cold War. Galling as it may be to Americans, it was not even the main theater of the struggle for Southeast Asia. Yet it was one of the most confused and emotional conflicts of the whole Cold War. For Americans, it was the most traumatic conflict since the Civil War. Apart from the loss of life and the disastrous results for the peoples of Indochina, the war was a shattering reverse for the Western side in the Cold War and the greatest defeat in American history.

Many accounts of the war have perpetuated the confusion of the war years, either through failure to examine the false ideas that arose during the war—which produced a mythology almost as great as the rest of the Cold War put together—or through being narrowly focused. Most writing on the war can be divided into two schools. The "counterinsurgency" school treats the struggle as a simple guerrilla war or internal uprising in South Vietnam. The other school of thought (which often seems to work backwards from the outcome of the war in 1975) treats it as a slightly modified conventional war between the two Vietnamese states.[1] But the confusing thing about the Second Indochina War is that, quite unlike any other war, it combined both these aspects in succession. What was originally a guerrilla struggle turned into a primarily conventional struggle, not as in other wars, by the development of a successful guerrilla force into a conventional army, but through the *defeat* of the guerrillas and their replacement by a conventional army, invading from the other zone of a divided country. And how and why that transition took place is still imperfectly understood.

On hearing of the Treaty of Versailles, one French leader exclaimed, "This is not peace, but an armistice for twenty years." But the peacemakers at Versailles outdid their successors at Geneva in 1954. The Franco-Vietminh agreement, the only binding agreement signed at Geneva, which ended the First Indochina War, was a military armistice. It established two zones into which the military forces of each side, and any civilians who so wished, would be moved, prior to "elections" whose nature and timing were left unspecified. All this was to be supervised by an international commission of representatives of Canada, India and Poland. The arrangements for what was likely to be a large-scale transfer of population should have suggested that Vietnam was being permanently partitioned. But the participants at Geneva refused to admit that they had failed to produce anything better than a simple agreement to divide Vietnam, as Germany and Korea had been divided. They issued—no one signed—a pretentious "Final Declaration" that asserted that the division would be temporary and that elections would be held in both zones in 1956 to establish a government for all Vietnam.

At Geneva, the British and Americans had favored a position similar to the one they had taken in Germany and Korea. There should be free elections in both zones, supervised by the United Nations or the Colombo group of neutral powers. Privately, the Americans fully understood that the Communists were in a very strong position in Vietnam and feared that they would win even genuinely free elections *if* they were held at an early date, so they wanted to set the date for such elections as far in the future as possible to enable the non-Communists to pull themselves together. (They did not, perhaps, really ponder the full implications of the fact that the Communists could win a free election at all—and the difficulty of reversing that situation.) But the Communist powers rejected UN or Colombo supervision, and the American government rightly believed that any election without supervision would be rigged in favor of the Communists, whose zone had a larger population than the south.

They and the South Vietnamese explicitly refused to be bound by the agreements at Geneva, including the Final Declaration, which, since it was unsigned, did not even bind the countries that issued it.[2]

In fact, neither side took the Geneva agreements too seriously. Although the United States had promised not to disturb the arrangements by force, it sent sabotage teams into the north to make the Communist takeover of their zone as hard as possible. The Communists violated the Franco-Vietminh armistice agreement on a far bigger scale. Disturbed by the massive flight of refugees (mostly Catholics) from their zone, they clamped down to stop more leaving. Several times the million persons who actually left might have gone south had movement been truly free. The Communists promptly violated the provisions restricting the size of their military forces and the introduction of military equipment. They increased their army from seven to twenty divisions, a force more than twice that in the southern zone.[3]

Generally speaking, however, the Communists' violations of the only real agreements reached at Geneva never made much impression on world opinion. Instead, attention later fastened on South Vietnam's refusal to participate in the elections "scheduled" for 1956, a refusal often wrongly attributed to American pressure. The Americans, in fact, wanted the South Vietnamese to engage in consultations with the Communists on the remote chance that really free elections could be arranged after all. Against their advice the South Vietnamese refused. In fact, the Communist leaders remained unwilling to allow the international supervision the Americans wanted, nor did they expect the South Vietnamese government to commit suicide by submitting to unsupervised elections. Although the Communists harped on the issue of the elections in their propaganda, the upper echelons of the party, north and south, were privately told not to expect them.[4]

The American government continued to attach great importance to halting further Communist advances in Indochina, although Secretary of State Dulles had stressed in May 1954 that the rest of Southeast Asia might be held without Indochina if a determined stand was made. The Eisenhower administration *did not* accept the domino theory developed during the Truman administration, and certainly not as it was understood in the 1960s. Its general attitude was that South Vietnam, Laos and Cambodia were difficult forward positions, in which it was worth investing considerable resources. But they were not vital—fortunately, because intelligence estimates in 1954 and early 1955 were anything but happy about the prospects for South Vietnam's survival. Secretary Dulles remarked to a National Security Council meeting in December 1954 that he himself was not optimistic about the future of the Indochina states. They were "very vulnerable. Yet if one looked at the other side of the picture, these countries are not really of great significance to us, other than from the point of view of prestige, except that they must be regarded as a staging ground for another forward thrust by the Communist powers." He and other officials spoke of "buying time" as the primary aim in the area.[5] These remarks should be remembered when it is argued that the whole policy of containing communism, or any involvement in Indochina, led *inevitably* to the massive American intervention in 1965.

It was decided to build up the military forces of the remaining non-Communist states. Dulles favored maintaining only a small army in South

Vietnam, designed to preserve internal security rather than trying to counter the growing North Vietnamese force. He sought to deter an open conventional invasion, which he deemed unlikely, by an alliance system and the threat of American retaliation against North Vietnam and China. The Joint Chiefs of Staff felt that Indochina was a low-priority area and were initially reluctant to get involved in training the South Vietnamese army at all; but they successfully insisted that it be enlarged and trained for a limited defensive role in the event of an invasion.

In September 1954, as part of his program, Dulles had constructed yet another alliance group, SEATO (Southeast Asia Treaty Organization) to deter any further Communist advance in Southeast Asia. Its composition was a curious one. The Indochina states were not members of SEATO, although they were "protocol states" whose territory was covered by the alliance. Burma and Indonesia, as neutrals, did not belong. Only Thailand and the Philippines, of the Southeast Asian countries, actually belonged to SEATO. Except for Pakistan, the other members were all Western states. The SEATO treaty was designed to operate less "automatically" than NATO (North Atlantic Treaty Organization), and Dulles made it clear that the United States did not intend to commit ground forces to the Southeast Asian mainland in any foreseeable event. SEATO was not a success and proved of little real importance. It did not cure the vulnerability of the non-Communist states in Indochina.

The "settlement" of July 1954 split former French Indochina into four parts: the two Vietnams, Laos and Cambodia. Geography made South Vietnam hard to defend against any sort of attack, conventional or otherwise. Most of it was thinly populated by primitive "Montagnard" tribesmen who detested the Vietnamese. The Vietnamese population was strung out along the coast in little depth except in the Mekong Delta area, which contained half the country's people. The critical parts of the country were close to vulnerable frontiers. The two northernmost provinces, which included Hue, Vietnam's third largest city and the country's traditional capital and cultural center, were poorly connected with the rest of South Vietnam by one road through a rugged mountain pass. The Northern provinces were far more accessible to North Vietnam. The Mekong Delta area bordered on Cambodia. Saigon was only thirty-five miles from Cambodia, and was connected to the sea only by a long, vulnerable river channel whose defense involved costly efforts during the Second Indochina War. The Americans would note nervously that if a large ship were sunk at any of several points, clearing the channel would be long and difficult, if possible at all.

Laos and Cambodia were ramshackle, poorly administered monarchies. Laos was hardly even a state, much less a nation. It was a political fiction created by the French, who had only recently nominally placed miscellaneous mountain tribes under the Laotian monarchy of the Mekong valley lowlands. It had ruled only the rump of the old Lao kingdom, most of which had been absorbed by Thailand. The Vietnamese Communists had created a satellite organization, the Pathet Lao, which already controlled two provinces of Laos in 1954. The Laotian government lacked the ability, and the Cambodian government the will, to prevent the North Vietnamese from using their territory against South Vietnam.

South Vietnam's internal situation was even worse. Although the Communists had always been much weaker in the south than in the north, they operated in a society even more fragmented and chaotic. South Vietnam never had well-organized non-Communist political parties. The normal differences between city and country were greatly exaggerated. The relation between the peasants and city dwellers, especially the middle classes, was one of mutual incomprehension at best. The government administration, which was poor in quality and low in morale, had little control over the countryside or army. In their last years, the French had let much of the real power in the South fall into the hands of groups often compared (perhaps flatteringly) to the warlords of Republican China. The Cao Dai and Hoa Hao religious sects had their own private armies, and controlled large chunks of the country. Saigon was dominated by the Binh Xuyen, a Mafia-like organized crime group. Few observers thought that the South Vietnamese regime had much of a chance to survive. Into this chaotic mess stepped the Americans and Ngo Dinh Diem.

Ngo Dinh Diem belonged to an old mandarin family close to the Imperial Court. A staunch anti-French nationalist, he had gone into exile rather than join either side in the First Indochina War. Although a civilian, he disconcertingly resembled Jiang Jieshi (Chiang Kai-shek) in many ways. Like Jiang, he belonged to a Christian minority, and was an old-fashioned autocrat. Patriotic, upright and personally austere, he was unable or unwilling to control corruption and self-seeking by his family and followers. Although out of tune with the modern world and the mass of the Vietnamese and uninterested in industrialization or land reform, he was a master of old-fashioned political maneuver. While in exile, he made many friendly contacts with prominent Americans, including liberals, conservative Catholic churchmen and the future president, John F. Kennedy. By a process of logic now hard to follow, these people decided that Ngo Dinh Diem was the best hope for democracy in South Vietnam.

Emperor Bao Dai appears to have appointed Diem as his prime minister simply because there was no other capable man whom he thought he could trust and had not yet been discredited. At first Diem controlled only part of Saigon. But in 1954–1956, helped by American economic aid, but often ignoring American advice, he accomplished things that had been widely believed to be impossible. He brought the army under his control, beat the sects and the Binh Xuyen, ended French influence, got rid of Bao Dai, and resettled the refugees from the north. He started a ruthless and partly successful campaign to tear up the Communists' underground network in the south. These achievements clinched the alliance between Diem and the Americans, who at first had had grave doubts about him.

Unfortunately they were just about the last accomplishments that he could boast. Having curbed the sects, he failed to reconcile them. After a tentative and reluctant stab at the land problem, he failed to resolve it, and he began destroying all non-Communist political opposition. As a substitute for normal politics, his brother, Ngo Dinh Nhu, built a strange semisecret elite party, the Can Lao, and a group of supporting organizations, all patterned on a Communist party and its typical front organizations. They expounded a little-known French-Catholic philosophy, "personalism," which few people understood. Officials had to join these groups to keep their jobs. The Ngo family was widely believed to favor their fellow Catholics in the distribution of government jobs, although this charge may have been exaggerated. By 1958, Diem and his family had alienated most South Vietnamese. This occurred despite much economic growth. In purely economic terms, Diem's regime, thanks to lavish American aid, outperformed the Communists.[6] All this reopened the way for the Communists, who had nearly seen the south slip out of their fingers. Ho Chi Minh, one of the ablest of all Communist leaders, brilliantly exploited it.

The Communist leaders in Hanoi had always aimed to unify Vietnam, and ultimately all Indochina, under their rule. But, contrary to what is widely imagined, they did not always plan a protracted guerrilla war in the countryside against the South Vietnamese regime. They hoped that would not be necessary, and that after a short period in which they would lie low, the political structure in the south could be brought to such a pitch of disintegration that a simple coup or an uprising, perhaps supported by a conventional military attack from the north, would secure a quick Communist victory. They concentrated a disproportionate amount of effort on building up an organization in Saigon.[7]

Diem's initially successful creation of an authoritarian regime and his campaign against the party destroyed these hopes. Moreover, the Communists had serious problems in their main base in the North. Newly reestablished in the cities and main concentrations of population, they faced serious administrative and economic problems. A drive to collectivize the peasantry encountered great resistance, culminating in a major peasant uprising in Nghe An province in November 1956. The Soviets and the Chinese probably also restrained the North Vietnamese. Given the international situation in the mid-1950s, neither Communist great power felt that completing the conquest of Indochina was either likely or important in the near future.

In the south the Communists were in a basically weaker position in their efforts to gain popular support than in the First Indochina War. Then the Communists had recruited much of their support from tribal peoples in the north and the lower middle class and the workers in the cities. But the tribal groups in the south did not respond much to Communist appeals. Most important, nationalism no longer worked much in the Communists' favor. Even Diem's worst enemies admitted that he was a Vietnamese patriot. Arguments that he was an American puppet lacked conviction. There were only a few hundred Americans in Vietnam in the 1950s, and throughout the war even Vietnamese who disliked Americans generally saw that they were not "imperialists" and that their motives and behavior differed radically from those of the French. (Their view was not entirely complimentary. Most educated Vietnamese respected French culture, but not that of the Americans.) Most people wanted Vietnam reunified, but not enough to fight for it.

The party had to use more parochial appeals; detestation of the Diem regime and the desire of the peasantry for land tenure reform, which had not been much of an issue in the First Indochina War. Diem's failure to make peace with the sects once their "warlord" positions had been broken enabled the Communists to form an alliance with the Cao Dai and the Hoa Hao, who had backed France in the First Indochina War. These groups included nearly a tenth of the population of the south. For a time they provided the bulk of the Communists' mass support and military recruits. Paradoxically, the Communists thus depended on a "right-wing" basis of support. The promise of land reform was a more permanent basis of appeal. It was also a limitation. The Communists never developed a strong position in the cities. The fight for South Vietnam resembled the proverbial clash between the whale and the elephant. The Communists could not get into the cities, the government into the countryside. Only a minority of the intelligentsia supported the Communists and organized labor resisted their appeals.[8] While the Communists' appeal in rural areas would be widespread in the late 1950s and much of the 1960s, it is doubtful that they ever won over a majority of the South Vietnamese people. It is also notable that, however badly the South Vietnamese Army may have fought, not one entire unit went over to the enemy. This was a notable contrast to the situation in the Chinese Civil War. Throughout the Indochina war, in fact, the South Vietnamese army suffered heavier losses from the enemy than did the Americans. But the government and army were permeated with spies.

During 1957 and 1958 the Communists engaged in sporadic terrorism. During 1958 the Soviets and the Chinese, despite their growing differences, became more willing to back a resumption of the revolutionary effort in South Vietnam, as long as Ho did not draw them into major risks. The Soviets, while not dropping the emphasis on supporting "nationalist" allies, now put more stress on revolutionary activities in Asia. In January 1959 the leaders in Hanoi decided that resentment against Diem was so great, and the international situation was such, that an "armed struggle" in the south was feasible.

This decision began the Second Indochina War.

In 1959 and 1960, some 4,000 southern veterans of the First Indochina War who had gone north in 1954 returned to the south to develop the party's organizations there. In a parallel effort, the North Vietnamese increased their support to the Pathet Lao in Laos. In May 1959 they formed Group 559, an organization that began work on the Ho Chi Minh Trail, a complex system of paths through the "panhandle" of Laos to South Vietnam. At this early date it was relatively easy even to cross the narrow demilitarized zone between the two Vietnams. During 1960 the Communist forces in the south, mixing effective propaganda, organizational work and terrorism, grew tremendously. In December 1960, a new front organization, the "National Liberation Front" (NLF) appeared as an overall umbrella for the party and its military forces. Contrary to a later widespread myth, the NLF was always under the secure control of the Southern Bureau of the Communist party. The NLF issued a typical Communist-front "minimum program" promising democracy, land reform and the elimination of Diem, skillfully designed to offer something to most South Vietnamese. The NLF nominally was a "united front" supposedly including two parties other than the Communists; but they existed only on paper.

The Communists built up an elaborate military organization like that used in the early stages of the war against the French. On the village level, there were "militia" units of part-time guerrillas, usually forming squads and platoons, and occasionally companies, which normally operated close to home. More mobile "regional troops" were organized up to battalion-size in each province. The regional troops supplied men for forming the main force of regular troops. By the end of 1960, the Communists already had a force of 30,000 guerrillas and 5500 "main force" regular troops in South Vietnam. They concentrated on ambushes and attacks on small, exposed government positions. A massive campaign of assassinations was waged against government officials.[9]

The Communists struck into a double gap in the defenses of the south. The Americans had trained the South Vietnamese army to oppose a conventional invasion from across the 17th parallel, not fight guerrillas. Diem had done just enough in the direction of land reform to fool some Americans and make his own people feel cheated. Two-thirds of the South Vietnamese were tenant farmers, a majority or near majority owned no land at all. The Eisenhower administration at least seemed to realize the crucial nature of the land issue. It dispatched Wolf Ladejinsky, the American expert most responsible for the successful land reform in Occupied Japan, to South Vietnam. Dulles expressed concern when Ladejinsky reported Diem's basic disinterest in the land issue, but he failed to follow up with the necessary action. Diem had seized Bao Dai's crown lands; some of them were used, not very efficiently, to resettle refugees from the North. In 1956 Diem announced land reform laws, first assuring security of tenure and rent reduction to tenant farmers, and later decreeing redistribution of large holdings (over 100 hectares). The upper limit was high compared to those imposed in similar conditions in Japan, Taiwan and Korea. But except for the law ensuring security of tenure, the land reform was a dead letter. Rent reduction was only occasionally enforced. While some landlords' properties were confiscated, only a portion were redistributed. The rest fell into the hands of government administrators who lived by the old principle that any new law can be made into a new source of graft. In the early years of the war, government troops reoccupying Communist-held areas even helped landlords retake land the Communists had redistributed—an excellent advertisement for the Communists. The Communists themselves gave peasants only provisional titles to redistributed land, making it clear that the new owners retained the land only at the party's pleasure.

It is an ironic fact that the conservative Eisenhower administration tentatively recognized the importance of land reform, even though it failed to get one carried out, while the liberal Kennedy and Johnson administrations, with incredible consistency, ignored the crucial nature of the land issue until 1967, although there was ample evidence that it was the greatest source of Communist appeal.[10] A general land reform took place only in 1970.

Thousands of soldiers were to pay with their lives for this stupidity. The blindness of the American government on this issue is hard to explain. In many other respects, the political situation in Vietnam was unique, or at least uncharacteristic of post-World War II Asia, and if the Americans can be faulted it is for not seeing and adjusting to its peculiarities. The land question, however, was different. It would only have been necessary to apply the solutions previously used in similar situations in Japan, Korea and Taiwan.

In supporting Ngo Dinh Diem and continuing to do so well after his limitations should have become obvious, the Americans made a disastrous error. As Dennis Duncanson commented, they backed a personal leader in preference to impersonal programs in the erroneous belief that this would be more conducive to stable government. It was a mistake, however, of a sort that they had made before and were to make again and again in other underdeveloped countries.

During 1960 the Eisenhower administration became aware that American policy was failing. Eisenhower commented in May 1960 that Diem was becoming arbitrary and blind. Secretary of State Christian Herter considered using aid as a lever to force Diem into line. Elbridge Durbrow, the American ambassador in Saigon, and other officials urged considering finding an alternative to Diem.[11]

But the new Kennedy administration, if anything, backed Diem even more uncritically than Eisenhower ever had.

6

The Kennedy Administration, Vietnam and Laos

The obviously deteriorating situation in South Vietnam along with Khrushchev's speech of January 6, 1961, pledging to support "wars of national liberation," led to some changes in American policy. Although it contained nothing really new, Khrushchev's speech impressed the new administration, which was fascinated by guerrilla warfare and "counterinsurgency," although it did not understand these things too well. Soviet pressures on Berlin, the embarrassing failures at the Bay of Pigs and the Vienna Summit, and reverses in Laos and elsewhere were additional pressures in favor of demonstrating American power somewhere, although it would have been hard to find a worse place than Vietnam to demonstrate either American power or "counterinsurgency" doctrine. In fact, Maoist-type guerrilla warfare in Southeast Asia had been repeatedly smashed before, and it would have been in the interests of the West to emphasize this fact instead of making South Vietnam a "test case." Instead, as the war went on, many American leaders were increasingly obsessed with the ludicrous notion that Vietnam was the place to stop "wars of national liberation." In an infantile way they believed that "if we stop them here, we will stop them everywhere."

To be sure, the danger they saw was hardly imaginary. Apart from the Chinese activities discussed earlier, they were deeply worried about Latin America, which had once seemed a quiet rear area for the Western side in the Cold War. They feared that the Cuban dictator Fidel Castro and his supporters would duplicate Cuba's revolution on the mainland of the Americas, now recognized as a tinderbox of poverty, misrule and potential revolutionary situations.

Castro, uneasily allied with the Soviets (who periodically plotted to replace him with a more traditional Communist leader) did try to spread his revolution. He aided some Latin American Communist parties, and separate pro-Castro groups, recruited mostly from recently radicalized moderates, which were sometimes allied, but often at odds, with the "Moscow" Communists. They tried to start revolutionary guerrilla wars in many countries; the Castroites' confused theories held that lengthy preparations of the sort Mao Zedong and Ho Chi Minh had made were not needed. "Revolutionary situations" could be created by guerrilla action and not just exploited.

But, as Moscow's own experts and many of its older Latin American followers had feared, Castro's success could not be duplicated. It had been due as much to Batista's collapse, and the efforts of democratic urban opposition groups whom Castro later outmaneuvered, as to Castro's widely advertised efforts. And Castro, until well after his victory in early 1959, had seemed to be (and probably was) a non-Communist. The new rebels were openly Communist from the start and forfeited the deception or treachery vital to Castro's success. Nor were the upper and middle classes of other Latin American countries quite as feckless and stupid as their Cuban counterparts. In fact, most of Latin America was not really vulnerable to rural guerrilla war. Even in the most backward countries people and power were concentrated in the cities. The United States was alert and strongly backed the Latin American governments with aid and advisers. Although several of the guerrilla wars, notably in Venezuela, Colombia and Peru, lasted a long time, only that in Nicaragua eventually led, after many ups and downs, to a Communist victory.

LAOS

During 1961–1962, the Kennedy administration lavished much attention—albeit ineffectively—on events in Laos. Much aid and effort had already been expended on an attempt to prop up the Royal Laotian government. During the mid-1950s the Americans had unsuccessfully tried to build a strong Laotian army and prevent the development of any coalition government that included the Communists. The Laotian right, assisted by Thai and American agents, tried to rig elections and exclude popular neutralist elements. This backfired. An attempt to integrate the Communist Pathet Lao forces into the Royal army collapsed in 1959; the Communists renewed their struggle against the government with the help of North Vietnamese troops.

In Laos the neutralists were more popular and efficient than either the right or the Communists. In December 1960 neutralists in the army revolted against the right. When forced to flee the capital they formed an alliance with the Communists. The Soviets then intervened, airlifting arms and equipment to the neutralists and the Pathet Lao, and helping to supply the North Vietnamese forces sent into Laos to assist them. The Communist-neutralist alliance defeated the demoralized Royal army. During early 1961, the Kennedy administration seriously considered a major intervention in Laos. Admiral Arleigh Burke, the Chief of Naval operations, was a strong adherent of the domino theory and argued that Laos was vital to prevent the loss of Thailand, and probably the rest of Southeast Asia. But, as in 1954, the Army Chief of Staff and the marine commandant strongly opposed intervening. They regarded American strength, and ability to supply forces in Laos as insufficient. And when the leaders of Congress were consulted, they strongly opposed such a move. Kennedy decided to negotiate at Geneva and seek a truly neutral buffer state. He sent American troops to Thailand primarily to bolster the anti-Communists' negotiating position. A settlement, reached during 1962, disguised an effective partition of Laos which achieved the main North Vietnamese objective of securing the Ho Chi Minh Trail.

The widely advertised Laotian settlement soon broke down. Its only benefit for the anti-Communist side was to end the neutralists' alliance with the Communists. The latters' aggressions soon forced the neutralists to fight them. From 1963 until the end of the Second Indochina War—and even after—there was a bloody seesaw campaign in Laos, a sideshow to the main fighting of the Second Indochina War. During each dry season, the Pathet Lao and the North Vietnamese advanced across central Laos. During the rainy seasons, when their supply trails were blocked by mud, the Laotian government forces pushed them back—but a little less each year; and in 1967 the Communists began building all-weather roads. The Royal Lao army remained of little value, and most of the fighting was done by Hmong (then usually called Meo) tribesmen supplied and directed by the CIA, and supported "covertly" by Thai forces. The Communist position in the panhandle and the Ho Chi Minh Trail remained secure throughout. But the Hmong resistance was important, for it tied down large North Vietnamese forces that could have been used in South Vietnam and enabled the Americans to maintain sophisticated navigational aids far forward, assisting the bombing of North Vietnam. From 1964 onward American planes blasted the countryside into crater fields, but they could not stop advancing infantry. The Hmong were brave fighters but were outnumbered. Without a decisive victory elsewhere in Indochina there was nothing to prevent the luckless Hmong from being bled white; and that was what happened.

Although the Hmong were heroically fighting a classic guerrilla war to defend their homes against invaders, they got little attention or sympathy from the rest of the world. It was hard to fit them into the overall stereotype that developed of events in Indochina, and it was claimed that they were merely "mercenaries" of the CIA. In 1969 a furor developed as it was claimed that the war in Laos was a "secret" one waged by the CIA without congressional authorization—a claim advanced by senators who had been briefed by the CIA years earlier. Yet, there was something dirty about the Laos struggle; the Hmong had long depended on raising and selling opium. The American government turned a blind eye to this; some Americans, although probably not the CIA as an organization, took a hand in the growing drug traffic.[1]

KENNEDY AND COUNTERINSURGENCY

Although the American government was often to complain about the North Vietnamese infiltration through the Laotian panhandle, it had essentially decided in the course of 1961 to make a decisive stand in South Vietnam instead of Laos. The new American ambassador in Saigon, Frederick Nolting, was told to get along with Diem, using persuasion and trust. Such tactics had already failed, just as they had failed with Jiang Jieshi in the 1940s.

Counterinsurgency became a fad which absorbed considerable time and resources. The army's Special Forces, originally designed to operate behind Communist lines in a future conventional war, were reoriented to become a strategically defensive, antiguerrilla force. The navy formed the SEALs (sea, air, land) for counterguerrilla operations in rivers, canals and narrow waters; the air force formed a "Jungle Jim" unit of obsolete propeller-driven planes to support counterinsurgency operations. All these units soon wound up in Vietnam. Up to 1964, many in the administration seem to have thought that combatting guerrillas could be left to such small, specialized forces.

But some of the apparent interest in counterinsurgency was mere lip service on the part of the armed forces. Such lip service was well-advised, for President Kennedy fired General George Decker, the Army Chief of Staff, who openly opposed the new emphasis, partly on strategic grounds. He, and probably most army officers, regarded it as a diversion from the army's main job—defending Europe against Soviet invasion—and, with less reason, believed that if a counterinsurgency effort were needed, the army's existing capabilities could easily tackle it. Conventionally minded officers controlled and continued to fill the relevant appointments, especially in Vietnam. And even the supposed experts within the administration, like Roger Hilsman and Walt Rostow, did not understand counterinsurgency too well. There was an overemphasis on the purely military and external aspects of the problem, particularly by General Maxwell Taylor, who seemed to be Kennedy's most trusted adviser in such matters. Rostow, chief of the State Department's policy planning staff, and later President Johnson's national security adviser, particularly overstressed the external factors—"active sanctuary" and infiltration from the outside—instead of the internal situations that allowed guerrillas to recruit, supply themselves and operate. Rostow belittled the importance of popular support in guerrilla war situations. While it was true that guerrilla war, or any other sort of civil war, was not an "armed election" the more popular side would automatically win, Rostow virtually ignored the critical political problems. He was, however, one of the few Americans to make any reference at all to land reform in Vietnam.

Insofar as Kennedy's advisers studied previous experience with Communist guerrillas, too much attention was paid to the example of the British in Malaya, despite the warnings of some in the administration, like General Lyman Lemnitzer, that conditions in Malaya differed greatly from those in Vietnam. The Americans did not seriously analyze the bases of Communist appeal and concentrated on developing "psychological warfare," military and police capabilities in South Vietnam.[2]

By late 1961, things were so bad that committing American ground combat troops to South Vietnam was already under serious discussion. In the end, this was rejected. Instead, it was decided to expand the South Vietnamese Army, which was to be reorganized and retrained. A "civic action" program for rural areas was started, while Diem was to be persuaded to initiate reforms aimed at appeasing urban middle-class groups. More American advisers, Special Force and other antiguerrilla outfits and helicopter units were sent to Vietnam. In early 1962, Americans entered combat, flying helicopters and fighter-bombers against the Vietcong. Kennedy attempted to conceal this until the news media exposed his lies. The navy started patrolling the South Vietnamese coast to stop maritime infiltrators, without success. It also launched preparations to provide the South Vietnamese with motor torpedo boats to carry out covert raids against North Vietnam in retaliation for its support of the guerrillas. But, like the similar raids the Kennedy administration had the CIA conduct against Cuba, the program was slow to get underway; when the raids finally began in 1964 they had little effect. An even more dubious innovation was "defoliation"—using powerful weed killers to deprive the enemy of cover and prevent ambushes. The British had used this on a small scale in Malaya against guerrilla gardens. Defoliation often contaminated Vietnamese crops, and the Vietnamese peasants hated it—with reason, as Americans who served in Vietnam would discover.

The advisory group in Vietnam was upgraded to become "Military Assistance Command Vietnam" (MACV), a title that was absurdly retained even when there were half a million Americans in the country. General Paul Harkins, a conventional officer, and not one of the few available experts on guerrilla warfare, was put in charge.

Diem ignored suggestions for reform in military and civil affairs. There was no real pressure on him; Kennedy's pompous national security adviser, McGeorge Bundy, typically made it an objective to increase Diem's confidence in the Americans rather than make him agree to American demands—an odd attitude to take to a leader utterly dependent on American aid. In February 1962 Roger Hilsman, the head of the State Department's Bureau of Intelligence and Research, and later an assistant secretary of state, and widely advertised as one of the officials more knowledgeable about guerrilla warfare, actually urged easing pressure for reforms. Like many others who later claimed to have seen through Diem, he remained optimistic about developments in Vietnam through most of 1963.

Like Jiang Jieshi, Diem appointed officers for political loyalty, not military ability. Authority was carefully divided to protect the regime against a coup. Diem insisted on holding isolated, untenable outposts for prestige reasons, so the Communists overran them again and again.

The regime's only real effort to save itself was the strategic hamlet program begun in February 1962. Inspired by the "New Villages" in Malaya, the rural population was to be regrouped into fortified villages to sever the link between the Vietcong ("Vietnamese Communists," as the National Liberation Front and its forces were called) and the peasants. But the peasants hated the strategic hamlets; they were forced to work on their construction without pay and received no recompense in increased services or help in moving from their old homes. Some strategic hamlets were so poorly sited and defended that they were easily captured, while much of the program was never carried out. Although it was widely believed that the Communists suffered reverses in 1962, it is uncertain if such claims were true. Any success was due to the appearance of helicopters and other new military equipment from the United States. But the Communists soon acquired antiaircraft weapons.

Some outside observers, notably Bernard Fall and a growing number of newsmen, were worried by events in Vietnam. But few American officials were skeptical about the course being followed, although Saigon's ambassador in Washington (who was Ngo Dinh Nhu's father-in-law) warned the U.S. government as early as June 1962 that Diem was in deep trouble and would probably be overthrown. In March 1963 the ambassador bluntly told the Americans that the war could not be won with Diem in the saddle.

The sole strong official advocate of a basic change in course in this period was Undersecretary of State Chester Bowles. Bowles' views were suspect, and readily ignored, because he (like Adlai Stevenson) was an old-fashioned sort of liberal, and was not a "Kennedy" man, and was regarded, with some reason, as being a "soft" in the Cold War. But, like Stevenson, Bowles occasionally saw some hard facts that eluded the purportedly tough minded and more fashionable elements in the administration. Early on, Bowles pointed out the importance of land reform. His pet idea was a large-scale settlement to "neutralize" all of mainland Southeast Asia, but preserving South Vietnam as a separate non-Communist state, and backed by guarantees and the use of force should the Communists violate the settlement. Alone of top officials, he was skeptical of claims of progress in 1962. In March 1963 he noted that one premise on which optimistic estimates were based—that the enemy would not commit Northern troops to the south—was dangerously false.

THE DOWNFALL OF THE NGOS

By early 1963 it was becoming apparent to some newsmen and lower level advisers in Vietnam that things were actually deteriorating. But high-ranking officials remained optimistic, and they expected to be able to remove most Americans by the end of 1965.

But the Americans finally became fed up with Ngo Dinh Diem and his family. Ironically, this was not caused by their real faults, which had been apparent for years, but by trumped-up charges that Diem had been persecuting Buddhists—one folly of which he was innocent. In fact, Diem was the victim of unscrupulous Buddhist leaders who hated him for political reasons, but the charge of religious persecution was widely believed. Diem's rapid descent to demonic status, however, did not prevent American leaders from remaining fantastically overoptimistic about the basic situation. As late as October 1963, Secretary of Defence McNamara and General Taylor returned from a visit to South Vietnam to announce that the major part of the American task in the country would be finished by the end of 1965. By then a few people in the State Department were uneasy about the accuracy of the optimistic estimates.

The U.S. government, which had previously discouraged a military coup against Diem, now gave the go-ahead to a group of plotters—although the latter sometimes had such a fit of nerves that the Americans had to push them along. Apparently there was no attempt to make American approval conditional on an agreement on Diem's successor and what policies would be followed. The Americans seemed to assume that once the monster Diem was disposed of all would be well. That proved an invitation to disaster. On November 1, 1963, a military coup overthrew the Saigon government. To the distress of the Americans, the rebels murdered Ngo Dinh Diem and Ngo Dinh Nhu.[3]

For a short time, the Americans thought everything would be all right. By mid-December, however, Washington began to realize that something was wrong. On December 23, CIA Director John McCone gave the new president the worst Christmas present of his life. There was, he warned, no organized government in South Vietnam, and it was now "clear that the statistics received over the past year or more from the GVN (Government of Vietnam) officials and reported by the U.S. mission on which we gauged the trend of the war were grossly in error."[4] Johnson did not know it, but he had already read the epitaph of his career. He showed a remarkable forbearance, which he would later regret, in dealing with those who had been so wrong for so long.

The destruction of the Diem regime was later regarded by many people as a mistake; but Diem had long since become a liability. That the situation got even worse after his death was due to the failure to form a stable successor regime. The initial impact of Diem's overthrow was actually unfavorable to the Communists. The coup was popular, and contrary to their statements for public consumption the Communists were sorry to see Diem go. They had no respect for him as an opponent, and they had lost the primary target of their propaganda. The Cao Dai and Hoa Hao, their reason for fighting gone, defected to the government, and many individual members of the National Liberation Front (NLF) broke away. The worried Communist leaders reasonably assumed that the Americans, having intervened to get rid of Diem, would now secure an efficient regime that would cooperate with them.[5]

Much to their relief, that did not happen. Instead, for a year and a half, coup followed coup. Chaos resulted, until the Americans finally put their foot down in 1965. Security in the countryside vanished. Although the Reds had lost their previous "right-wing" allies, the opening up of the political situation in Saigon let them keep the situation there stirred up by indirect means. The Dai Viets, the right-wing secret society of northern refugees that had originated under the Japanese occupation, had strongly influenced Bao Dai's government before Diem. It used the political chaos in the south to regain influence. There is reason to believe that at least some of the Dai Viet group, which included "Marshal" Nguyen Cao Ky, the ruler of South Vietnam from 1965 to 1967, were manipulated by Communist agents, who helped steer the southern regime into destructive and self-defeating policies, perpetuating the follies of the Diem regime.[6]

There has been much futile speculation about what President Kennedy would have done about Vietnam had he not been murdered. Some later claimed that before his death he had become disillusioned with the struggle and had decided the war could not be won, and planned to withdraw U.S. forces—after he was safely reelected. There is no contemporary documentary support for this claim. The evidence suggests that he thought that things were going well at least until mid-1963, and that once Diem was removed the war could be won. He never saw, or expected, the terrible dilemma that faced Lyndon Johnson. Kennedy was a particularly strong believer in the most extreme version of the domino theory. He insisted, several times, that should South Vietnam go Communist, all Southeast Asia must inevitably follow; and he publicly endorsed this idea just six weeks before his death. His only known doubts about the domino theory stemmed from an even more fatalistic notion; in October 1961 he told Arthur Krock that China would dominate Southeast Asia as soon as it got nuclear bombs. He not only made no attempt to prepare the public for failure but as late as October 1963 pressured the *New York Times* to transfer David Halberstam, the newsman who had done most to expose the failings of U.S. policy and the Diem regime.[7]

The almost certainly false claims about his plans to withdraw from Vietnam and speculation about what he might have done, obscured the damning fact that Kennedy and those around him never had any understanding of what was going on in Vietnam at any time, and that all their actions were based on miscalculations. Indeed, for all the terrible blunders other presidents made in Vietnam, it is doubtful that any of them were as completely out of touch with what was going on as Kennedy. He had raised the number of Americans from 800 to 16,000 and brought American forces into limited combat. He died at a convenient moment for his fantastically inflated reputation.

7

Crisis and Massive American Intervention

Despite the shrinkage of their popular base, and some signs of strain, (the Vietcong, previously dependent on volunteers, now had to draft men) the Communists went from strength to strength during 1964. Three-fourths of South Vietnam fell under their control. Having used up their southern cadres, the Communists began sending northerners south, and began arming the Vietcong with late-model Soviet weapons or Chinese copies of them. They greatly increased seaborne smuggling. The war was entering the third or conventional stage of Mao's classic pattern. Late in 1964, the Vietcong formed division-sized units. And the northern regime decided, some time in 1964, to do what Bowles had suggested they might—send a regular North Vietnamese unit, the 325th Division, to the south. It believed that would enable it to quickly finish off the South Vietnamese regime. Hanoi assumed that the United States would probably not send in its own ground forces to stop it.

Despite their quarrel, both Communist great powers backed Ho. He tried to remain neutral while reconciling his patrons. The Western world misread Ho's position as pro-Chinese, although if anything he was probably pro-Soviet. In 1963 the Soviets made clear that the Vietnamese struggle was an approved "war of national liberation." From 1965 onward, the Soviets and Chinese blasted each other for "sabotaging" aid efforts, but ensured that North Vietnam's war effort wanted for little. The Chinese stationed some 50,000 troops between the Chinese border and Hanoi to operate and defend the railroads, while the Soviets helped build the strongest air defense system in history. The American leaders, obsessed with the pursuit of "detente" with the "moderate" Soviets, and the idea that a "militant" China was the real threat to peace, stubbornly refused to grasp that the USSR really backed North Vietnam and was in fact its main supplier. North Vietnam, however, never fully accepted the advice, much less dictation, of either of its patrons. When the Americans intervened in strength with ground troops, the Chinese advised conserving forces and reducing the effort in the south to a lower level of guerrilla activity. The Vietnamese Politburo ignored this. The Soviets seem to have been less inclined to offer advice on military strategy, but urged a more flexible negotiating position on the Vietnamese. Instead of demanding major concessions such as a complete halt to American bombing before opening talks, the Soviets favored a combination of "talking and fighting."[1]

PLANNING, RAIDS AND RESOLUTIONS

During the first half of 1964 the Americans recognized that the situation in South Vietnam and Laos was deteriorating. Already there was "contingency planning" for air attacks on North Vietnam. Many in the U.S. government believed that the Communists might back down to save the small industrial base in the north. The Johnson administration drafted a congressional resolution patterned on the Formosa and Middle East Resolutions of the 1950s, designed to marshal support for its efforts and deter the Communists.

The long-awaited South Vietnamese naval raids (called "34-A Operations") against the north finally started. Few really expected drastic results, although some hoped—not too realistically—that such covert operations might even cause North Vietnam to break with the big Communist powers and become an Eastern Yugoslavia. Many in the American government had come to recognize, by this time, that North Vietnam was not a Chinese satellite; they hoped, unrealistically, that its distrust of China was such that they would be reluctant to let Chinese troops enter Vietnam. But most were also still sure that a Vietcong victory would lead to a general collapse and Chinese domination of Southeast Asia.

Henry Cabot Lodge, the ambassador in Saigon, already favored secret, unannounced air attacks on Laos and the north. President Johnson warned congressional leaders, on May 15, that even with increased U.S. aid, the prospect in Vietnam was not bright. Two days later, he authorized American air reconnaissance over Laos, not only to gain intelligence but demonstrate American resolve to the Communists. After a plane was shot down, fighters armed to suppress antiaircraft fire escorted the photo planes. When another plane was lost, the air force launched a retaliatory strike against Xieng Khouang in Laos on June 9—the first openly American air attack of the Second Indochina War. It was hoped that would "send a message" to Hanoi.[2]

The 34-A raids soon provoked a major incident. For years, U.S. destroyers had occasionally patrolled close inshore, but in international waters, off China, North Korea and North Vietnam to collect electronic intelligence. The missions off Vietnam gathered data for the 34-A raids, but were not directly involved with them. On August 2, 1964, North Vietnamese motor torpedo boats attacked the destroyer *Maddox* in international waters while it was on one of these intelligence missions. A South Vietnamese force had just attacked nearby islands. The North Vietnamese attack was repulsed.

A second destroyer joined the *Maddox* and the patrol continued. On the night of August 4 the two destroyers reported another attack. It has never been clear whether this second attack really happened or, as seems more likely, was a figment of the imagination of the destroyers' crews. There was no doubt about the reality of the *first* attack. It occurred in broad daylight.

Although Secretary of State Rusk and CIA Director McCone believed that the North Vietnamese thought the destroyer patrols were directly related to the 34-A raids, and the Communist attacks were defensive reactions, the administration led the public to think that the North Vietnamese actions were completely unprovoked. Although Senators Richard Russell and Wayne Morse disclosed the South Vietnamese raids to the public, their remarks got little attention at the time. (The administration told the relevant congressional committees of the raids in executive session.)

President Johnson ordered a retaliatory air attack against North Vietnamese naval bases and fuel tanks. He used the attacks in the Gulf of Tonkin as the occasion to submit a joint resolution to Congress. The Southeast Asia Resolution (often misnamed the "Gulf of Tonkin Resolution") essentially gave the president the functional equivalent of a declaration of war. Johnson hoped it might deter any further North Vietnamese action and associate Congress with any actions he might later find necessary to stop the Communists.

But using the convenient circumstances the Gulf of Tonkin incidents seemed to provide, efforts to obtain congressional support ultimately backfired. Tying, or seeming to tie, the basic issues involved in Vietnam to incidents subject to ambiguous interpretations proved a capital mistake. When the South Vietnamese raids received greater publicity, it became clear that the first attack on the *Maddox*, although incontestably genuine, was not quite the unprovoked act of madness it had seemed. It also emerged that there were grave doubts about whether the second attack had taken place, although Johnson apparently thought that it had when he submitted the resolution. Johnson laid himself open to the charge of using duplicity to secure its passage. It was even suggested that the raids and patrols had been deliberately arranged to provoke incidents. Actually, the navy had not expected the Communists to attack. There was no plot. Such charges seem to have been as baseless as similar charges about the responsibility for Pearl Harbor. But they helped obscure the fact that the real issue before Congress had been whether or not to support the defense of South Vietnam, and not what had happened in the Gulf of Tonkin on August 4, 1964.[3] Later, when the war and President Johnson became violently unpopular, it suited many people to pretend otherwise, and claim that Johnson had "lied" the country into the war. But the evidence shows that in 1964 and 1965 when the crucial decisions were made Congress and public opinion were squarely behind doing what was necessary to prevent a Communist takeover of South Vietnam. It was not, however, popular to point out such things. Johnson was not a likable man, and, especially after his death in 1973, he was a very convenient scapegoat for mistakes shared by many other people.

Johnson did not follow up the Southeast East Asia Resolution with immediate action, despite the advice of the Joint Chiefs of Staff, who urged air attacks on North Vietnam. Whether because 1964 was an election year, or because he genuinely hoped that something would turn up, he made no decision to enlarge the American effort in Vietnam until well into the following year. But no miracle occurred to save the Americans from their dilemma.

Arguments for temporizing were not lacking among the president's subordinates. Discerning the difference between wishful thinking, rationalizations designed to aid his reelection, and serious ideas is hard even in retrospect. Dean Rusk, though a firm believer in the domino theory who would stick with the war long after many of Johnson's other advisers had run for cover, seems to have been especially inclined, in 1964–1965, to delay a full-scale American combat commitment until it was absolutely certain that nothing less would save South Vietnam. On September 9 he advised Johnson to hold off action, suggesting that the Soviet-Chinese conflict was deepening and the forthcoming December meeting of Communist parties should make it even worse, inhibiting the Communists' ability to make trouble in Southeast Asia. Maxwell Taylor, who had replaced Lodge in Saigon, and General William Westmoreland, the new commander of Military Assistance Command in Vietnam (MACV), opposed bombing the North until there was a more stable government in the South. (Later they completely reversed this line of argument!) On November 3, Taylor modified his position, urging retaliation for a Vietcong attack on U.S. planes at Bien Hoa. But he characteristically suggested that "too much" in coercing the north could be as bad as "too little." "At some point we will need a relatively cooperative leadership in Hanoi willing to wind up the Viet Cong insurgency on terms satisfactory to us and our South Vietnamese allies. What we don't want is an expanded war in Southeast Asia and an unresolved guerrilla problem in South Vietnam"—an interesting example of the idea, common among the civilian officials of the administration, though not Taylor's fellow soldiers, that the use of force could be fine-tuned or closely controlled.[4]

On December 1, Johnson indicated that he would bomb North Vietnam if things got worse. On December 12, he approved air attacks on infiltration routes in Laos. Those attacks began on December 17, but remained small and infrequent—and without visible effect. Johnson himself was not confident about the probable results. He indicated, in December, that he did not think that eliminating North Vietnam's intervention would in itself end the war in the south; nor did he think that the war could be won from the air.[5] Strangely, the Laotian air attacks drew little attention from the public at the time or from later historians; both suffered from the defect of vision that reduced all Indochina, or even all of Southeast Asia, to Vietnam.

THE DECISION FOR MASSIVE INTERVENTION

Early in 1965, it became clear that something had to be done. Either the Americans must commit their own forces on a large scale, or let South Vietnam fall. But, despite a few exceptions, it seems to have been generally accepted by officials at all levels that a Vietcong victory meant not just the fall of all of Indochina to the Hanoi regime, but the loss of all of Southeast Asia to Communist forces aligned with China. The Secretary of Defense held a particularly extreme view, holding that not only would all Southeast Asia go Communist, but Greece and Turkey would retreat into neutrality. (A Communist takeover of Indonesia seemed likely whatever the United States did in Vietnam.) During 1964, the CIA's Board of National Estimates, and elements in the National Security Council, had once or twice suggested that repercussions outside Indochina might not be as immediate or automatic as the "domino" analogy implied, but even the most optimistic assessments given President Johnson held that they would be terribly damaging to the Western position in Asia, and not just Southeast Asia. And Johnson, by his own account, was highly conscious of the "pincer threat" from Indonesia as well as North Vietnam.[6] Nearly all saw the strategic issues in

Southeast Asia, which was rightly viewed as important, in all-or-nothing terms. Despite all the talk about counterinsurgency, most in the administration seem to have conceived of the Vietnam situation as analogous to the Korean War.[7] This was perhaps promoted by their knowledge—as yet not public—that the Northern regime was sending its own troops south. They did not reflect that that was hardly the cause of the main problem.

The alternative of a strategic retreat, of writing off South Vietnam, and occupying a backstop position somewhere in the area was not seriously considered. The muddled political situation in Saigon would have afforded a good excuse for withdrawal. Such a move should not have been inconceivable. In fact, it would have continued the previous pattern of American actions, or rather retreats, on the Asian mainland. Despite its general commitment to containing communism, the United States had always been very reluctant to commit its forces to the Asian mainland. It had accepted serious reverses in China in the 1940s, in Vietnam in 1954, and Laos in 1962, rather than send in American ground troops. Under the spell of a strange rigidity of ideas, the American government stumbled towards disaster.

It is notable, however, that many of the older veterans of the Truman administration, who either worked in the Johnson administration or were consulted by Johnson—Dean Acheson, Robert Lovett, John McCloy and, possibly, Clark Clifford—were markedly unenthusiastic about a massive commitment in Vietnam even in 1965, while George F. Kennan openly opposed the war as a mistake. The facts noted above, along with the views of the Eisenhower administration noted in Chapter 5, show that it is simplistic in the extreme to argue that the war was just the logical and inevitable result of the whole containment policy.[8]

THE BOMBING OF NORTH VIETNAM

In February 1965, a Vietcong attack on an American helicopter unit based at Pleiku in the Central Highlands of South Vietnam provided the occasion for the Americans to begin bombing North Vietnam. The first two attacks on the north were launched as specific acts of retaliation for the Pleiku incident and a subsequent attack on Americans; on February 11, Johnson switched to a continuing air campaign. The shift from "retaliation" to systematic attack was blurred and helped give a (false) impression of deception.[9] The campaign's purpose was vague and unclear; it was supposed to encourage the disintegrating South Vietnamese, make the enemy pay a price for his aggression, and hamper the infiltration of men and supplies to South Vietnam. It was conducted in a confused and hesitant manner under tight control from Washington. The Joint Chiefs of Staff wanted a massive attack on all important North Vietnamese targets to try to break the country's ability to wage war, but they were ignored. Instead, President Johnson listened to those civilian advisers who advocated a "graduated," restrained approach. Initially modest attacks would gradually increase in intensity. Bombing was seen almost as a symbolic act; the threat it posed, especially to the Communists' industries (which were not yet attacked), was seen as important as the actual damage done. "Graduated response" was supposed to reduce the danger of intervention by the major Communist powers. Instead of designing a whole air campaign with explicit military objectives, the president approved piecemeal "packages" of bombing attacks on a weekly or biweekly basis. Not only targets, but attack routes and even armaments were dictated by the president and Secretary of Defense McNamara. The bombing concentrated on interdiction targets to damage North Vietnam's ability to move troops and supplies south. Hanoi, Haiphong and the northeast, which contained most of the ports and facilities for transporting supplies from China, were off limits to bombing.

Probably not even an unrestrained massive assault would have had any early effect on the struggle going on in South Vietnam. These poorly thought out pinpricks were bound to fail.[10]

THE DECISION TO COMMIT GROUND TROOPS

But even as the bombing started, the administration knew that it alone would not be enough. By the spring of 1965, the 200,000 Communist troops (still almost all South Vietnamese) fighting in the south were chewing up the South Vietnamese army at the rate of a battalion a week. They made excellent progress toward the enemy command's objective—cutting the country in two by an attack through the Central Highlands.

In March 1965 the president approved landing a Marine brigade in South Vietnam. Initially it had the limited job of defending a vital air base at Danang. Early in April, Johnson decided to send more Marines and let MACV use them more offensively. This decision was kept secret, and its existence was even denied, but reporters inevitably noticed what was going on. This episode, although probably the only serious example of "duplicity" by the administration, fed the myth that the country had been led into the war by trickery and deception. General Harold Johnson, the Army Chief of Staff, had warned the president as early as mid-March that winning the war would take half a million men and five years. By contrast, the secretary of defense advised Johnson in late April that it would take a year or two to demonstrate enemy failure in the south, which would be needed before there could be a negotiated settlement.

During April, McNamara, General Westmoreland (the commander in Vietnam) and the Joint Chiefs of Staff were agreed that a far larger force would have to be sent. In effect, a full-scale army was needed. Although the decision to bomb North Vietnam and land combat troops at Danang would seem to logically imply a full-scale commitment requiring whatever was needed to prevent the fall of South Vietnam, this was not the case—or, at least that was not how the American leaders saw things. Johnson characteristically put off a final, clear-cut decision for a major ground commitment for a considerable time. The military's proposals encountered some resistance. Johnson's able vice president, Hubert Humphrey, urged withdrawing from Vietnam. Humphrey pointed out the implicit contradiction between the administration's essentially optimistic, detente-oriented evaluation of the world situation (which he shared) and engaging in a war, and warned Johnson that there would be strong and growing opposition to the war effort from the left. Johnson ignored Humphrey's warnings of what would happen, and cut him out of the foreign policy debate. Maxwell Taylor had briefly favored withdrawal early in 1965 out of despair at the bungling of the Saigon government. But he soon dropped that idea, although for a time he opposed introducing American ground forces. In June 1965 he finally admitted that that was the only way to prevent a Communist victory.

Undersecretary of State George Ball had favored bombing North Vietnam, but only as a last-ditch measure and as a way to secure a bargaining position from which the Americans could make a face-saving agreement. He did not really think that the bombing would be effective and basically did not want to fight over Vietnam. Even Ball, however, found it hard to admit that he was willing to accept a Communist victory. He titled one of his memoranda on the subject a "Compromise Solution for Vietnam," although in it he wrote more frankly of "cutting our losses." Ball strongly opposed a major commitment of ground forces (he admitted that the war must be lost without them) with arguments of varying quality. He argued that the enemy was determined that the war would become unpopular and was basically unwinnable. American forces, or "white Western troops," could allegedly not defeat guerrillas or fight effectively in jungles. Ball expressed fears that China might intervene, and opined that the Communists could actually win a free election in South Vietnam. He only belatedly attacked the domino theory, and so harped on the theme that the Americans would be in the same situation as the French that some were offended by his comparison between Americans and those disreputable imperialists. Only some of his ideas were well-based or vindicated by experience and some were clearly wrong; on the whole, Ball's arguments were less well formulated than Hubert Humphrey's. Still, he was a clearer thinker than many of Johnson's advisers.

Johnson heard Ball out, but in July 1965 he approved the Defense Department's recommendations for a major commitment of ground troops. In other respects, however, Johnson refused to listen closely to most of his advisers. They warned that the war would be a long one. General Greene, the commandant of the Marine Corps, endorsed General Johnson's view that it would take a half a million men and five years to win the war. The chairman of the Joint Chiefs of Staff declared that he hoped to make definite progress in three years, but that it was unreasonable to expect victory in a year. McNamara, however, gave the president a preposterous "statistical assessment" of the chances of victory—20 percent by 1966, 40 percent by 1967, and 50 percent by 1968.

Johnson recklessly gambled that the war would be *less* arduous than his advisers feared. Refusing to mobilize the reserves, he followed a "guns and butter" policy. His Council of Economic Advisers assured him that this was viable. The war must coexist with a major program of social reforms and without the imposition of economic controls. Johnson did not expect the war to become basically unpopular; he expected attacks on his policies to come from the right, as had the attacks on Truman's policies in Korea, from those demanding stronger policies and less restraint on the use of force.He did little to rouse popular support for the war, fearing that an effort to do so would arouse an hysteria that would turn against the limits he wished to impose.[11]

Johnson's seeming blindness was not unique. It was left to Secretary McNamara to make the incredible remark that "The greatest contribution Vietnam is making—right or wrong is beside the point—is that it is developing an ability in the United States to fight a limited war, to go to war without the necessity of arousing the public ire."[12] As usual, McNamara was wrong; ultimately the "public ire" was aroused—against the American government instead of its enemies.

The administration evasively presented Communist actions as a clear-cut, if novel, form of international aggression. This was a very partial truth, for in 1965 and for some time after, the struggle in South Vietnam was still a genuine, domestically based revolution, albeit one directed and supported from the Communist zone of a divided country. The Vietcong could not have lasted more than a few weeks had they not been able to get men and supplies within South Vietnam and capitalize on genuine grievances there.

Contrary to what was often said later, the arguments flourished in public hardly differed from what the administration leaders themselves thought. Johnson and others stressed the threat of Chinese expansion and compared the struggle to the Korean War. To back away from the challenge would amount to another Munich, or a return to the appeasement policies that had failed in the 1930s. Earlier presidents had committed the United States and its credibility was at stake. Occasionally it was suggested—inaccurately, to put it kindly —that the SEATO treaty obliged the United States to intervene. The domino theory and the specter of a Vietcong victory encouraging more "wars of national liberation" were invoked.[13]

These arguments were enough—in the short run. Americans might not know much about Southeast Asia, but most were still firmly anti-Communist and disposed to believe what a president said about foreign affairs. There was a general presumption—though not an inflexible rule—that Communist advances should be resisted. Even if the circumstances were obscure, a war against a Communist power was probably justified. The reputation of those who had opposed American intervention in World War II and Korea, the only wars most people remembered, was not good. A young soldier neatly summed up the general view at the time when he remarked that "It never occurred to me that America would go to war without a good reason."[14]

Johnson proved a terrible war leader. A skillful parliamentary politician of a sort who rarely becomes president, he was not popular, although perhaps it was a good thing that he lacked the aura of phony glamor that had draped his predecessor. He knew little about military affairs; distrusting his military advisers, he made no attempt to replace them with better men. He relied on the advice of a single retired officer, Maxwell Taylor, who had been a good field commander in World War II and Korea but was a man of singularly poor judgment in other matters, and the same civilian officials who had bungled the conduct of Vietnamese affairs earlier.

Astonishingly, Washington failed to formulate an overall strategic plan for the conduct of the war. Despite General Johnson's horseback opinion, there was no estimate of the forces needed to win the war, the tasks that had to be performed to accomplish this, or the time and losses involved. In fact, just what winning the war meant was never too clear. It was generally expected that the war would end in some sort of negotiated settlement, but what the minimum acceptable terms would be was not decided. Many officials vaguely spoke of frustrating the enemy, of making clear that the

Communists could not win, as constituting an American victory, apparently assuming that once the Communists were convinced they could not win they would settle. Secretary McNamara and McGeorge Bundy thought for a time that bombing and the American military presence might be used as bargaining counters and could be traded for a North Vietnamese agreement to pull all Communist forces out of the South—a truly fatuous notion. Later McNamara resorted to a characteristic "solution" to the problem; he urged avoiding "color" words such as "winning" or "victory," speaking, instead, of a "favorable settlement."

Washington was more definite about what it would *not* do. It rejected a naval blockade of North Vietnam or closing its ports with mines. There would be no invasion of North Vietnam or enemy "sanctuaries" in Laos or Cambodia, at least by ground troops. American leaders feared Soviet or Chinese intervention, and this deterred them from strong measures. These fears were almost certainly exaggerated. While the Chinese warned that they would intervene if the Americans invaded North Vietnam (indeed they already had troops there), it was never likely that any other action would evoke such a response. The rejection of relatively bloodless actions like a naval blockade or other measures to seal North Vietnam's ports, while waging a less effective bombing campaign bound to be far more costly in lives, was a particularly bizarre decision. It was a notable contrast with the policy followed in the Korean War; then North Korea was blockaded from the start.

The leaders of the armed forces disliked these limitations, and they made that clear to the president. But they did not warn Johnson, or, indeed, believe, that the war would be lost if they were imposed. All seem to have assumed that American power, however crudely or inadequately applied, must triumph over North Vietnam and the Vietcong in the end. It was left to the command in Vietnam to design a strategy for the war—such as it was.

General Westmoreland, who had commanded in Vietnam when the American role was still largely advisory, remained in charge. He proved a mediocre leader, although he had a very difficult job—Eisenhower once told a startled Lyndon Johnson that Westmoreland's job was harder than the one he had faced in World War II. Working within the limits assigned by Washington, Westmoreland visualized a three-phase strategy of attrition, requiring several years.

In the first phase, in 1965 and early 1966, he would protect vital installations and stop the Communists from cutting South Vietnam in two. After this, the Americans, leaving pacification operations and security duties largely to the South Vietnamese, would strike the enemy's regular forces and base areas in "search and destroy" missions. Westmoreland reasoned that this would keep the enemy regular forces away from populated areas, and let the South Vietnamese deal with the local guerrillas based there. The Americans could use their greater firepower freely without hurting civilians, and keeping Americans away from civilians would reduce friction with the Vietnamese. In a final phase the remnants of the guerrillas would be mopped up. Westmoreland hoped to eventually get permission to clean out the enemy sanctuaries in Laos and Cambodia, but he did not deem such actions vital to victory. In practice, pacification and counterguerrilla activities would take second place to a conventional struggle against the enemy's regular units, which were to be worn down in a war of attrition. Westmoreland had little interest in "counterinsurgency" and did not aim primarily at fighting guerrillas at all, a point frequently misunderstood then and later. With the war within South Vietnam entering the third, conventional phase of Mao's classic pattern, and the guerrillas forming division-sized units (and being joined by other such units from the North) this was almost certainly necessary in 1965. But Westmoreland fundamentally misunderstood the enemy, and his approach landed the Americans in difficulty later.[15]

8

Buildup and Decision
1965–1968

In 1965–1966, Westmoreland skillfully directed the buildup of American forces and their logistics base—the latter was a feat rarely appreciated. The Communist threat in the Central Highlands was so great that he had to rush in American combat units at the expense of their normal logistic support. Despite much opposition from General Giap, who favored reverting to Mao's second phase and smaller-scale guerrilla warfare, the Communist commander in the south, Nguyen Chi Thanh, was allowed to persist with the plan to cut South Vietnam in two.

HELICOPTER WAR

The North Vietnamese ran right into a new kind of American unit, an "airmobile division."

The American 1st Cavalry Division was entirely carried and supported by its own helicopters and light planes. The airmobile concept had originated in the 1950s as a new way to stop a Soviet attack in Europe, not fight guerrillas. Its development, and the broader use of helicopters in general, was one of McNamara's few contributions as secretary of defense. It was also costly; the army not only had to procure thousands of vehicles requiring tedious maintenance (helicopters needed several hours of maintenance for each hour flown) but quickly train thousands of pilots to fly craft that were harder to handle than fixed-wing planes. Helicopters had already been used in Korea to evacuate wounded, where they had saved many lives, and they had enabled the British to move into the mountain spine of Malaya and prevent the Communists from forming a fall-back base there. And the French had used hundreds of them to carry forces into combat in Algeria. Indochina, however, would be the helicopter war par excellence. Thousands would be used and they would shape the whole war.

In the early 1960s, much had already been learned, sometimes the hard way, about using transport helicopters and armed attack helicopters ("gunships") by the small units supporting the South Vietnamese. As it became clear in early 1965 that a major commitment of ground forces to Vietnam was likely, the experimental division testing the airmobile concept was hastily turned into an operational unit and sent to Southeast Asia. General Douglas Kinnard, its commander, proposed basing it in Thailand rather than Vietnam, to operate against the Ho Chi Minh Trail. That imaginative course would probably have caused the enemy more trouble than any other. (Although the Americans would have found that the enemy was not as dependent on the trail as they then supposed, that discovery alone would have been valuable.) But this proposal conflicted with national policy, and Westmoreland sent the division to block the enemy frontally in the Central Highlands of South Vietnam—and into the first large-scale encounter with the North Vietnamese.

In close-fought battles in the Ia Drang river valley, American spoiling attacks stopped the North Vietnamese with heavy losses to both sides. The Americans won, but committed serious blunders and once or twice came close to losing whole battalions to fierce attacks on defensive perimeters or ambushes. They found that the North Vietnamese forces might lack heavy weapons, but were tough opponents, well-trained and armed with plenty of automatic weapons and ammunition, and skilled at using camouflage and minimizing the American advantage in firepower by "hugging their enemy." Although, surprisingly, the North Vietnamese Army's training was conventional enough, and unlike some of the luckier Americans, they had received little specialized training in jungle fighting, they had learned to handle themselves well enough on the way south.

The Americans were disturbed by their heavy casualties, especially "nonbattle casualties"—injuries and sickness. They found that their gunships alone could not stop determined enemy attacks that got to close quarters. Although the American command drew optimistic conclusions from the Ia Drang campaign, the enemy learned much. They would not fight on such unfavorable terms again. The battles were as much a lesson in the limitations of the airmobile force as their value. Even in 1962–1963 it had been apparent that transport helicopters needed escort and fire support by specialized gunships carrying machine guns, rockets and grenade launchers. An attack near a dug-in enemy needed the support of air force planes as well. Although helicopters were surprisingly resistant to damage and reduced their exposure to enemy fire by skillful maneuvering and flying close to the ground and making use of terrain, they were vulnerable when landing. Complete surprise was hard to attain; the noisy craft could be heard far away, and finding a place to land was often hard.

The enemy found counters to the helicopter. They sometimes used men as bait to trick gunships into flying into "helicopter traps" laced with antiaircraft guns. That was a dangerous practice, for the gunships' firepower was fearsome; and the Americans learned to call down artillery fire on likely ambush sites. The Communists learned to spot probable landing zones, and noted in advance where to site machine guns and mortars to cover them. Sometimes they were mined, or booby-trapped with salvaged American bombs, or stakes were hidden in tall grass to rip through the bellies of helicopters as they landed. The Americans countered this by elaborate preparatory bombardments, at the cost of surprise. Later on the Americans blasted their own landing zones out of the jungle with bombs weighing up to 15,000 pounds. Alternatively, helicopters lowered engineers on ropes through the trees to flatten out new landing zones with demolition charges.[1]

THE MEN ON THE GROUND

The helicopter made the rapid and deep thrusts of Westmoreland's strategy possible. But once American soldiers set foot on the landing zone, they found that the fighting was not drastically different from that in other wars. It was merely the setting that was unusually unpleasant.

The Americans sent to Vietnam did not represent a cross-section of American society. The draft, which had been quite fair until the late 1950s, tended to scoop up poor and working-class boys. In the early years of the war the army's combat units (especially the elite ones) were disproportionately black. Although the army took steps to change that potentially dangerous situation (ironically, race relations worsened later, after that problem was fixed), it remained unrepresentative in terms of class and (what has been far less remarked) in terms of geographical background. (Men from farms, and villages of under 1,000 people, which had 2 percent or less of the U.S. population, were nearly a tenth of those who died in the war.) Student deferments, which actually acted as effective exemptions rather than postponements of service, and later on, (but far less noted) phony medical exemptions, kept most middle-class and upper-class men out of the armed forces. (Student deferments were particularly skewed against the lower class since they did not cover part-time students.) A less-than-brilliant policy devised by the Kennedy administration used the military to "reha-bilitate" the poor by lowering minimum requirements for draftees. This brought in many men who would have been rejected as mentally unfit earlier, and was a source of trouble. The unfairness of the draft, growing draft evasion by the middle and upper class and the failure to call up the reserves made the U.S. army in Vietnam very different from the force that fought in World War II and Korea. It was distinctly split between older career men and a mass of very young draftees of 18 or 19 (averaging considerably younger than those in earlier wars).

Americans arriving in Vietnam—increasingly as lonely replacements rather than members of complete units—were shocked at what they encoun-tered. Unbearable heat, humidity, rats and loathsome insects, a near-univer-sal stench compounded of excrement, rotten plants and nuoc-mam sauce offended them. The army made no attempt to prepare soldiers for the people they would deal with, so soldiers were often disconcerted by minor social customs that could easily have been explained in advance. The dirty habits of lower-class Vietnamese, particularly their defecating in public and chew-ing of betel nut, and the near-universal poverty disgusted Americans. They quickly sensed that they were not wanted, and relations between Americans and Vietnamese civilians were usually bad, although there were a fair number of exceptions. (We shall discuss an important one later in this chapter.)

Soldiers who served in combat units were generally dissatisfied with their training. The infantrymen, even more heavily overloaded than usual, found themselves in a war of long, exhausting patrols in dreadful heat, in search of an elusive enemy. When not marching up and down over rough ground or through thick forest, they had to pass through dense, knife-edged elephant grass, or wade through flooded rice paddies or swamps, attacked by leeches and other vermin. Heatstroke, malaria, infected bites and trench foot were common. The fear of mines and booby traps was ever present. The standard American rifle, the M-16 was, at least initially, unreliable and many never liked it.

When the enemy was found, it was usually the other side that fired first, in an ambush or surprise night assault. When an enemy force was "found and fixed" helicopter assaults under fire were often followed by attacks on a well dug-in enemy occupying stoutly built bunkers. Captured ground was usually given up. A general sense of "going around in circles" began to eat away at soldiers' morale. The South Vietnamese forces, even more than civilians, were generally held in contempt, even more than they deserved.[2]

The enemy, however, was generally respected, even when he was hated. American soldiers often praised the fighting ability of the North Vietnamese and Vietcong. They were astonished by their high morale and their ability to come back again and again after staggering losses; a product of good training and fierce indoctrination emphasizing nationalist themes and fear of the Americans. Many northerners believed that the Americans not only killed prisoners (as they sometimes did) but ate them, or alternatively, had a machine that turned them into Negroes. (While many Vietcong became fed up, few North Vietnamese surrendered.) Both Vietcong and North Vietnamese impressed Americans with their ability to use stealth, move silently and far during the night, and make use of terrain and booby traps. Both were excellent at laying large, complex and deadly ambushes, often baited with human decoys. A characteristic tactic was to attack a small Allied unit to draw a relief force into an ambush. The North Vietnamese tended to be better shots and better at maneuvering than the Vietcong; the Americans were also impressed by the effectiveness of their mortars.

The Communists put great emphasis on careful preparations for battle and "preparing the battlefield" by prepositioning supplies and studding an expected battlefield with fortifications of the sort that protected their permanent base camps. They characteristically built dual belts of mutually supporting well-camouflaged bunkers covered by dirt and logs, similar to those favored by the Japanese in World War II. The bunkers were usually proof against anything but a direct hit by a bomb, a heavy shell, helicopter rocket or tank gun—and they were often sited so that the latter weapons could not be brought to bear. Attacks on bunker lines were so costly in lives that the Americans learned to stand off and slowly pound them with supporting fires; many of the defenders got away. The difficulty of maneuvering through jungle or the other difficult terrain the enemy usually chose to fight in meant that it was very hard to completely destroy an enemy force. Usually the enemy could break off action and slip away before any ring closed in on them. In their own attacks on American prepared positions, the enemy often achieved surprise, but this usually did not help them much. The enemy never overran a sizable American force or base and usually suffered staggering losses—a ratio of five to one or more—when they tried. Although not "banzai" charges of the sort launched by the Japanese in World War II—they were usually carefully prepared and supported to the extent possible, they had much the same effect. As the war went on American commanders deliberately dangled small units in seemingly exposed positions to tempt the enemy into such self-destructive attacks.[3]

ALLIES

Americans and Vietnamese were not the only combatants in the war. Other Asians and Westerners participated on the Allied side, although generally on a small scale. The only countries to send major forces to South Vietnam were Thailand, Australia and South Korea. The small Thai division proved worthless and more intent on black marketeering than fighting. The Australians' brigade-sized force was, if anything, more effective man for man than the Americans, and seemed to get along better with the Vietnamese. But Australian antiwar sentiments and morale followed the same downward curve as the Americans', and the unit became less effective. The two Korean divisions, the largest Allied contingent, were very effective in combat, but their commanders were also very cautious. The Koreans also had a bad reputation for brutality; the Vietnamese often complained about them to the Americans.[4]

STRATEGY AND CAMPAIGNS

In 1965, the enemy attempt to split the country in two, and snatch a military victory before enough Americans could arrive to prevent, had failed. The encounter with American forces was an unpleasant experience for the Communists, who were rocked by other measures. Naval patrols of the South Vietnamese coast cut the enemy's seaborne supply line, forcing reliance on the Ho Chi Minh Trail, and supplies brought through Cambodia. The latter was actually more important than the route through Laos, but the Americans were slow to realize this. Patrol boats on navigable rivers helped disrupt the enemy supply system within South Vietnam and hampered their troop movements.

In 1966 Westmoreland started major "search-and-destroy" operations designed to invade the enemy base areas and catch and smash North Vietnamese and Vietcong main-force units. These operations hurt the enemy. But large operations could not be kept secret, especially when the South Vietnamese played a role. Often alerted well in advance, the enemy often left before the Americans arrived. If fighting took place, it was still at times and places chosen by the Communists, as they ambushed leading elements or tried to wipe out seemingly exposed detachments.

Because of American firepower, battles did cause heavy enemy losses, and attacks even on evacuated base areas cost the Communists painfully acquired supplies. But it was doubtful whether such operations really paid off. The enemy regular forces' main supply routes and bases stayed out of reach in Laos and Cambodia, where their units retreated when hard-pressed. The Americans did not realize, for many months, the true importance of the Cambodian sanctuary. While the Ho Chi Minh Trail carried the enemy's manpower south, most of his supplies came through Cambodia. While Laos could be bombed, ground forces could not pursue the enemy into either country, and bombing could not stop soldiers and porters from marching along jungle trails and carrying the relatively modest quantities of supplies needed by the enemy troops—infantrymen supported by mortars, recoilless rifles and rocket launchers. Even in 1968, the enemy needed to import only a hundred tons a day into South Vietnam to keep going. Not only the Vietcong but the North Vietnamese got most of their food, and much else, within South Vietnam. There was nothing to stop the North Vietnamese from sending men into the South; they paid a price in losses to air attack, but it was not one that they could not afford. The American forces were like a dog at the end of a leash. They were trying to attack enemy forces as they poured out of the end of the pipeline from the north, instead of cutting the pipeline. And the American command failed to find a sensible way to measure the progress of its strategy. It relied heavily on counting the enemy dead. But this "body count" soon became an object of derision; it was neither honest nor accurate. It has been suggested that enemy losses were only half those officially estimated.

Moreover, as many authorities on guerrilla war, and the marine generals serving under Westmoreland, warned, the "search-and-destroy" efforts had little effect on the Vietcong guerrillas who were based in the populated areas. The marines, following "orthodox" counterinsurgency theory, urged concentrating on pacification and providing security in populated areas. They argued that the real war was the struggle for the villages. If enemy main force units launched attacks to support the guerrillas, superior American firepower and mobility would crush them before they did much damage. Ultimately the guerrillas would dry up, and Vietcong main force units, denied recruits from the villages, wither away.[5] This, of course, would not deal with the threat posed by the North Vietnamese Army, but that force, while growing, did not yet seem truly formidable.

The marines developed a novel method of pacification, the "combined action program." A marine rifle squad composed of selected volunteers, was coupled with a Vietnamese Popular Forces (militia) platoon, and the resulting Combined Action Platoon was permanently assigned to a Vietnamese village. What were usually termed "villages" were really townships; they averaged 3,500 persons, spread out in several hamlets. The marines and militiamen lived in the village, got to know its residents, provided security against the Vietcong and encouraged self-help projects to improve the local economy. The project was a wonderful success. The belief of Westmoreland (and many others) that American soldiers could not get along with Asian peasants was disproven—if the men involved were properly prepared and led. By the end of 1967, seventy-nine Combined Action Platoons, including 1200 Americans, were pacifying an area containing 250,000 people. Participants and observers were sure that the program could be greatly expanded, but the army generals turned up their noses at the marines' success. The American command had been handed the key to pacification and victory over the guerrillas, but chose not to use it.[6]

All in all, the Americans fell between two stools. As the marines realized, they were not dealing effectively with the guerrillas; letting the enemy use Laos and Cambodia as sanctuaries—immune from a ground invasion, the only sort of attack that could cut the enemy's supply lines—the Americans denied themselves victory over the enemy's main forces.

While Westmoreland sought to grind down the enemy's "big units," the Communists tried to turn the effects of attrition around. While trying to evade attacks on their major base areas inside South Vietnam, the Communists engaged the Americans wherever circumstances were at all favorable, seeking to cause losses that would sap support for the war at home. During 1966 and 1967, the North Vietnamese opened a new front across the demilitarized zone between the two Vietnams. They may have hoped to secure an area in which they could establish a "capital" for the National Liberation Front. They failed to obtain that, but drew Allied forces into a conventional struggle where their own supply lines were short, and diverted Allied units from opposing the guerrillas. Violent battles in which both sides used plenty of artillery resulted. The scale of the forces committed by both sides and the intensity of the fighting grew steadily. The American force in Vietnam (still absurdly known as MACV) was built up to a force of nine divisions and over half a million men—a force bigger than that committed in the Korean War. The Communist forces in 1967 were bigger than ever before. But the enemy command was beginning to become worried.[7]

POLITICS AND BLACK MARKETS

1965 had seen the end of the coups, while in 1966 an attempted revolt by the militant Buddhists was crushed; after that there was a precarious political stability. During 1967 the Allied political position in the south showed some signs of improvement, and there was, perhaps, slight progress toward pacification, although not nearly as much as was imagined. In May

1967, the United States finally formed a single agency under civilian control—"Civil Operations and Revolutionary Development"—to direct pacification. With the Vietnamese, they initiated a new "Revolutionary Development" program. It put fifty-nine-man armed teams in rural areas to counter the local guerrillas and assist the peasants with economic improvements. Steps to improve the police and militia started.

The astounding fact that Vietnamese peasants, like peasants elsewhere, wished to own the lands they farmed finally sank in. President Johnson appears to have played an important role in the new interest in land reform—an important exception to his generally sorry record as a war leader. The South Vietnamese government began tentative steps toward land reform, although at first it did no more than confirm some land titles. There were steps toward democratic government. Elections were held, although their success at expressing the popular will was doubtful. A slate of military candidates triumphed over ten civilian rivals. General Nguyen Van Thieu, who had fought on both sides in the First Indochina War, replaced Ky, completing a rise to power in which he had proven himself a clever intriguer. Thieu was in some ways an able man, but he was never really popular. The elections, although generally honest, afforded little comfort to observers. They confirmed the military's ascendancy in South Vietnamese politics, and, even worse, the politicization of the military. A "peace candidate" associated with the Communists won nearly a fifth of the vote.[8]

South Vietnamese society suffered more and more from large-scale corruption, fueled by the blundering distribution of U.S. aid. Enormous amounts of material were diverted from American warehouses and PXs to the black market, and thence to the enemy. The Americans failed to guard or properly supervise unloading or storing supplies. Saigon became a thieves' paradise. The American Commercial Import Program, which brought civilian goods into Vietnam, became a plaything for corrupt officials. This was not only demoralizing, but helped the enemy. The enemy forces in the Saigon area supplied themselves entirely from Allied Sources except for their weapons and ammunition. (In fact, they could even obtain those things on the black market, but they preferred Soviet-type weapons.) The American Embassy and MACV seem to have looked on this state of affairs with indifference. Far from playing a "colonial" role in Vietnamese affairs, an antiwar propagandists all over the world claimed, the Americans were incredibly indulgent, often truckling toward the South Vietnamese government in humiliating ways. Although it was utterly dependent on American help, the Americans rarely applied pressure to get what they wanted. Ironically, the American leaders shared the obsessions of their critics; there was a near-paranoid fear of playing a "colonial role." The Americans even failed to demand a joint command giving them control of the South Vietnamese armed forces—something they had secured in the Korean War without anyone complaining.[9]

THE AIR WAR AGAINST NORTH VIETNAM

While the military and political struggle raged in the South, the Americans continued an air campaign against North Vietnam, conducted largely by four air force fighter-bomber wings based in Thailand and navy aircraft flying from carriers stationed in the Gulf of Tonkin. Against the strenuous warnings of the armed forces and the CIA (which was skeptical of the decisiveness of any bombing campaign against the North) the administration continued to refrain from an all-out blitz, although it gradually attacked a wider range of targets to interdict the flow of men and supplies to the south, hitting bridges, marshalling yards and other transportation targets. But much of the North remained off limits to attack, including Hanoi, Haiphong, and the transportation routes between Hanoi and China. It was thus easy for the Communist great powers to continue their aid to North Vietnam, while the gradual expansion of the air effort made countermeasures simpler. Attacks on the enemy's fuel storage, originally highly concentrated and vulnerable, were allowed only in June 1966, after it had been dispersed to relative safety. It was characteristic of the war that bombing such facilities could become the subject of a major intragovernmental dispute lasting for months instead of being undertaken as a matter of course. Later attacks were allowed on industrial targets and the electric power system. The Soviets helped North Vietnam build an air force and a strong air defense system, including surface-to-air missiles as well as old-style antiaircraft guns. In one of the most ludicrous episodes of the war, the Americans were not allowed to attack enemy's surface-to-air missile units for many months. When the air force requested permission to hit the missile sites then under construction, Assistant Secretary of Defense McNaughton scoffed at the idea that the North Vietnamese would actually use them, arguing that they were just a political ploy by the Soviets. Unfortunately, the enemy did not think along the lines of the political "strategists" in Washington; they fired the missiles. Fortunately, the missiles proved less effective than anyone had expected, but they forced American planes to fly lower, exposing them to the fire of conventional antiaircraft guns. Attacks on the enemy's airfields were banned until April 1967. The large areas closed to attack made the flight paths of American planes readily predictable and simplified things for the defenders.

While the senseless restrictions made the air campaign more costly in lives and planes, it is by no means clear that they made the difference between success and failure. And in terms of its aims the air campaign failed. The enemy's supply requirements in South Vietnam were so small that even tremendous destruction of vehicles, bridges and railroads did not and could not prevent enough material from getting through. It is doubtful whether the damage to the enemy counterbalanced the loss of planes and pilots. The ultimate sources of North Vietnam's ability to make war lay largely outside its borders: the Vietnamese Communists ran an agricultural economy and depended on imported weapons and fuel. True strategic bombing of enemy war production, as seen in World War II, was almost impossible in Indochina. The only strategic air attack possible against the North would have been to blast the system of dykes that made possible the irrigation of North Vietnam's rice fields. This would have forced North Vietnam to import food to prevent famine, and would probably have prevented it from maintaining forces in the south. Although less ruthless than some Allied actions in World War II, such a policy does not even seem to have been considered. Alternatively, a naval blockade combined with concentrated attacks on the supply routes between China and Hanoi might have choked off most of North Vietnam's outside supplies. But that too was ruled out. The Haiphong dock area, by far the most vulnerable point in the enemy's supply system, remained safe. By October 1967, 200,000 tons of goods lay in and around Haiphong while American planes raced around attacking tiny supply dumps.

The enemy's countermeasures were effective. The North Vietnamese devoted half a million men to keep their battered internal transportation system going, using many of the same devices used by the Germans in Italy in World War II and by the Communists in the Korean War to fight Allied air interdiction. Repair materials were kept at regular intervals; bicycle brigades ferried cargo between trains across the gaps blown in the lines. Trucks and trains moved only at night or in bad weather; by-passes and alternate routes were built, along with underwater bridges. Storage areas were widely scattered. Though under strain, North Vietnam kept going.

The critical military route through Laos was also kept open with more and more engineers, trucks, guns and finally missiles. Ultimately 50,000 men or more ran an increasingly complex system of roads and trails; by 1968 they used as many as 3,000 trucks. The trucks ran at night; to beat infrared sensors they drove slowly, their engines shielded by mats. Troops tried to move by less-obvious paths. The maze of trails was cleverly camouflaged; the North Vietnamese planted additional trees and bushes to hide them. They maintained a network of rest stops at intervals of ten to twenty kilometers.

The inherent difficulty of a successful air campaign in Indochina, enemy countermeasures and the stupid restrictions imposed were not the only causes of failure. The air force and navy had not prepared very well for a limited war with conventional weapons. Since Korea, the services had been oriented toward an all-out war or a European struggle in which tactical nuclear weapons would be used. American conventional ordnance was inadequate; guided bombs were not available and the ground-to-air missiles the Americans did have were inaccurate and too light to smash important targets such as bridges. The low-level tactics originally favored proved too dangerous; with rare exceptions, dive-bombing was the only way to deliver bombs accurately and survive. Underrating the importance of air combat, and overrating the effectiveness of air-to-air missiles, the Americans had dispensed with cannon on most of their fighter planes. The ratio of enemy planes shot down to American losses in the air fighting was depressingly low compared to that achieved in Korea. U.S. Air Force tactics were stereotyped and inflexible, and the proper evaluation of damage done to the enemy was often ignored. To satisfy bureaucratic requirements and keep up "sortie rates" during a bomb shortage, planes flew with light loads. Men were needlessly exposed to being shot down for no good reason—some were even sent to strafe bridges with cannon. On the whole, the story of the first air campaign against North Vietnam reflects little credit on anyone on the American side. It also exacted a high political price. Although the Americans did not attack major cities, and were rather careful about sparing civilian lives, a tremendous propaganda campaign was unleashed against the bombing of North Vietnam. It convinced many people all over the world that huge numbers of civilians were being slaughtered.[10]

OPPOSITION TO THE WAR

Propaganda against the bombing merged into a vaster attack on American policy, which stemmed mostly, but by no means exclusively, from the left wing of the political spectrum and won many adherents of other political currents.[11]

At least at first, few outside the extreme left suggested that the United States should simply pull out and accept losing the war. There was much vague talk of a "negotiated settlement" or a "political solution." In 1965 and 1966 (and sometimes even later) it was often hard to discern a clear dividing line between moderate criticisms of American policy and the avowed policies of the Johnson administration, which itself proclaimed that it did not seek victory but rather negotiations. The attitude of most early critics was typified by Senator William Fulbright's speech of June 15, 1965, which rejected military victory as too costly and unconditional withdrawal as endangering American credibility. Moreover (a point often later misunderstood) for many "moderates" like Fulbright the *war was not the real issue*. They regarded the war in Vietnam as just an example or even merely a symptom of America's alleged "overcommitment" or excessive American intervention in the "Third World" or the world in general. They had little interest in the war per se and were slow to focus their attention on the issues immediately involved.[12] (Although his own arguments against the war were not very impressive, as chairman of the Senate Foreign Relations Committee, Fulbright held hearings that did much to make opposition to the war respectable.) It is perhaps worth mentioning, in this context, that the present author was, and still is, a "moderate" opponent of the war. But I believe that it would be quite misleading to cite only, or even stress, those criticisms of the war that were sensible or justified, or that nowadays seem socially acceptable.

As time passed and the war dragged on, timid critics grew bolder, and the ranks of the extreme left grew. Increasingly many, perhaps most, vocal opponents of the war were not satisfied to suggest that the war was imprudent, or simply a mistake, or even just wrong. Increasingly, many insisted that the war was totally evil and immoral, comparable to the very worst episodes in history.

A vast variety of arguments was used by opponents of the war, ranging from unpleasant and vital truths that the Johnson administration had chosen to evade to lies as vile and fantastic as any ever uttered by the Nazis. Some stressed "practical" arguments, most particularly that the war, whether just or unjust, could not be won. This argument was probably the most popular of all and increasingly convinced many people, especially after the Tet offensive in 1968. Some critics insisted that Vietnam, or even all of Southeast Asia, was of little real importance. Others demonstrated the inadequacy of the domino theory and that the whole region was not really at stake. Some rightly pointed out that North Vietnam was not a Chinese satellite and its victory would not help Chinese expansion. Alternatively "defeatists," like Walter Lippmann and Hans Morgenthau, insisted that Chinese domination of all Southeast Asia was inevitable. The same people tended to argue that the attempt to stop this must lead to war with China and perhaps the USSR as well. This was perhaps the "maximalist" argument against the war, corresponding to the domino theory, or its most extreme versions, on the other side (and of course proved equally unjustified). Yet another maximalist argument, advanced by Robert Heilbroner and others, accepted that revolution was sweeping the Third World; the West could not stop it, and had no right to try. Some argued that the conflict between the USSR and China had made containing communism, previously vital, less necessary or unnecessary; other critics—"revisionist" historians of the Cold War and those who heeded them—maintained that the whole Cold War was a mistake or the result of Western aggression.

Many argued that the struggle in Vietnam was a civil war in which the United States had no business intervening. This particular argument came in at least two different versions. The first stressed that the war was really a civil war *within* South Vietnam. The second version, employed more frequently as North Vietnamese forces took over the burden of the fighting on the Communist side, argued that Vietnam was a single nation, and, therefore, that fighting between North and South constituted a civil war. Some critics pointed out that the South Vietnamese regime was undemocratic and corrupt, while other critics alleged that the United States was fighting to impose its own values on an Asian nation that did not want them. Vietnamese support for the Vietcong was emphasized (and often wildly exaggerated). Some opponents of the war argued that the North Vietnamese regime was the one true representative of Vietnamese nationalism and, therefore, should not be opposed. (Nationalism in "Third World" countries, although not advanced Western ones, was treated as a holy cause.)

The past was interpreted or revised to discredit American policy. Ho Chi Minh, it was frequently said, would have become a "Titoist," friendly to the West, if the United States had only been nice to him in 1945. The United States was "guilty" of having supported French colonialism. The Americans and South Vietnamese, not the Communists, had broken the Geneva Agreements. President Johnson had led the nation into war by duplicity and lies. (This, in fact, was the biggest lie of all.) American methods of waging war were slaughtering civilians and laying the country waste. Anyhow, the money expended in the war should be spent on the poor at home.

As the war continued, truly manic charges appeared. The United States was guilty of imperialism, aggression, even genocide. Its actions were equated with those of Nazi Germany. Such bizarre attitudes were not limited to the far left; in November 1967 Senator Robert Kennedy told an audience, "Don't you understand that what we are doing to the Vietnamese is not very different than what Hitler did to the Jews?"[13] The struggle over Indochina was absorbed into a growing neurotic obsession over the relations between the West and the "Third World" and between white and nonwhite peoples; the war was now often seen as simply another episode of Western imperialism or as "racist." By the end of the 1960s, the general tendency was unmistakably to emphasize the most extreme and dishonest arguments. There was a powerful need to believe the worst, even to roll in the muck. In a way hard to analyze, the war and the growing opposition to it both fed on and powerfully reinforced the growing mood of demoralization, self-contempt, and moral disintegration that was a marked feature of the Western world in the late 1960s and early 1970s, and which never really dissipated thereafter.

The development of widespread criticism of the war, and the growing disillusionment of public opinion must be distinguished from the growth of organized activism against U.S. policy, the so-called antiwar movement. That term was a double misnomer. For its extreme wing, at least, was not "against the war" because they were pacifists, or because they wanted to end the struggle or American involvement in it at any price; it wanted an enemy victory. And some radical leaders actively enjoyed the war (as they later incautiously admitted) and reveled in the opportunity it offered to turn people against a society the war "exposed" as evil and oppressive. For them, in fact, the war was not the real issue (just as it was not the real issue for some moderates either), rather it was the struggle against American capitalism and imperialism. It cannot be stressed too strongly that people opposed American involvement in Indochina for many different reasons. There was no similarity between the motives and beliefs of say, Norman Thomas and George Kennan—to name two upright and intelligent, but otherwise very different older critics of American policy–and those of the "Chicago Seven."

The antiwar organizations were torn behind the scenes by bitter disputes for control between the Trotskyite Socialist Worker's Party and the New Left. The latter element, never too coherent at the best of times, tore itself apart in sectarian squabbles and was infiltrated by Maoists. It became increasingly violent. Those antiwar leaders sincerely devoted to civil disobedience found it harder and harder to prevent their demonstrations from degenerating into pointless violence. Many involved in antiwar demonstrations seemed to be acting out their own psychological problems rather than trying to persuade others to oppose the war; many of their quirks—such as waving Vietcong flags, burning American flags, and spitting on returning veterans (even nurses!) were not calculated to win people over. They were an embarrassment to those seriously opposed to the war; and they seemed to become more and more hysterical even as most Americans came to accept the moderate antiwar position, and saw the war as a mistake. The radicals often seemed to hate "mainstream" opponents of the war like Senators McCarthy and Kennedy as much or more than they did Johnson (which is saying a good deal). A minority finally descended into terrorism, although they often seemed more efficient at blowing themselves up rather than their intended targets. They continued to quarrel among themselves; the Weatherman faction of Students for a Democratic Society (SDS) debated seriously over whether killing white babies was politically correct.

Against the growing opposition, the Johnson administration seemed nearly helpless. Johnson, for reasons quite apart from the war, and which in retrospect had little to do with his real vices and virtues, became very unpopular. Until 1968, he seems to have worried mainly about the attacks on his policies by "hawks" who urged a tougher line, mostly arguing in favor of heavier bombing of North Vietnam. (For a time, in 1966–1967, this group may have been stronger than the opponents of the war.) Johnson himself, perhaps, was so naive a patriot that at first he found it hard to believe that many people could take the antiwar arguments seriously. Later, he became quite bitter, and, by some accounts, gave vent to amazing outbursts, in private. He sent not only the Federal Bureau of Investigation (FBI), but (illegally) the CIA to seek the links he believed existed between his opponents and the Communists. But he did not counter his critics strongly in public. To the extent that he tried to rally opinion, he tried to stress that things in Vietnam were going well, a theme particularly prominent in the fall of 1967, when General Westmoreland indicated that American troops could begin withdrawing in two years. Johnson still avoided trying to whip up popular emotion; on the few occasions he tried this, he spoke in terms of an old-fashioned "rally round the flag" patriotism that might have gone over well in his native Texas but did not impress people who imagined that they were more "sophisticated." He neglected moral arguments or an emphasis that real national interests were involved. Those fields of argument were left to his enemies. This was a self-inflicted defeat. Had Johnson seized the moral high ground, by emphasizing the evil nature of the Communist regime and its alliance with America's main enemy, the Soviet Union, and played up Vietcong atrocities—and he need have said nothing but the truth about those subjects—he might, at least, have slowed the growth of the opposition to the war.

But in the last resort, it is not surprising that he did not do these things. For Johnson and his administration actually shared much of the outlook of their more moderate critics. Johnson saw himself not as a crusader against communism, but as striving for detente, as "building bridges to the East" in the catchphrase of the era, and he himself had eschewed decisive action against the enemy from the start. If the war in Indochina made any sense at all, morally and strategically, which was highly doubtful, it was only within the framework of a prolonged struggle against Communist totalitarianism, seen as an unmitigated evil. But to arraign North Vietnam as a Soviet cats-paw contradicted the administration's basic policy and would have made nonsense of the fashionable optimism about relations with the USSR. The administration rationalized, of course, that China, not the Soviets, was the real enemy behind North Vietnam, but that claim was increasingly hard to sustain. In truth, to preach the virtues and imminence of detente and simultaneously wage war made no sense. Thus Johnson was caught in a tangle of contradictions. Probably he never appreciated the irony of the fact that he increasingly depended on men like his old enemy, Barry Goldwater, who backed the war but had little use for his general approach to foreign policy.

In 1967 the growth of opposition was still at an early stage, but there was much evidence that support for the war was soft and flabby, and that it was eroding and was not liable to survive a perceived reverse.

Already, polls showed that more people considered the war a mistake than not. Surveys of congressional opinion in September and October 1967 showed a major shift from support of the administration's policy to "seeking a way out." Few however, openly admitted that they favored accepting defeat; many pretended—perhaps even to themselves—that there was some middle course between victory and defeat. (It was not only the extremists, in this era, who were disingenuous.) This shift was generally based on the perception that the president's policy was failing, not yet on questioning the morality of the war or the basis of the policy of containment. But it was symptomatic that failure was seen as a reason to abandon the war effort, rather than demanding a change in policy or personnel to obtain success.

Often, it should be noted, supporters of the war turned into opponents for reasons having less to do with their recognizing some previously ignored reality than with the collapse of their own baseless fantasies that the war could be quickly ended (fantasies the administration had not encouraged) or that it could be "managed" with a minimum of inconvenience. Senator Thruston Morton of Kentucky, explaining his change of heart, declared that he had been "all for the bombing. I thought once we started, the war would be over in six months." The influential Luce publications, despite their reputation for hard-line anticommunism, became shaky in 1967 because Henry Luce and his editor-in-chief felt that Vietnam might be "worth

50-100,000 American troops but not much more."[14] Lyndon Johnson made many disastrous mistakes, but it is hard not to feel sympathy for a man faced with the defection of "supporters" like these!

During 1966–1967 there was disillusionment within the administration as well, notably on the part of Secretary of Defense McNamara and his civilian subordinates. McNamara, originally more optimistic than the professional soldiers, apparently began to jump to the opposite extreme as early as late 1965. He and his associates suspected, with reason, that, American strategy in South Vietnam was not working, and that bombing the north was not "cost-effective." Some, like Henry Luce, felt that the war had just become too big, as Alain Enthoven put it, "I fell off the boat when the troop level reached 170,000."[15] Many of these men, it should be noted, including McNamara himself, were at odds with members of their own families over the war; some of their children held quite extreme views. In October 1966 McNamara decided that the American commitment should be "levelled off" at 470,000 men and the current level of bombing. He hoped to make bombing the North unnecessary by building an "anti-infiltration barrier" between the two Vietnams. Apparently inspired by the "Morice Line" used by the French in the Algerian War, it was to consist of obstacles and minefields peppered with electronic sensors that would direct covering fire and counterattacks. The barrier would be partly extended into Laos with sensors and air-laid mines. (McNamara still opposed ground operations there.) Since everyone knew that most infiltrators entered South Vietnam through Laos, not across the DMZ, even ground-force officers who thought the bombing of North Vietnam ineffective regarded the barrier as ridiculous. An attempt to set up positions from which it could be built cost many lives. Aside from the abortive barrier scheme, McNamara had no real idea of what to do. He told President Johnson that "we must improve our position by getting ourselves into a military posture that we credibly could maintain almost indefinitely."[16] The notion that keeping half a million men in South Vietnam indefinitely was a credible posture must be one of the most laughable misappreciations of the war. It was not only the optimists who were out of touch with reality.

The Joint Chiefs of Staff were not rich in ideas either. They admitted in late 1967 that the war could not be won within the next two years although, unlike McNamara, they believed that progress was being made and accepted Westmoreland's March 1967 estimate that he was reaching the crossover point where enemy losses were exceeding infiltration and recruitment in South Vietnam, and that pacification was making progress. The Joint Chiefs did favor mining North Vietnam's ports as well as increased bombing. But McNamara, as did his successor, flatly rejected reconsidering the limitations agreed on in 1965.[17]

THE TET OFFENSIVE

Although the American leaders were far too optimistic, the Communist leaders had become worried by mid-1967. (The reader should be warned that assessing the actual situation in 1967, even in retrospect, is an unusually complicated and difficult issue.) While Westmoreland's concentration on the enemy's big units and massive search and destroy operations was not the most effective possible strategy, and he overestimated the results attained, it probably was not as totally ineffective as the exponents of "orthodox" counterinsurgency doctrine tended, then and later, to assume. Helicopter-assisted mobility, and the Americans' massive firepower, made his blows more effective than similar operations in previous wars. The Americans inflicted heavy losses, and deprived the enemy of effective control of some population and territory, even if less than Westmoreland supposed. The search-and-destroy operations did not succeed in trapping and destroying entire enemy units, but the invasion of his base areas did disrupt the enemy supply system. In the northern provinces, the Marines prevented the enemy from getting his usual share of the rice crop there. More important than the loss of control over some areas and the people living there, from the enemy point of view, was the flight of more than a million people as refugees into areas, especially cities, already held by the Allies, where they could no longer support the guerrillas.

The Communists feared that time, after all, might not be on their side. They had taken heavy losses, and the American forces were strong. If the war dragged on, the Americans might become impatient and take drastic actions, or even apply their forces more intelligently. Had the Vietnamese Communists been doctrinaire "Maoists," as they were widely believed to be in the 1960s, they might have fallen back to a lower level of guerrilla warfare, as the Chinese had urged for some time. But while the Vietnamese leaders had been forced by circumstances to resort to Maoist-type guerrilla warfare in both Indochina wars, their military ideas were not identical to Mao's. Their takeover of Vietnam in 1945 had been attained by a general uprising, while victory in 1954 had been clinched by defeating the French in a conventional battle. While Dien Bien Phu was not militarily decisive— only a small fraction of the French forces in Indochina had been lost—it had broken the French will to fight on. The Communist leaders sought a short-cut to victory by reproducing these earlier successes against the

Americans and the South Vietnamese. They convinced themselves that the massive flight of refugees from the countryside into the cities, and friction between Vietnamese and the "imperialists," had created a revolutionary situation in the cities. An attack on the cities would start a general uprising like that of 1945. The South Vietnamese army and regime would collapse; and the Americans, left flat-footed, would leave.

During the latter half of 1967, the Communists, mainly using North Vietnamese units, attacked in border areas, to lure American units well away from the cities. Since MACV was already inclined to fight in the border area, the Communist effort succeeded. One CIA analyst, Joseph Hovey, fully grasped the enemy scheme, but everyone else assumed that the Communists would adhere to orthodox Maoist doctrine, or that the idea of an uprising was absurd, or the enemy was not desperate enough to try such a stunt.

In early 1968, as Tet, the Vietnamese lunar new year holiday, approached, the North Vietnamese presented a major threat to a marine force at Khe Sanh, an isolated plateau that was the Western anchor of the projected "McNamara Line." A situation deceptively like the siege of Dien Bien Phu seemed to develop, attracting attention throughout the world, but the reality was different. The marines held the high ground. They were much closer to supporting forces than the French, and were backed by immensely greater airpower. It is unclear whether the Khe Sanh move was simply a feint. It is more likely that the enemy was carrying on a "wheels-within-wheels" plan, in which the move against Khe Sanh was mainly a diversion, but a decisive battle would be sought if the situation developed favorably. Westmoreland welcomed a major battle there. He wanted to draw the enemy into a classic conventional battle and crush them. He hoped to get permission to follow such a victory up by a drive from Khe Sanh into Laos to cut the Ho Chi Minh Trail. The sensors developed for the "McNamara Line" proved useful, guiding fantastically intense air and artillery bombardments that shattered the North Vietnamese force and discouraged or prevented a full-scale assault.

General Westmoreland and his staff were looking to the north. They expected a general enemy offensive, but not one of the size and extent which occurred. They did not expect an attack on the cities. The Americans knew of calls for a "general uprising," but, except for Hovey, dismissed them as propaganda; they were sure that the South Vietnamese would not rise and assumed that the enemy knew this too. Nor did they believe the enemy would actually strike on the day of Tet, the greatest Vietnamese holiday. But General Frederick Weyand, one of Westmoreland's ablest subordinates, who commanded the American corps in the Saigon region, was worried. He did not foresee the whole enemy plan, but expected attacks on cities and enemy installations in his area. He persuaded Westmoreland to let him keep some units scheduled to be moved to the north, and pulled some of his troops closer in to Saigon.[18] This proved to be a very, very fortunate decision. And a breakdown in Communist planning caused some units to strike prematurely, giving some advance warning elsewhere.

Vietcong units had slipped close to or actually inside most of South Vietnam's major cities. On January 30, 1968, they attacked, trying to bypass major military units and seize government installations and positions in the hearts of cities and towns. Special operations were supposed to take Radio Saigon, the principal headquarters and air bases in the Saigon area, and the American Embassy. Once the Saigon broadcasting station was in their hands, the Communists planned to announce the fall of the government and the collapse of the South Vietnamese armed forces.

Fierce fighting erupted all over the country. North Vietnamese units seized most of Hue, the old capital, and were thrown out only after a month of heavy fighting. At least 2800 civilians were massacred by the Communists. But in most places the enemy was ejected in a relatively short time. The Communists had miscalculated. So had Westmoreland, who reacted sluggishly to the attacks. At first he continued to think that the attacks on the cities were a diversion, and he was grossly overoptimistic about the situation at Hue.

The South Vietnamese did not collapse, and there was no popular uprising. Backs to the wall, the South Vietnamese Army and police fought courageously as never before. The attack on the cities on a sacred holiday enraged people. The Vietcong suffered terrific losses. Of 67,000 men perhaps half were killed or captured, while many enemy agents and leaders were exposed. Far from scoring a decisive victory, the Communists suffered a shattering defeat. Their guerrilla forces were permanently crippled.

It had, however, been a close shave for the Allies. If not for General Weyand's precautions, the enemy might have overrun most of Saigon for a time; even so the defense of some major points was a touch-and-go affair. The great airfields in the Saigon area, Tan Son Nhut and Bien Hoa, were poorly defended; only luck and gross blunders by the enemy saved them from capture, and prevented the loss of hundreds of planes and helicopters. Tan Son Nhut, which was also the site of MACV and the South Vietnamese Joint General Staff headquarters, was saved by the presence of South Vietnamese troops who were supposed to have been moved elsewhere and were there by mistake, the heroic crews of a few American gunships, and the timely intervention of a U.S. armored cavalry unit that arrived just in time to take the attacking force in the flank. This little-noted battle, rather than the bloodier and more-publicized fighting around Hue and Khe Sanh, was the truly decisive battle of Tet. It may have prevented the early loss of the war and all the consequences that might have flowed from a quick and open, humiliating defeat of the United States. Everything that happened throughout the war shows that the Communist hope of a popular uprising was a pipe dream. But had the Vietcong captured the South Vietnamese headquarters and broadcast their planned proclamation over Radio Saigon they might have triggered at least a partial collapse of South Vietnamese resistance.

As far as the *internal* struggle in South Vietnam was concerned, the Communists had shot their bolt. Vietcong main force units could no longer replace their losses from within the south; northern soldiers began to fill their ranks. The South Vietnamese army and government were jolted into taking actions that were long overdue. National mobilization was proclaimed. The pacification program, which temporarily collapsed, was quickly revived and accelerated. Land seized by Diem's government but never distributed was finally parcelled out.[19]

The Tet offensive was a decisive reverse for the enemy. It spelled the defeat of communism as a revolutionary movement inside South Vietnam. The main burden of the war on the Communist side now fell on the North Vietnamese army, and the war became a primarily conventional war.

It might be thought that the United States would have no great trouble winning this simpler, more understandable struggle. In a rational world the enemy defeat might have been followed up by a determined attack into Laos and Cambodia. But things did not work out that way.

DECISION FOR DEFEAT

At home, there was an explosion of opposition to the war. The enemy's ability to launch a powerful surprise attack on South Vietnam's cities was a terrific shock. There was much leaping to conclusions; Governor George Romney of Michigan, a Republican presidential candidate, expressed a widespread view when he declared that Tet showed that the South Vietnamese people supported the enemy. The Johnson administration's and General Westmoreland's optimistic statements of the fall seemed exposed as utter folly, and whatever they said henceforth, even if well-founded, would be generally ignored. The Tet offensive became one of the worst-reported events of a poorly reported war. The fact that the Communists had failed just did not register. And many in Washington flew into a near-panic. It was not the case, as was often said later, that the news media alone misrepresented the outcome; indeed commentators like Walter Cronkite, who declared that the war was a stalemate, were far more sober than some in the administration. In retrospect, it is clear that the Americans' will to fight had already been soft. Instead of reacting to a perceived defeat with anger and renewed determination to win, as in previous wars, the tendency was to throw in the towel. In a short time nearly a fifth of the electorate switched from supporting the war to opposing it. President Johnson exerted little leadership and did little to shape public opinion or explain the facts in this critical period; although he was so unpopular by then that any greater effort on his part might have backfired. (Troops of hecklers followed him everywhere, chanting "Hey, hey, LBJ, how many kids have you killed today?") Moreover, an attempt by the chairman of the Joint Chiefs of Staff to secure a massive increase in U.S. forces and restock the depleted strategic reserve boomeranged. He got Westmoreland, who wanted a modest reinforcement, to request 206,000 more men, and presented the request to Johnson as though Westmoreland wanted the whole force for himself. And even he did not share Westmoreland's optimistic assessment of the Tet fighting. The request quickly leaked to the public, where it was naturally misinterpreted as showing that the situation was desperate. Johnson viewed the troop request without enthusiasm. Even within the administration there was a general, and understandable, distrust of Westmoreland's judgment, and a belief that "enough was enough," no more resources should be sunk in the war. Even hard-liners like Paul Nitze feared that the war was undermining America's position in the world. A few men, like Walt Rostow and Johnson's friend, Supreme Court Justice Abe Fortas, urged sending in more troops and "taking the gloves off" with the bombing; Fortas urged Johnson to rouse the public.

A major reassessment of American policy developed. Many officials favored ending or reducing the bombing of North Vietnam. Many also urged a shift to a "population control" strategy like that long favored by the marine corps. But they did not get their way, at least immediately; indeed this idea, three years overdue, was perhaps no longer appropriate. Clark Clifford, the new secretary of defense, decided that military victory was impossible and urged negotiations, although he recommended no real strategic alternative to the present course; he saw no end in sight whatever the Americans did. In March 1968, at Clifford's suggestion, Johnson reconvened the "wise men," an advisory group of prominent former officials and generals of the older generation, such as Dean Acheson, Omar Bradley and Matthew

Ridgway, as well as former officials of his own administration. Although they disagreed among themselves at least as much as his usual advisers, the president was much impressed by the pessimists among them, especially former Secretary of State Acheson. Acheson's arguments were particularly frank and well-reasoned, even if they were not always soundly based. Acheson maintained that given the trend of public opinion and international circumstances, there was no longer the time nor the possibility of applying enough resources to win the war. Public opinion and our interests elsewhere required disengaging within a year. Acheson frankly doubted that the South Vietnamese would be up to taking over the war effort in that time. No one else seems to have concluded that Vietnam should be abandoned, although either Rostow and Fortas were right, or Acheson was right—there was no middle course.

Johnson did not fully accept Acheson's gloomy conclusions, but decided to send only 22,000 more men to Westmoreland's command. Although no explicit ceiling was imposed, it was clear that that would be the last increase in the number of troops. In a program apparently initiated by Westmoreland (but which Clifford and Nixon both claimed credit for) the South Vietnamese forces would be improved and reequipped (they were still fighting with World War II-era weapons against an enemy with modern small arms). There was, however, no decision for a new ground strategy. Johnson ordered a partial bombing halt, ending attacks on North Vietnam above the 20th parallel.

In the same speech in which he announced these moves, Johnson declared that he would not run for the presidency again. It was widely supposed that the antiwar movement had "driven" him from office, and this became one of the war's enduring myths. In fact, Johnson had privately decided not to run in 1967; the heart condition that finally killed him meant that he could not survive another term.

Although the Communists had earlier demanded a complete end to the bombing before any negotiations, they agreed to "peace talks" in Paris. This inspired widespread foolish hopes. But the negotiations proved even more disastrous than the truce talks at Panmunjom in the Korean War and failed to produce agreement. Later in 1968, all bombing of North Vietnam ended. The attack shifted to the Ho Chi Minh Trail in Laos, and it became somewhat more effective in interdicting enemy supplies than the earlier air campaign.[20]

9

American Withdrawal

In retrospect, it seems clear that in the spring of 1968 the United States lost the Second Indochina War, although for seven years costly and devoted efforts were made to evade or ignore this and postpone defeat. While neither the Johnson administration nor its successor were really willing to do what was necessary to win the war, neither was reconciled to losing it, either.

The new president, Richard Nixon, proved an even worse leader than Lyndon Johnson. It is probably true, as many have said, that he understood world affairs and conflict better than Johnson, but his psychological quirks and other limitations were such that this was of little help to anyone. His administration was a labyrinth of Byzantine intrigues and dissension. Even more than Kennedy and Johnson, Nixon and his principal foreign policy adviser, the slippery National Security Adviser Henry Kissinger, were obsessed with images and the surface of things rather than reality.

During the election campaign, Nixon had claimed to have a "secret plan" to end the war. This, alas, did not exist. Nixon and Kissinger appear to have privately believed in 1968 that the war could not be won, and that probably the best that could be accomplished was a "decent interval" between a peace agreement, an American departure and the fall of South Vietnam. This, they supposed, would be less humiliating, and have less drastic effects on international and domestic politics, than an immediate departure from Indochina. But they probably hoped for something better, and finally proved as incapable as their predecessors of a realistic and dispassionate evaluation of the situation. They rejected the course of rapid withdrawal favored by Secretary of State William Rogers and Secretary of Defense Melvin Laird.

They tentatively tried to bluff the North Vietnamese into thinking that they planned a massive air assault to blast them into submission. But the Communists saw through them; and if they ever seriously considered carrying out their threats they had dropped the idea by late 1969. Although rejecting any attempt to actually win the war, they, in effect, chose to sacrifice other commitments to devote American strength to Indochina. They underrated the enemy's determination and the difficulty of negotiating with North Vietnam. They began accepting excessively optimistic evaluations of the situation in South Vietnam.

Nixon announced a policy of "Vietnamization," of preparing the South Vietnamese to take over the war while American forces were gradually reduced. In fact, this was a fancy name for the policies inaugurated under Johnson. By June 1969, the situation had improved sufficiently so that some American troops could leave.

Westmoreland's successor, the able General Creigton Abrams, had shifted to a "one-war" strategy. Improving the South Vietnamese forces and population security had equal priority with hunting the enemy's big units. Abrams ordered a major transfer of American forces from the north to the Saigon area; the marines were allowed to quietly evacuate Khe Sanh and adopt the more mobile defensive tactics they had long wanted. Different tactics were adopted for offensive operations. Abrams aimed more at finding the enemy's supplies than destroying units. There was a mass of operations based on small, briefly occupied firebases (often used as bait for enemy attacks); American companies and platoons spread out widely to seek out small enemy caches and set up ambushes along the trails from Cambodia.

On top of the Tet defeat, the new strategy, pacification and other measures caused the Vietcong to visibly shrivel. Roads were opened, and villages freed from attack. The Communists' few attempts to launch serious attacks misfired, and during 1969 they adopted a policy of conserving their forces and outwaiting the Americans. In 1969–1970 the government finally carried out a real land reform. A new South Vietnamese militia, the People's Self-Defense Force, was formed, and in a year or two more than a million civilians were armed. The South Vietnamese armed forces unquestionably improved. But they remained weak in many ways. The general level of leadership was poor, and the gap between the largely upper- and middle-class officers and the peasant enlisted men remained enormous. The army depended on American transportation and air support as well as supplies. The government remained under military domination (all provincial governors were soldiers) and was permeated by corruption and unpopularity.

Nor did Thieu resist the temptation to reverse progress toward local self-government at the village level. Most South Vietnamese people did not like the Communists, but few respected their non-Communist rulers. Knocking out the Communists as a revolutionary movement did not mean that a solid structure capable of fending off the Northern regime had been built.[1]

In the United States, support for the war continued to decay. Even to many who had strongly supported it earlier, and who rejected all the arguments against it, it seemed an epic dreariness without meaning or end. While most people were willing to give gradual disengagement, and preparing the South Vietnamese to take over, a chance, many were not so patient. Some now openly favored a Communist victory. Opposition to the administration's policy intensified. Much as public opinion had dumbly accepted even the most dubious arguments of the Johnson administration in 1965, now even the most absurd attacks on the war received a respectful hearing.

The disclosure, in late 1969, of the My Lai massacre was a further blow to national morale. In March 1968, troops of the "Americal" Division had murdered several hundred Vietnamese civilians at My Lai. It was widely argued then, and even much later, that this was somehow typical of the conduct of American troops. There were certainly other cases of Americans murdering Vietnamese civilians; relations with them were usually bad. Insults, beatings and the killing of domestic animals were common. There were cases where firepower was used recklessly or worse. Tankers sometimes replied to a single sniper shot from a village by indiscriminately firing high explosives or white phosphorus into the place. When men in one cavalry unit were killed or wounded, some pilots ran amok and "blew away every person and village in their path."[2] Still, such behavior was not characteristic, and Vietnamese were not usually afraid to be around Americans. While many—far too many—Vietnamese were killed accidentally or as incidental by-products of military operations, it is doubtful that Vietnam was worse in this respect than World War II or Korea.

My Lai, in extent at least, was almost certainly unique. Nothing has come to light in the last twenty-five years to suggest that any crime similar in scale was committed by American troops. It was perhaps characteristic of the war that while My Lai received enormous publicity in the United States and throughout the world, a similar massacre committed by South Koreans at about the same time—not to mention the far more numerous and planned massacres committed by the Communists—got little attention. It seems likely that the astigmatism caused by obsessions with race was responsible. It was news if "white men" massacred "yellow people" but not if "yellow people" massacred each other.[3] My Lai securely established the picture of Vietnam veterans as psychotic killers; they would be ritually degraded on movie and television screens for the next two decades. But even those who regarded My Lai as utterly atypical were sickened, and no one wanted any part of a war where such things could happen. In this already depressed atmosphere, the Allied raid into Cambodia in 1970 caused an explosion.

CAMBODIA

The Americans had never completely respected Cambodia's phony neutrality. Units fighting along the border occasionally falsified map coordinates to bring air attacks and artillery down on enemy troops seen crossing the border, and senior officers had winked at this. In planned operations, special forces and SEALs occasionally entered Cambodia to observe enemy activities, snatch prisoners for interrogation, or sabotage installations.

Since 1969 the Americans had bombed enemy bases in border areas of Cambodia. The bombings were not announced in order to spare Cambodia's erratic ruler embarrassment. Increasingly afraid of his Vietnamese "guests," Prince Sihanouk agreed to turn a blind eye to the bombing if the attacks received no publicity. It is characteristic of much commentary on the war that this "secret bombing" was later held up as more evidence of government duplicity. In fact, it was an "open secret," reported in the *New York Times* shortly after it began. It is equally characteristic of the Nixon administration that, even after the "secret" was exposed in the world's greatest newspaper, it tried to suppress information about it!

Cambodians, or at least the town-dwelling educated minority, had turned violently against both Sihanouk's corrupt and arbitrary rule and the Vietnamese Communist presence in Cambodia. In March 1970, Lon Nol, the leader of the Cambodian army, overthrew Sihanouk, and proclaimed a republic. The Cambodians celebrated Sihanouk's downfall by massacring Vietnamese civilians who had long been residing in the country. The new rulers quickly proved as incompetent as the old ones. Lon Nol was a dizzy character quite out of touch with reality; and throughout the agonizing struggle for Cambodia, the Americans made no serious attempt to ensure that their aid was properly used.

The North Vietnamese quickly struck out of the sanctuaries to clear their rear, and began forming a Cambodian Communist force to overthrow Lon Nol's government. The Cambodian army, a parade-ground sinecure for the upper class, gave them little trouble.

The Nixon administration had little interest in saving the Cambodians, nor any expectation of this. But it saw the new situation as a chance to strike a major blow against the enemy and win more time for "Vietnamization." At the end of April, American and South Vietnamese forces drove into Cambodia. Nixon announced the attack in a poorly written speech that made even senior officers enthusiastic about the operation cringe; he led people to think that the attack was aimed at capturing the enemy headquarters, which the planners had regarded as no more than an outside chance and called it an "incursion." At least as far as American forces were concerned, it was only a prolonged, large-scale raid; but, as usual, the American government's preference for overcomplicated doubletalk simply helped to land it in more trouble. Opposition to the war in the United States burst out in an explosion of hysterical rage, as the administration was accused of "expanding the war." Nixon hastily limited the American forces to a penetration of only thirty kilometers into Cambodia, and the American forces withdrew in eight weeks. The South Vietnamese stayed longer. Congress quickly passed legislation to prevent American soldiers from operating in either Cambodia or Laos.

The results of the operation were mixed. The South Vietnamese performed well. Angry at the massacres of their fellow countrymen, they ruthlessly plundered the Cambodians. The operation seemed to vindicate "Vietnamization," but in fact the successes had been scored by unusually well-led units carefully babied by the Americans. The Allies captured huge amounts of supplies, probably forcing the enemy to postpone a major offensive in South Vietnam for a full year, and came close to winning a really great victory. Despite some advance warning, the leaders of the National Liberation Front and many elite units barely escaped encirclement. The operation showed what might have been accomplished had a full-scale attack into Cambodia with larger forces been executed in previous years. As it was, however, most of the enemy forces got away. They had just been pushed deeper into Cambodia, where neither a limited operation nor Lon Nol's army could deal with them.

In just four months, the North Vietnamese and their Cambodian Communist allies overran half the country, including almost the whole area east of the Mekong River, and wrecked the Cambodian army. While the North Vietnamese carried on the bulk of the fighting, they created an effective Cambodian Communist force, the "Khmer Rouge." Before Sihanouk's overthrow, they had refrained from aiding the Cambodian Communist guerrillas, who had based themselves among the Khmer Loeu hill people, a backward minority group. Now, however, the Communists had a broader appeal. Sihanouk formed a royal government-in-exile and acted as their front man. The Communists played on the peasants' traditional reverence for the royal family to gain support—an ironic foundation for what was to become the most fanatically revolutionary of all Communist regimes.[4]

THE COLLAPSE OF MORALE

Before the Cambodian affair, American morale had fallen almost to zero. Now it sank below zero.

Feeling against the war reached such a pitch of fanaticism that even normally "moderate" individuals openly gloated when an attempt to rescue American prisoners of war in North Vietnam in November 1970 failed.

The armed services, or at least the army, were in a state of near collapse. This disintegration may have begun as early as 1968; it was visibly catastrophic by 1971. Men refused to fight; officers were murdered. Tremendous tension developed between draftees and regulars, and between whites and blacks. Drug use was rife, although, like racial conflict, it was far worse in the rear than in the field. Marijuana use had become common in 1968; heroin use exploded in 1970. Indeed with the drug problem, the U.S. forces passed from what can reasonably be described as demoralization to something else, for which no satisfactory term has been devised. Armies that are "merely" demoralized, like the Russian Army in 1917 or those of the Central Powers a year later, do not behave this way. In this orgy of mass self-destructiveness, it was not "every man for himself" but almost "every man against himself."

Moreover the rest of the army was sacrificed to keep the force in Vietnam going. Combat units in Europe and Korea were largely ineffective, and those at home became little more than holding units for men going to and from Vietnam. The United States was very, very lucky that it was not forced into another war in the late 1960s and early 1970s.

Several factors were involved in this dreadful collapse. There has been a curious reluctance to peer into this situation and how it came about, or at least look beyond obvious elements internal to the military forces. Probably the main factor was influence from the larger society. The armed forces could not be sealed off from antiwar sentiments and the feeling that people at home did not support them, or the general demoralization so common in the Western world in that period.

But unsound military policies, some dating back many years, had a major impact. American tactics and training were poorly adapted to Vietnam and soldiers soon sensed this. The policy of sending enlisted men to Vietnam as individual replacements, "rotating" them after one-year tours, harmed the cohesion in military units. Worse, officers served tours of only six months, ensuring that many were less experienced than the men under them. This widened the gulf between officers and enlisted men. Moreover, the ranks of the officer class had become both inflated and caste-ridden. The proportion of officers in the army (15 percent) was more than twice that in World War II. An emphasis on business-style "management" instead of traditional combat leadership in the training of officers left them less able to conduct themselves in battle and win the respect of their men. Rampant careerism among the officer class and career non-commissioned officers (NCOs) was known to extend to avoiding their share of combat. Some experts, such as S.L.A. Marshall, considered the army's policy of drafting men at eighteen— a policy with all sorts of unhappy social consequences—a serious mistake, holding that, contrary to what the army assumed, men in their twenties made better and more resilient soldiers than teenagers.[5]

TOWARD A PSEUDOPEACE

The South Vietnamese continued to take over the burden of combat. But when they tried to duplicate the Cambodian "incursion" in Laos in 1971 without direct American support, there were clear signs of the limits of "Vietnamization." The Laos attack was a disaster; although suffering heavy losses, the Communists launched a counterattack with massed tanks that routed the South Vietnamese force.

The Communists prepared a major offensive for 1972. By striking in an election year, when American ground forces had already largely departed, they hoped to avoid any strong American reaction; while if the offensive succeeded, South Vietnamese resistance might collapse. A serious defeat might discredit Nixon and cause his defeat, or force an end to American involvement in Indochina. The Soviets provided ample supplies of heavy equipment; this was to be a straightforward conventional offensive, launched by the North Vietnamese regular army.

The Allies expected an attack. But, as usual, its precise timing and strength proved a surprise. On March 30 the North Vietnamese struck in the north, across the demilitarized zone and out of Laos. In the following month two new attacks began, one out of Cambodia aimed at Saigon and the other in the Central Highlands, designed to cut the country in two. There was furious fighting and a critical situation developed.

President Nixon, however, reacted resolutely. Whether or not his policy was truly based on saving South Vietnam, he was determined to avoid an open, humiliating defeat. On April 6 intense air attacks began against North Vietnam. Using new laser- and television-guided bombs, the new air campaign was far more effective than its predecessor. The enemy's transportation system was heavily damaged. On May 8, the Americans began mining North Vietnam's ports. The Communist great powers grumbled, but neither took any counteraction, much to the anger of the North Vietnamese, who openly abused their patrons. Neither the USSR nor China was willing to disturb their new relationships in a way that might work to the other's advantage. They may also have perceived that what was going on would not be decisive. Even if the North Vietnamese lost this round it was hardly the end for them. The United States, in turn, did not even squawk about the enormous Soviet supply effort that had made the North Vietnamese offensive possible. The quest for detente put the Nixon administration in an absurd position. It raged about the acts of a minor Communist state, while professing the greatest optimism about relations with those who had made them possible. The international aspects of the Communist "Easter offensive" in Vietnam proved a preview of the consequences of detente.

In South Vietnam, the remaining American ground troops stayed in reserve, but the South Vietnamese received abundant supplies and tremendous support from American air attacks and naval gunfire. After desperate fighting, the Communists were brought to a halt. In June, the South Vietnamese launched a counteroffensive, although they were only moderately successful in regaining lost ground. The Communists had failed to decisively defeat the South Vietnamese forces, although perhaps only by a narrow margin. Some South Vietnamese units fought well, but others performed poorly. The country had been saved partly by enormous American air and naval support, which had inflicted perhaps half the enemy's heavy losses (they lost at least a hundred thousand men and half their tanks and heavy guns) and the enemy's mistakes. Whatever its limitations earlier, air interdiction was very effective against a conventional army dependent on a continuing flow of fuel, ammunition and other supplies. The Communists failed, or in the face of airpower were unable, to mass their forces for one decisive stroke, and they had failed to keep supplies moving to forward units after their initial successes. They did not use their masses of armor and artillery properly.[6]

The defeat of the Communist offensive and the bombing of the north broke the deadlock that had beset the peace negotiations. The public negotiations begun in 1968 had long been just a front for secret talks (publicly disclosed only in January 1972) between Henry Kissinger and the North Vietnamese. The Communists adamantly insisted that the Americans must not only remove all their forces from South Vietnam, but end aid to the South Vietnamese government and make Thieu step down. A coalition regime of Communist, anti-Communist and "third force" elements must be formed before a peace agreement. The Americans, by contrast, weakened. They initially demanded that North Vietnamese as well as American forces leave the south, but dropped this demand in 1970.

The talks were renewed in July 1972. In early September the Communists dropped the demand that the Americans themselves wreck the Saigon government and remove Thieu. In the next six weeks the Communists dropped the demand for an open coalition regime and their insistence that they be allowed to choose the third force elements that were to participate in the political talks in a "national council" that were to follow a cease-fire. Most major issues seemed settled by mid-October. Only the issues of releasing political prisoners held by Saigon, and regulating the entry of military supplies into South Vietnam after the cease-fire remained. While these points were dealt with, and others clarified, the Americans undertook to secure South Vietnamese agreement to the settled points.

The South Vietnamese government, which had been excluded from the talks, violently insisted that the North Vietnamese remove all their forces from the South. It opposed the National Council and any acknowledgment that Vietnam, North and South, formed a single nation. The southern leaders pointed out that the Americans had overlooked discrepancies between the Vietnamese and English texts which meant that the national council was conceded administrative responsibilities, in effect smuggling a coalition government in by the back door. Although Kissinger earlier had foolishly told the world that "peace is at hand," the Americans felt forced to pass the South Vietnamese demands to the Communists on November 20. This seems to have been a pro forma gesture; no one expected the Communists to make serious concessions. North Vietnam, meanwhile, agreed to the earlier disputed points. But it now backpedaled itself, withholding agreement on the issue of civilian prisoners, and threatening to hold back American prisoners of war until all Communist political cadres and agents were freed. The Communists introduced new political demands.

Nixon, infuriated, ordered the greatest air offensive of the war against North Vietnam. The attacks carefully aimed at military targets, caused relatively few civilian deaths, but set off furious opposition throughout the world. They were even criticized by the Pope. They were, however, effective. The North Vietnamese backed down and returned to the terms agreed on earlier, without the disguised coalition scheme. Thieu was persuaded to sign the "peace agreement" by promises of a vast quantity of supplies and secret assurances from Nixon that he would react strongly if there were "major violations" by the North Vietnamese. Thieu professed to swallow these assurances; perhaps he was foolish enough to believe them. In fact, given the state of American congressional and public opinion, those promises were valueless. Only a public declaration or treaty might have meant something. Nixon and Kissinger did not try to secure support for the use of American forces to enforce the peace. Presumably they knew what the public reaction would be.

The Paris agreement was greeted with fantastic hoopla. Kissinger and the North Vietnamese Foreign Minister, Le Duc Tho, were jointly awarded the Nobel Peace Prize; only the American accepted. (One wit suggested giving the next Nobel Prize for literature to Walt Disney.) In fact, like some other agreements negotiated by Kissinger, the Paris agreement was sloppily worded and contained contradictory provisions. Although the Nixon administration hailed it as a victory or at least "peace with honor," it did not register the attainment of American objectives. North Vietnam was conceded the right to maintain its forces—numbering at least 145,000 men and perhaps a great deal more—inside the frontiers of South Vietnam, and the agreement gave the Communists an active political role in the country. The arrangements to supervise the cease-fire were based on the same unanimity principle that had always failed before in dealing with Communist regimes.

In practice, all the Americans got was the return of their prisoners of war. The South Vietnamese got nothing, not even peace. In fact, they got less than nothing, for, on the chance that the agreement *might* mean something, the Communists launched a last-minute rush to grab as much territory as possible, provoking counterattacks by the angry South Vietnamese. The cease-fire not only never took effect, but proved the occasion for the most violent fighting in months. As Arnold Isaacs has commented, "Kissinger's peace was never anything but an illusion."[7]

There was no peace, not even for one minute.

10

The End of the Second Indochina War

Congress soon made clear that there would be no American response if the Communists tried to overrun South Vietnam. It cut off all funds for military operations in Laos and Cambodia—where the Americans had continued bombing since the Paris agreement. Congress also passed the War Powers Act, which (if constitutional, a point that has never been clarified) severely limited the president's ability to take military action anywhere. Contrary to what is often said, this was not a result of the Watergate scandal, but a logical and inevitable expression of the public mood that had arisen in the last five years. Congress and the public had reluctantly given the president considerable leeway to end the American role in the war in an orderly way. But, once the Americans were out, and a "peace agreement" signed, there was no support at all to go back in to enforce it.

THE FALL OF CAMBODIA

To the surprise of most observers, the Cambodian government survived the end of American air support, although it held only the capital of Phnom Penh and a few other major towns. An airlift and convoys up the Mekong kept it going. Despite monumental incompetence from top to bottom, the army fought on bravely. Perhaps it was held together by sheer terror at what the Communists would do if they won. The latter were already massacring people in captured areas.

Since 1972 the North Vietnamese, needing all of their forces for South Vietnam, had withdrawn most of their men to their bases near the border, turning over the bulk of the fighting to the Khmer Rouge. Although Cambodia fell under Vietnamese Communist rule, this came about in a more complex, and infinitely more horrible way than was generally expected at the time. Unfortunately for the Cambodians, the older, pro-Vietnamese leaders of the Cambodian Communists were replaced by fanatics led by Pol Pot (Saloth Sar). This faction was loosely aligned with China in international policy, but propounded a strange version of communism all their own. These supertotalitarians made the Stalinists in Hanoi look like humanitarians by comparison; they aimed to destroy all vestiges of traditional Cambodian society and Western and Vietnamese influence. Neatly standing Lenin on his head, they aimed to destroy urban life and build a new, totally regimented rural society.

Although Lon Nol's forces fought hard, they could not stop the Communist forces from slowly strangling Phnom Penh. The Communists finally sealed off the Mekong supply route with mines, and brought the airport under rocket attack. On April 17, 1975, the government forces surrendered. The civil war had cost perhaps 600,000 deaths. But the Khmer Rouge quickly demonstrated that their version of peace was worse than war. They celebrated their victory by burning every book they could find, and emptying the capital, whose population had swelled to three million persons, along with every other city, in a series of death marches into the countryside. Everyone associated with the old regime and all intellectuals outside the Communist leadership were exterminated when identified. Successive forced migrations, famines and massacres cost at least 1.2 million lives by January 1977.[1]

THE FALL OF SOUTH VIETNAM AND LAOS

During 1973 and 1974 the South Vietnamese position had steadily eroded. The North Vietnamese rebuilt the Ho Chi Minh Trail into an all-weather highway system, laying a fuel pipeline beside it. They reinforced their forces in the South, not only with more men, but tanks, heavy guns and antiaircraft missiles. Aid from the Communist great powers at first declined after the Paris agreement, but soon picked up again.

American aid to South Vietnam declined steadily, and the worldwide inflationary spiral that followed the 1973 oil crisis seriously damaged South Vietnam's economy. Thieu's harassment of critics, encroachment on local government, the rampant corruption in government, and inability to "deliver" peace or American aid made the government steadily more unpopular with a war-weary people. It seemed that there could be no end to the war other than a Communist victory. Even fiercely anti-Communist Catholics, Thieu's coreligionists, were disgusted by corruption. Although the "anti-war" movement in the United States, which now seemed simply a lobby in favor of a Communist victory, had apparently declined in 1971 and 1972, a very successful propaganda campaign was waged throughout the world against aid to the South Vietnamese government, whose oppressiveness was wildly exaggerated. Whether because of this campaign, or a desire to hear no more about Indochina, the cuts in aid to South Vietnam were popular with Americans. All polls showed that strong majorities opposed more aid by the time the Communist started their final offensive.

Already, in 1974, the South Vietnamese no longer received replacements for lost tanks and planes. Many planes, helicopters and vehicles were unserviceable for lack of spare parts. There is a prevalent misconception that, after a relative lull since 1973, South Vietnam suddenly fell apart, with little resistance, at the first blow in 1975. This is far from the case; there had been heavy fighting throughout the two years after the "peace" agreement. In 1973 the South Vietnamese suffered more casualties than in any previous year except for 1968 and 1972. And 1974 was much worse. Thieu tried to hold on to all the territory that had been under his control in January 1973. He refused to make strategic withdrawals or adjust to his straitened supply situation. In Washington, the Nixon administration remained ridiculously optimistic, even as it begged Congress not to cut aid. Because of a muddled system of reporting South Vietnamese battle statistics, the Administration did not realize how bloody the fighting really was in 1973–1974. The U.S. ambassador in Saigon, Graham Martin, was a fanatical supporter of the South Vietnamese cause. The fact that he had lost a son in the war made him anything but an objective reporter of the facts. Perhaps in a wrong-headed effort to counter the prevailing bias against Thieu's government, he submitted misleadingly rosy reports, suppressing more realistic evaluations by those under him. In general, however, American military observers were overoptimistic about the effectiveness of the South Vietnamese forces, as they had been throughout the war.[2]

In 1974, the Soviets apparently advised North Vietnam to finish off the south before it expended its last gold reserves to buy arms from non-American sources. A strong attack in December 1974 overran all of Phuoc Long province—the first South Vietnamese province entirely lost in the whole course of the war. When the Americans did not react, the North Vietnamese readied the final blow. Their ground forces were only about equal in number to those of the South Vietnamese, but had a two-to-one superiority in armored vehicles, and they were massed at critical points.

In early March 1975 a major attack began in the north. While attention was focused there, the Communists' main blow fell on Ban Me Thuot, a critical but poorly defended communications center in the south-central region. When Ban Me Thuot fell, Thieu decided to retake it. On March 14, finally recognizing that his forces were overextended, he decided to withdraw from the Central Highlands—a move that he had rejected earlier when it could have been executed without enemy interference—in order to free forces to retake Ban Me Thuot. He also decided to abandon the far north. Trying to catch the enemy off balance, the forces leaving the Central Highlands used an unfinished highway instead of the best road out of the area. The incompetent corps commander failed to arrange for local and regional forces to protect the line of retreat. Entangled in a horde of civilians, including the soldiers' own families, the retreating force fell apart. In the north, Thieu's last-minute troop movements also led to disaster. Even before Ban Me Thuot fell, Thieu had ordered the elite 1st Airborne Division transferred from the north, where it was a vital reserve, to the Saigon area. His best unit was thus in transit when the most critical fighting of the war began. The retreating forces in the north disintegrated under enemy pressure; an attempt to hold a beachhead around Danang collapsed. Senior officers fled to save themselves; their soldiers then dispersed, trying to find and protect their families. Two-thirds of South Vietnam was lost in three weeks. Tens of thousands of soldiers and civilians were evacuated by sea, amid horrible scenes as fleeing soldiers looted and murdered civilians. The defeat was so complete that the Communists found it hard to follow up the retreat.

By this point, nothing save direct and massive American intervention could have stopped the North Vietnamese. Nevertheless, the Ford administration sent a military mission to Vietnam and continued to request aid from Congress to rebuild the South Vietnamese forces. But it even found it hard to get Congress to support the use of American forces in an evacuation of South Vietnam or accept South Vietnamese refugees in the United States. Ambassador Martin claimed that the rump of South Vietnam was viable; supported by Henry Kissinger, now Secretary of State, Martin failed to make arrangements for an evacuation until the last minute. The relative success of the evacuation was due to the fact that he was bypassed by more realistic subordinates and the military commanders involved. The final North Vietnamese offensive hit surprisingly tough resistance at Xuan Loc, but it could not be stopped. The crazed illusion that defeat could be avoided, or made more palatable, persisted to the end. Martin and Kissinger were entranced by the idea, dreamed up by the French ambassador in Saigon, that the Communists wanted a "political solution." They hoped that once Thieu was replaced, the Communists would negotiate a cease-fire with the Saigon government, and arrange a coalition regime instead of an outright military conquest of the South. Thieu finally resigned, but the Communists demanded nothing less than total surrender. Saigon fell on April 30.[3]

For the people of South Vietnam this was only the beginning of a long ordeal which has not yet ended. The integration of a region that had developed in a very different way into the Communist system proved difficult. Perhaps as many as 300,000 South Vietnamese found themselves in concentration ("reeducation") camps. Many others were forced to move to new resettlement zones. The religious sects were suppressed, and the montagnards forcibly resettled and assimilated into Vietnamese society. The south's other minority, the Chinese, were harshly treated; they formed a large proportion of the boat people who tried to follow in the wake of those evacuated by the Americans in 1975.

Predictably, the fall of South Vietnam did not end the fighting in Indochina. Laos fell to the Pathet Lao, and became a Vietnamese satellite state. Hundreds of thousands of Hmong fled to Thailand, some going on to the United States. The Khmer Rouge began a nasty little border war with Vietnam, while they massacred Vietnamese (and other) minorities in Cambodia. Exasperated by Cambodian actions, or gauging that Pol Pot's massacres had softened up Cambodia sufficiently, the Vietnamese decided to finish the conquest of Indochina. On December 25, 1978, 200,000 North Vietnamese troops, supported by a rising led by Heng Samrin, a pro-Vietnamese Cambodian Communist, invaded Cambodia. The Vietnamese soon overran most of the country and installed Heng Samrin as a puppet ruler.

The Vietnamese had been increasingly pro-Soviet, and China's rulers were enraged by the conquest of Cambodia, as well as the Vietnamese mistreatment of their Chinese minority. Many of those in North Vietnam had fled to China itself. In February 1979 the Chinese invaded Vietnam. Their minimum objective was evidently to force the Vietnamese to let go of their conquest; but they may have hoped to force a reorientation of the Vietnamese government away from the Soviet Union. The invasion was poorly conducted. Although a huge force was employed, the equipment of the Chinese army was out-of-date. Failing to concentrate their forces, its elderly leaders launched blundering direct assaults on a wide front. The invasion was stopped dead. Fighting in Cambodia continued. Pol Pot's followers, and some weaker anti-Communist groups waged a bloody guerrilla war against the occupiers, who in turn raided the guerrillas' sanctuaries in Thailand. The Western powers put themselves in the horrible and absurd position of supporting the exiled Pol Pot regime as the "legitimate" government in opposition to the Vietnamese occupation. But the conquest of Cambodia was one of several of the last wave of Communist victories that could not be consolidated. Like the Soviets in Afghanistan and their client regimes in Ethiopia and Angola the Vietnamese were unable to destroy their opponents before the final crisis overtook Soviet Communism.[4]

On the Asian mainland, Communist guerrillas had little success outside Indochina. Since the early 1960s, several guerrilla efforts had sputtered in various outlying areas of Thailand. But these forces were based either on unpopular minority nationalities or in areas whose regional peculiarities and grievances were atypical of Thai society. The Communists could not move into the Thai heartland, and suffered from squabbles between pro-Chinese and pro-Vietnamese factions among their leaders.[5]

REFLECTIONS

By the end of the 1970s, the fears that had impelled the American leaders to try to "save" South Vietnam in the 1960s had thus partially materialized, but in an inverted form, although the domino theory was clearly incorrect. Instead of Southeast Asia being threatened by China and a pro-Chinese Vietnamese Communist regime, inspiring a series of Maoist-type guerrilla wars, Chinese influence had been ruined. The region faced a strongly armed pro-Soviet Vietnam, which harbored a Soviet naval base and posed a powerful threat of invasion toward its mainland neighbors. Only in the Philippines did a powerful Communist guerrilla force threaten a local government. It, too, wound up in the Soviet camp—as long as there was one. The collapse of the Soviet empire, not local events, finally ended the Cold War in Southeast Asia.

A number of factors led to the defeat of South Vietnam. Thieu's ghastly mistakes in ordering poorly conducted retreats and shuffling his best units from place to place enabled the Communists' final offensive to go much more smoothly than the Communists had ever expected. The collapse followed a long decline in American support and South Vietnamese morale. Widespread corruption was a powerful demoralizing element, as the South Vietnamese leaders later admitted. South Vietnamese society remained badly fragmented to the end. The Communists were not popular, but there were no strong and respected leaders forming a counterpole to the party.[6] The only strong leaders that South Vietnam produced, Diem and Thieu, were never popular, and both became widely hated.

It has sometimes been claimed that the cuts in American aid caused the fall of South Vietnam. They had considerable impact, and the actions of Congress in cutting American aid were not defensible. Whether or not the United States had a legal commitment to supply South Vietnam, it certainly had a moral one. But the actual effects of the cuts in aid should not be overstressed. Although "Vietnamization" was not a complete and immediate failure, the performance of the South Vietnamese forces in 1971 and 1972, and thereafter leave little reason to suppose that they could have gotten along with adequate American supplies but without American military participation. Right up to the end, American air intervention might have saved South Vietnam, but the South Vietnamese were incapable of doing so, no matter how lavish American logistical support was. More supplies might have prolonged the war but would not have changed the outcome. Only the "loan" of tactical nuclear weapons, which could have smashed the massed North Vietnamese forces, might have enabled the South Vietnamese to win.

Dean Acheson had been wrong in thinking in 1968 that the American government had just a year to get out of Vietnam, and the South Vietnamese, despite their final defeat, bore up better than he, or most observers, expected. Yet, in the long run, it does not seem that his estimate was basically mistaken. The South Vietnamese could never defend themselves, and the United States paid an enormous price in internal stress and morale for the sluggishness of its withdrawal, a policy that has aptly been described as an attempt to "crawl while standing up." At any rate, the loss of the war was not caused by American action or inactions after the Paris "peace" agreement, or even during the Nixon administration. It had been decided long before.

However, victory was not inherently unattainable. In fact, the paradox of the war, from an American point of view, is that the United States managed to defeat the Vietcong guerrillas, but failed to employ its power so as to prevent North Vietnam from overrunning the south in a conventional offensive. It succeeded, however belatedly and clumsily, at what had always (rightly) been regarded as a difficult and complex task, and failed at a straightforward conventional task which its power should have made easy. There can be few, if any, precedents for such foolishness. But, as we have seen earlier, American policy in Vietnam from 1950 onwards, and especially after 1960, was marked by blockheaded stupidity. With a modicum of common sense—the implementation of a land reform, along the lines that had proven sound elsewhere in East Asia, and the encouragement of sane leaders instead of a poor copy of Jiang Jieshi—a strong South Vietnam might have been built after the First Indochina War. The second war might have been prevented entirely. Most amazing was their blindness to the critical nature of the land issue, as though the Vietnamese peasants' desire to own their own land was not just an example of a universal desire. One need not sentimentalize over the Vietnamese peasants who joined the Vietcong—their willingness to be led by tyrants for whom land reform was a trick showed them to be, at best, credulous simpletons. But what can be said of the supposedly sophisticated Westerners who made no effort to understand the people whom they were dealing with?

While the American decision to intervene in a massive way in 1965 was based on an overestimation of the strategic importance of Indochina, our ability to fight there, and the patience of the American public, the war effort was not doomed to failure, even then.[7] The war was lost fundamentally because of poor political and military leadership at the top. President Johnson, his civilian advisers, and the military all share the blame, in varying degrees, for the failure to develop a sound military strategy. Such a strategy would have had to combine antiguerrilla measures oriented toward population security with offensive thrusts to cut the enemy's supply lines in Laos and Cambodia, and effective operations against the Communist rear in North Vietnam, which should have been blockaded. The failure to produce clear and unmistakable results (which a rational and successful strategy should have shown by 1967) and Johnson's failure to provide moral leadership led to the erosion, and then the collapse of the will to fight under the impact of a *perceived* reverse. At a further remove, a major factor in the loss of the war was a simple failure, or even refusal, to understand what was going on in Vietnam, or even develop a capability to do so. It had been apparent since 1950 that Indochina was a major theater of the Cold War; yet no body of expertise was created to deal with it. Even in the early 1960s only about thirty Americans spoke Vietnamese, and there were only two academic specialists on Vietnam in the United States.

Having stressed failures at the top, it is, however, necessary to point out that almost no element in American society performed well during the Second Indochina War. Ironically, just about the only exception was the much-abused Central Intelligence Agency, whose estimates of the situation were, generally speaking, fairly realistic. The behavior of the opinion-forming elements in American society, the news media and academia, was a spectacle of shambling incompetence. As the Australian correspondent Denis Warner remarked, "The Vietnam War threw up more imposters and charlatans in the name of war correspondent than I can remember in all the other wars I have covered put together."[8] But the influence of the news media should not be overrated. Until 1967 or 1968 the press and television generally supported the war without understanding it too well. It was the Johnson administration's failure to "produce," and its refusal or inability to convince people that the war was either just or winnable that allowed the "antiwar" movement to score successes. That movement seemed to succeed almost in spite of itself. The antics of its extremist elements, with their habit of carrying enemy flags, engaging in violence, and emitting a stream of continuous lies, were not calculated to make converts to their cause. The incoherence of the opponents of the war in some ways was a mirror image of the incoherence of American policy. Indeed, as has been suggested earlier, the difference between the two sides was not as extreme as might appear at first sight, either in terms of ideas or social distances. Many policy makers responsible for American intervention were not ardent about winning, and indeed considered those with strongly anti-Soviet or anti-Communist attitudes rather vulgar. And they often harbored bitterly antiwar elements within their own families.

It is worth noting the vast differences between the Second Indochina War and the other great military struggle of the Cold War era, the Korean War. Although it has recently been fashionable to lump the two conflicts together and claim that they were similar, that idea does not bear examination. The international situation had changed greatly between the two wars. The Korean War took place when the world situation was extremely tense, and its conduct cannot be understood unless it is appreciated that there were strong fears that a Third World War was imminent. The Cold War blocs, on both sides, were fairly solid. When major American combat forces were committed to South Vietnam, few feared world war in the near future. Rightly or wrongly, it was generally believed that the international situation was easing; American policy was based partly on a desire not to disturb this. The Korean War was a clear-cut case of aggression by a typical Stalinist satellite state created by Soviet occupation. While the South Korean government was imperfectly democratic, Syngman Rhee, despite his faults, was much abler than any of the rulers of South Vietnam. The South Korean government was in no danger of overthrow by the Communists within South Korea, and Koreans, unlike Vietnamese, were free from complexes about "Western imperialism." They had learned, the hard way, that there were other and worse sorts of imperialism. South Vietnam never quite escaped from being a mere rump left over from France's effort to suppress a Communist-led national movement. However, this point should not be overstressed. As we have seen earlier, some groups that fought for the French in the first war backed the Communists in the Second Indochina War, while many individual Vietnamese took the opposite course. The degree of continuity between the two Indochina struggles is often exaggerated.

The Korean and Indochina wars were fought differently, and had different results. The restrictions imposed on American forces in the Korean War, whether or not they were wise, were simple and rational given the perceived need to subordinate the war in Korea to a global effort to meet a Soviet attack. Many restrictions imposed in Indochina were exceedingly complex, and made little sense. Despite Vietnam's supposedly even lower priority in world affairs, the American leaders wound up subordinating almost all other commitments to the war effort there. In 1951, General Omar Bradley had called the Korean War the wrong war, in the wrong place, and with the wrong enemy; but the United States was at least engaging, effectively, the second power of the Communist world. In crude, inhuman profit and loss terms, that war imposed severe costs on the Soviets and the Chinese, especially economically. It hardened the system of anti-Communist alliances and aroused intense anti-Communist sentiment. Western armed forces were built up and improved.

The American engagement of a third-class Communist state in the 1960s had diametrically opposite effects. For relatively small outlays the Soviets tied down large American forces at enormous economic and psychological cost to the West, not to mention the costs in lives. As the American general Theodore Mataxas noted, the United States had entered the Korean War with a bad army; in Vietnam it went in with a good army, and came out with a bad one. Where Korea had reinforced hostility to totalitarianism in the free countries, the Second Indochina War nearly destroyed it. The reputation of the United States, not only in the eyes of much of the world, but of a large section of its own people, was shattered, and has never fully recovered. The task of opposing the Soviet Union, which was growing stronger militarily, was made immensely more difficult by the double mistake of intervening in Indochina, and then failing to fight there in a sensible and effective way.

Contrary to widespread belief, the Second Indochina War was neither inevitable nor unwinnable. Nor was it necessary, as events showed, for the United States, or the anti-Communist side in the Cold War, to hold South Vietnam or Indochina. But it was only within the context of the Cold War that it made any sense. If it was not a noble cause, as one American president would later suggest, neither was it a high crime, as many would continue to insist. It was merely a horrible blunder that made no contribution toward winning the larger struggle.

Notes

CHAPTER ONE

1. Ritchie Ovendale, *The English-Speaking Alliance* (London: George Allen and Unwin, 1985), pp. 145–146.

2. F. C. Jones, *Japan's New Order in East Asia* (Oxford: Oxford University Press, 1954); *Southeast Asia Under Japanese Occupation*, edited by Alfred W. McCoy (New Haven: Yale University Southeast Asian Studies, 1980).

3. Gary Hess, *The United States Emergence as a Southeast Asian Power 1940–1950* (New York: Columbia University Press, 1987), pp. 48–158, 186; Christopher Thorne, *Allies of a Kind* (New York: Oxford University Press, 1978); Charles Cruickshank, *SOE in the Far East* (New York: Oxford University Press, 1985), esp. pp. 137–150.

4. United States Department of State, *Foreign Relations of the United States 1947 Volume II* (Washington: Government Printing Office, 1972), pp. 887–888 (hereafter, individual volumes in this series will be abbreviated as FRUS after their first mention); *1947 Volume IV* (Washington: Government Printing Office, 1972), pp. 552–553, 557, 562–564; *Soviet Views on the Postwar World Economy*, edited by Leo Gruliow (Washington: Public Affairs Press, 1948); Philip Jaffe, "The Varga Controversy and the American Communist Party," *Survey* (Summer 1972), pp. 138–160; Robert Conquest, *Power and Policy in the USSR* (New York: St. Martin's Press, 1961), pp. 63–73; Gavriel Ra'anan, *International Policy Formation in the USSR* (Hamden, Conn.: Archon, 1983), pp. 63–73; Frederick Barghoorn, "The Varga Discussion and Its Significance" *American Slavic and East European Review* (October 1948), pp. 214–236; Dana Adams Schmidt, *Anatomy of a Satellite* (Boston: Little, Brown, 1952), pp. 100–101; Trevor Barnes,

"The Secret Cold War: The CIA and American Foreign Policy in Europe 1944–1956 part I" *Historical Journal* 2 (1981), pp. 407–408.

5. Andrei Zhdanov, *The International Situation* (Moscow: Foreign Languages Publishing House, 1947); Charles B. McLane, *Soviet Strategies in Southeast Asia* (Princeton: Princeton University Press, 1966), pp. 351–357; Ra'anan, *International Policy Formation in the USSR*, pp. 110–111.

6. Traditional interpretations of the 1948 Southeast Asia uprisings held that the Soviets ordered the uprisings via the Calcutta conference. J. H. Brimmell, *Communism in Southeast Asia* (Oxford: Oxford University Press, 1959), pp. 252–263, 271; *Marxism and Southeast Asia* edited by Frank N. Trager (New York: Praeger, 1959); Hugh Seton-Watson, *From Lenin to Khruschev* (New York: Praeger, 1960), pp. 304–314, 317–318. McLane, *Soviet Strategies in Southeast Asia*, pp. 253–280, 345–349, 357–360, 371–373, 385–387, 417–418, rightly questioned the Calcutta conference's importance but not Soviet direction, save perhaps in Burma. In accordance with a later fashion to exculpate the Soviets for responsibility for Communist rebellions, or to project backward the disintegration of the Communist camp, some writers denied that the Soviets prompted the Southeast Asian rebellions. (E.g., see William McCagg, *Stalin Embattled* (Detroit: Wayne State University Press, 1978), pp. 309–310, 401n 58, 403n 20; Tanigawa Yoshihiko, "The Cominform and Southeast Asia" in *The Origins of the Cold War in Asia*, edited by Akira Iriye (New York: Columbia University Press, 1977), pp. 362–377. These arguments are unconvincing; the evidence for each country, discussed in Chapter 3, confirms the older writers.

7. Marshall Shulman, *Stalin's Foreign Policy Reappraised* (Cambridge: Harvard University Press, 1963), pp. 35, 43–45, 108–120; Conquest, *Power and Policy in the USSR*, pp. 95–104; A. Doak Barnett, *Communist China and Asia* (New York: Vintage, 1960), p. 90, 153–154; Tang Tsou, *America's Failure in China*, Vol. 2 (Chicago: University of Chicago Press, 1963), pp. 523–524, 563–564.

8. Hess, *The United States Emergence as a Southeast Asian Power*, pp. 229–250, 286, 306–309, 341, 342–343; Robert Blum, *Drawing the Line* (New York: Norton, 1982), pp. 3–4, 108, 111–123; *Foreign Relations of the United States 1947 Volume VI* (Washington: Government Printing Office, 1972), pp. 1099–1101; *Foreign Relations of the United States 1950 Volume VI* (Washington: Government Printing Office, 1976), pp. 741–757; Ovendale, *The English-Speaking Alliance*, pp. 157, 163–166; Tsou, *America's Failure in China*, vol. 2, pp. 498, 506–509, 513–518; Michael Schaller, *The American Occupation of Japan* (New York: Oxford University Press, 1985), pp. 149, 151, 161, 213–235.

9. Hess, *The United States Emergence as a Southeast Asian Power*, pp. 314–316, 322–324; *Foreign Relations of the United States 1949 Volume VII, part I* (Washington: Government Printing Office, 1976), pp. 282–32, 39–45, 101–102; *The Pentagon Papers: Senator Gravel Edition*, vol. 1 (Boston: Beacon Press, 1971), pp. 30–34, 38–40, 63, 197–198, 361–374; *Containment*, edited by Thomas

Etzold and John Lewis Gaddis (New York: Columbia University Press, 1978), pp. 251–276; Blum, *Drawing the Line*, pp. 108–123, 204–217; Leslie Gelb and Richard Betts, *The Irony of Vietnam* (Washington: Brookings Institution, 1979), pp. 40–48; Ovendale, *The English-Speaking Alliance*, pp. 148, 157–166, 169–172; Ronald Spector, *Advise and Support* (Washington: Office of the Chief of Military History, 1983), pp. 107, 196.

10. James Schnabel, *Policy and Direction* (Washington: Office of the Chief of Military History, 1972), p. 63.

11. *Foreign Relations of the United States 1948 Volume IV* (Washington: Government Printing Office, 1974), pp. 735–736; *FRUS 1947 Vol. IV*, pp. 17, 24, 29–31, 51, 6–62, 96–98, 110–114, 575.

12. *Foreign Relations of the United States 1951 Volume VI* (Washington: Government Printing Office, 1977), p. 569; *Foreign Relations of the United States 1952–1954 Volume XIII, part 1* (Washington: Government Printing Office, 1982), pp. 117–118.

13. *FRUS 1950 Vol. VI*, pp. 569, 958–963, *FRUS 1951 Vol. VI*, pp. 27–31; *FRUS 1952–1954 Volume XIII*, pp. 865–874, 981–982; *Foreign Relations of the United States 1952–1954 Volume XVI* (Washington: Government Printing Office, 1981), pp. 472–475.

14. *Foreign Relations of the United States 1950 Volume I* (Washington: Government Printing Office, 1977), p. 438; *FRUS 1950 Vol. VI*, pp. 744–747; *FRUS 1952–1954 Vol. XIII*, pp. 238–34; *Foreign Relations of the United States 1951 Volume I* (Washington: Government Printing Office, 1979), pp. 67–68.

15. *Foreign Relations of the United States 1952–1954 Volume XII* (Washington: Government Printing Office, 1981), pp. 26–32; *FRUS 1952–1954 Vol. XIII*, pp. 115, 971; *FRUS 1951 Vol. VI*, pp. 10–12.

16. *FRUS 1952–1954 Vol. XIII*, pp. 82–89.

17. Ibid. pp. 53–60; 714–717, 1146–1148; *FRUS 1952–1954 Vol. XII*, pp. 45–51; *FRUS 1951 Vol. VI*, pp. 16–26.

18. *FRUS 1952–1954 Vol. XII*, p. 32.

19. *FRUS 1952–1954 Vol. XIII*, pp. 83–84, 361–362; *FRUS 1952–1954 Vol. XII*, pp. 45–51.

20. *FRUS 1950 Vol. I*, pp. 298–305.

CHAPTER TWO

1. Douglas Pike, *History of Vietnamese Communism* (Stanford: Hoover Institution Press, 1978), pp. 1–39; William Duiker, *The Communist Road to Power in Vietnam* (Boulder: Westview, 1981). The view that French rule was especially bad is common among American scholars; e.g., Ellen Hammer, *The Struggle for Indochina* (Stanford: Stanford University Press, 1966). Later research, notably that of Robert Sansom, *The Economics of Insurgency in the Mekong Delta* (Cambridge: MIT Press, 1970), pp. 46–51, supports the arguments of more pro-French

writers like Bernard Fall, *The Two Vietnams* (New York: Praeger, 1963); Donald Lancaster, *The Emancipation of French Indochina* (Oxford: Oxford University Press, 1961); and Jacques Dalloz, *The War in Indochina* (New York: Barnes and Noble, 1990), pp. 1–27.

2. Huynh Kim Khanh, "The Vietnamese August Revolution," *Journal of Asian Studies* (August 1971), pp. 768–769; Hammer, *The Struggle for Indochina*, pp. 28, 95–101, 145; Pike, *History of Vietnamese Communism*, pp. 45–54; Duiker, *The Communist Road to Power in Vietnam*, pp. 82–103; Edgar O'Ballance, *The Indochina War* (London: Faber and Faber, 1964), pp. 38–53; Dalloz, *The War in Indochina*, pp. 30–50.

3. Earl Mountbatten, *Post Surrender Tasks* (London: Her Majesty's Stationery Office, 1969), pp. 285–289; Hammer, *The Struggle for Indochina*, pp. 106–127; Peter Dennis, *Troubled Days of Peace* (New York: St. Martin's Press, 1987), pp. 19–54, 164–179; Lancaster, *The Emancipation of French Indochina*, pp. 129–130. Philip Ziegler, *Mountbatten* (New York: Harper and Row, 1985), pp. 330–333; Bernard Fall, *Street Without Joy* (New York: Schocken, 1972), pp. 26–32.

4. Duiker, *The Communist Road to Power in Vietnam*, pp. 111–123; Hammer, *The Struggle for Indochina*, pp. 131–188; Lancaster, *The Emancipation of French Indochina*, pp. 142–169; McLane, *Soviet Strategies in Southeast Asia*, pp. 254–255, 266–273; O'Ballance, *The Indochina War*, pp. 35–80; Dennis Duncanson, *Government and Revolution in Vietnam* (New York: Oxford University Press, 1968), pp. 161–166; Donald Zagoria, *Vietnam Triangle* (New York: Pegasus, 1967), pp. 37–39; Robert F. Turner, *Vietnamese Communism* (Stanford: Stanford University Press, 1975), pp. 45–62, 69–72; Spector, *Advise and Support*, pp. 37, 42–57, 66–67; Dalloz, *The War in Indochina*, pp. 52–82.

5. Chalmers Johnson, *Autopsy on People's War* (Berkeley: University of California Press, 1973); Douglas Blaufarb, *The Counterinsurgency Era* (New York: Free Press, 1977), pp. 3–11; Arthur A. Cohen, *The Communism of Mao Tse-tung* (Chicago: University of Chicago Press, 1964); Jerome Chen, *Mao and the Chinese Revolution* (New York: Oxford University Press, 1965), pp. 216–224.

6. Duiker, *The Communist Road to Power in Vietnam*, pp. 121–130; Lancaster, *The Emancipation of French Indochina,* pp. 142–169; O'Ballance, *The Indochina War*, pp. 134–138, 192–194, 205–206; Dalloz, *The War in Indochina*, pp. 83–113.

7. *FRUS 1951 Vol. VI*, p. 396; *FRUS 1952–1954 Vol. XIII*, pp. 209–210, 598; King Chen, *Vietnam and China* (Princeton: Princeton University Press, 1969), pp. 187–195, 217–222, 240–270; Bernard Fall, *The Two Vietnams*, p. 111; O'Ballance, *The Indochina War*, pp. 103–118; Duiker, *The Communist Road to Power in Vietnam*, pp. 128–130; McLane, *Soviet Strategies in Southeast Asia*, pp. 432–441; Lancaster, *The Emancipation of French Indochina*, pp. 219–220, 254–256; Peter Calvocoressi, *Survey of International Affairs 1951* (London: Oxford University Press, 1954), p. 456; Dalloz, *The War in Indochina*, pp. 147–148.

8. *FRUS 1949 Vol. VII, part 1*, pp. 28–32, 39–45, 101–102; *The Pentagon Papers: Senator Gravel Edition* vol. 1 (Boston: Beacon Press, 1971), pp. 30–34, 38–40, 63, 197–198, 361–374; Blum, *Drawing the Line*, pp. 108–124, 202–217; Spector, *Advise and Support*, pp. 77–87, 110, 128–133, 150–152, 194; Hess, *The United States Emergence as a Southeast Asian Power*, pp. 202–207, 323; Leslie Gelb and Richard Betts, *The Irony of Vietnam* (Washington: Brookings Institution, 1979), pp. 40–48.

9. Fall, *Street Without Joy*, pp. 33–47; O'Ballance, *The Indochina War*, pp. 121–195, 198; Hammer, *The Struggle for Indochina*, pp. 253–254, 263–265; Geoffrey Fairbairn, *Revolutionary Guerrilla Warfare* (New York: Penguin, 1974), pp. 198–202; *FRUS 1950 Vol. VI*, pp. 958–963; *FRUS 1951 Vol. VI*, pp. 27–31, 332–333, 345, 352, 359, 383, 409, 420–421, 452, 469–475, 500, 503, 509; Dalloz, *The War in Indochina*, pp. 116–137; Duiker, *The Communist Road to Power in Vietnam*, pp. 148–154; T. Turner, *Vietnamese Communism*, pp. 78–81.

10. *FRUS 1951 Vol. VI*, pp. 432–437, 447–449; *Foreign Relations of the United States 1952–1954 Vol. I* (Washington: Government Printing Office, 1982), pp. 186–196, 589; *FRUS 1952–1954 Vol. XIII*, pp. 131–144, 243–249, 311–312, 556, 592–602, 865–874.

11. *The Pentagon Papers*, vol. I, pp. 391–399, 405–407; O'Ballance, *The Indochina War*, pp. 196–236; Chen, *Vietnam and China*, pp. 273–275, 285–290, 297. Bernard Fall, *Hell In a Very Small Place* (New York: Vintage, 1968) is the best account of Dien Bien Phu.

12. *FRUS 1952–1954 Vol. XIII*, pp. 551–552, 949; Spector, *Advise and Support*, pp. 170–172, 184.

13. *FRUS 1952–1954 Vol. XIII*, pp. 1141–1144, 1158–1160, 1173, 1182–1183, 1220–1224, 1238–1241, 1250–1264, 1280–1281; *FRUS 1952–1954 Vol. XVI*, pp. 437–442, 485–486, 553–557; *Pentagon Papers*, vol. I, pp. 88–91, 97–98, 104–105, 377, 436–443, 455–460, 467, 471–472, 593–598; Sherman Adams, *First Hand Report* (New York: Harper, 1961), pp. 117–118; Fall, *Hell In a Very Small Place*, pp. 293–313; John Prados, *The Sky Would Fall* (New York: Dial Press, 1983), esp. pp. 86–148; Spector, *Advise and Support*, pp. 197–220; James Cable, *The Geneva Conference of 1954 on Indochina* (New York: St. Martin's Press, 1986).

14. *FRUS 1952–1954 Vol. XVI*, pp. 720–726, 772; Duiker, *The Communist Road to Power in Vietnam*, pp. 164–165; O'Ballance, *The Indochina War*, pp. 208–209, 235–245, 250–256; Fall, *Street Without Joy*, pp. 185–243; R. B. Smith, *An International History of the Vietnam War* (New York: St. Martin's Press, 1983), pp. 19–24, 59–60; Johnson, *Autopsy on People's War*, pp. 47–50; George Modelski, "The Viet Minh Complex" in *Communism and Revolution*, edited by Cyril Black and Thomas P. Thornton (Princeton: Princeton University Press, 1964), pp. 185–214.

CHAPTER THREE

1. J. H. Brimmell, *Communism in Southeast Asia*, pp. 252–254; McLane, *Soviet Strategies in Southeast Asia*, pp. 345–367, 376, 385, 417–418. Cf. Anthony Short, *The Communist Insurrection in Malaya* (New York: Crane, Russak, 1975), pp. 43–53; Ruth McVey, "The Southeast Asian Revolts" in *Communism and Revolution*, edited by Cyril Black and Thomas P. Thornton (Princeton: Princeton University Press, 1964), pp. 145–184, which minimize, although they do not disprove, the element of Soviet involvement.

2. George M. Kahin, *Nationalism and Revolution* (Ithaca: Cornell University Press, 1952) is the best account of the Indonesian independence struggle, albeit excessively pro-Indonesian. Cf. also Benedict R. O'G. Anderson, *Some Aspects of Indonesian Politics Under Japanese Occupation* (Ithaca: Cornell University Press, 1961), pp. 8–98, 105–106, 114–118; Charles Wolf, *The Indonesian Story* (New York: John Day, 1947).

3. Kahin, *Nationalism and Revolution*, pp. 141–158; Mountbatten, *Post Surrender Tasks*, pp. 289–310; F.S.V. Donnison, *British Military Administration in the Far East* (London: Her Majesty's Stationery Office, 1956), pp. 332–334, 339–341, 421–433; Dennis, *Troubled Days of Peace*, pp. 67–142, 180ff; *Foreign Relations of the United States 1945 Volume VI* (Washington: Government Printing Office, 1969), pp. 1158–1163, 1169, 1173, 1176–1181; Hess, *The Emergence of the United States as a Southeast Asian Power*, pp. 186–188.

4. Kahin, *Nationalism and Revolution*, pp. 155–249; Wolf, *The Indonesian Story*, pp. 32–132; Hess, *The Emergence of the United States as a Southeast Asian Power*, pp. 190–193, 277–298; Hubertus van Mook, *The Stakes of Democracy in Southeast Asia* (New York: Norton, 1950), pp. 187–259; Leslie Palmier, *Communists in Indonesia* (New York: Anchor, 1974), pp. 105–129.

5. Kahin, *Nationalism and Revolution*, pp. 249–301, 333ff.; Palmier, *Communists in Indonesia*, pp. 130–137; McLane, *Soviet Strategies in Southeast Asia*, pp. 401–410; Anthony Reid, *The Indonesian National Revolution* (Longman: London, 1974), pp. 102, 129–146.

6. Lucian Pye, *Guerrilla Communism in Malaya* (Princeton: Princeton University Press, 1956) is the best account of the social background of Malayan communism. The wartime and immediate postwar periods are described in Cheah Boon Kheng, *Red Star Over Malaya* (Singapore: Singapore University Press, 1983); Edgar O'Ballance, *Malaya: The Communist Insurgent War 1948–1960* (London: Faber and Faber, 1966), pp. 19–66; Short, *The Communist Insurrection in Malaya 1948–1960*, pp. 24–25, 34–36, 39–41; Donnison, *British Military Administration in the Far East*, pp. 378–387; F. Spencer Chapman, *The Jungle is Neutral* (London: Chatto and Windus, 1949).

7. Brimmell, *Communism in Southeast Asia*, pp. 199–209; O'Ballance, *Malaya: The Communist Insurgent War 1948–1960*, pp. 67–86; Short, *The Communist Insurrection in Malaya 1948–1960*, pp. 25–94, 499; Kheng, *Red Star Over Malaya*, pp. 62, 249, 265 ff.; Richard Clutterbuck, *Riot and Revolution in Singa-*

pore and Malaya (London: Faber and Faber, 1973), pp. 45–56, 265, 273; M. R. Stenson, *Industrial Conflict in Malaya* (London: Oxford University Press, 1970). Short guardedly minimizes the impact of external Communist advice or instructions on the Malayan Communist decision to make war; but cf. McLane, *Soviet Strategies in Southeast Asia*, pp. 308–313, 385–387; and Cecil Sharpley, *The Great Delusion* (London: Heineman, 1952), pp. 110–111.

8. Brimmell, *Communism in Southeast Asia*, pp. 325–326; Short, *The Communist Insurrection in Malaya 1948–1960*, pp. 75ff., O'Ballance, *Malaya: The Communist Insurgent War 1948–1960*, pp. 67–168; Richard Clutterbuck, *The Long, Long War* (New York: Praeger, 1966); Julian Paget, *Counterinsurgency Operations* (New York: Walker, 1967), pp. 43–78.

9. Fairbairn, *Revolutionary Guerrilla Warfare*, pp. 156–161, 173; Douglas Blaufarb, *The Counterinsurgency Era* (New York: Free Press, 1977), pp. 47–48.

10. Eduardo Lachica, *The Huks: Philippine Agrarian Society in Revolt* (New York: Praeger, 1971), pp. 6, 24–25, 35–117; Alvin Scaff, *The Philippine Answer to Communism* (Stanford: Stanford University Press, 1955), pp. 6–27; Alfredo Saulo, *Communism in the Philippines* (Manila, Philippines: Ateneo, 1968), pp. 40–44; Luis Taruc, *He Who Rides the Tiger* (New York: Praeger, 1967), pp. 5–25.

11. Scaff, *The Philippine Answer to Communism*, pp. 27–136; McLane, *Soviet Strategies in Southeast Asia*, pp. 417–432; Lachica, *The Huks*, pp. 119–136, 309–312; Edward Lansdale, *In the Midst of Wars* (New York: Harper and Row, 1972), pp. 7–121; Blaufarb, *The Counterinsurgency Era*, pp. 22–49; Taruc, *He Who Rides the Tiger*. pp. 25–115; Jay Taylor, *China and Southeast Asia* (New York: Praeger, 1974), p. 259; *FRUS 1950 Vol. I*, p. 130; *FRUS 1950 Vol. VI*, pp. 1428, 1444, 1461, 1474; Hess, *The Emergence of the United States as a Southeast Asian Power*, pp. 229–250.

12. F.S.V. Donnison, *Burma* (New York: Praeger, 1970), pp. 122–142; Donnison, *British Military Administration in the Far East*, pp. 71–73, 335–373; Frank N. Trager, *Burma: From Kingdom to Republic* (New York: Praeger, 1966), pp. 61–96; Ziegler, *Mountbatten*, pp. 317–322.

13. Brimmell, *Communism in Southeast Asia*, pp. 187–191; McLane, *Soviet Strategies in Southeast Asia*, pp. 316–334; McVey, "The Southeast Asian Revolts," pp. 160–174; Trager, *Burma*, pp. 96–97.

14. Brimmell, *Communism in Southeast Asia*, pp. 190–193, 308–312; McLane, *Soviet Strategies in Southeast Asia*, pp. 371–383; McVey, "The Southeast Asian Revolts," pp. 174–175; Trager, *Burma*, pp. 97–130; Donnison, *Burma*, pp. 142–145; Taylor, *China and Southeast Asia*, p. 194.

15. Trager, *Burma*, pp. 114–115, 319–321, 428–429 n. 32; Donnison, *Burma*, pp. 146–147, 154.

16. Andrew F. Krepinevich, *The Army and Vietnam* (Baltimore: Johns Hopkins University Press, 1986); Larry Cable, *Conflict of Myths* (New York: New York University Press, 1986).

CHAPTER FOUR

1. Uri Ra'anan, *The USSR Arms the Third World* (Cambridge: MIT Press, 1969); William Shinn, "The 'National Democratic State'—A Communist Program for Less-Developed Areas," *World Politics* (April 1963), pp. 377–389; Richard Lowenthal and J. M. van der Kroef, "On National Democracy," *Survey* (April 1963), pp. 119–134.

2. Harold C. Hinton, *China's Turbulent Quest*, rev. edition (Bloomington: Indiana University Press, 1972), pp. 68–77, 107, 112, 117–118, 137, 143–144, 147–150, 243–244; Johnson, *Autopsy on People's War*, pp. 21–23, 35–38, 64–68, 76–85; Taylor, *China and Southeast Asia*, p. xi; Bruce D. Larkin, *China and Africa 1949–1970* (Berkeley: University of California Press, 1971); Lyndon Johnson, *The Vantage Point* (New York: Popular Library, 1972), pp. 134–137, 150–151; Harold C. Hinton, *Communist China in World Politics* (Boston: Houghton Mifflin, 1966); Donald Zagoria, *The Sino-Soviet Conflict 1956–1961* (Princeton: Princeton University Press, 1962).

3. Howard P. Jones, *Indonesia: The Possible Dream* (New York: Harcourt, Brace and Jovanovich, 1971), p. 47.

4. Palmier, *Communists in Indonesia*, pp. 157–173; Arnold Brackman, *The Communist Collapse in Indonesia* (New York: Norton, 1969), pp. 13, 20–28, 43, 140.

5. *Foreign Relations of the United States 1955–1957 Vol. XXII* (Washington: Government Printing Office, 1989), pp. 322–327, 334, 339, 351, 354, 370–373, 401–404, 412–414, 421–422, 429–431, 436–440, 533, 548; Palmier, *Communists in Indonesia*, pp. 173–187; James Mossman, *Rebels in Paradise* (London: Jonathan Cape, 1961); Ra'anan, *The USSR Arms the Third World*, pp. 175–218; Joseph B. Smith, *Portrait of a Cold Warrior* (New York: Ballantine, 1981), pp. 216–240; John M. Allison, *Ambassador from the Prairie* (Boston: Houghton Mifflin, 1973), pp. 301, 305, 337.

6. Palmier, *Communists in Indonesia*, pp. 185–214; Arnold C. Brackman, *Southeast Asia's Second Front* (New York; Praeger, 1966), pp. 91–114; Jones, *Indonesia, the Possible Dream*, pp. 174–215; J.A.C. Mackie, *Konfrontasi* (Kuala Lumpur: Oxford University Press, 1974), pp. 98–102; *Khrushchev Remembers: The Last Testament* (New York: Bantam, 1974), pp. 353–355.

7. *Khrushchev Remembers: The Last Testament*, pp. 353–374.

8. Ra'anan, *The USSR Arms the Third World*, pp. 235–239; Justus M. Van der Kroef, "The Wages of Ambiguity" in Thomas T. Hammond, *The Anatomy of Communist Takeovers* (New Haven: Yale University Press, 1975), pp. 534–562; Palmier, *Communists in Indonesia*, pp. 223 ff.

9. Mackie, *Konfrontasi*, esp. pp. 1–8, 104–279; Brackman, *Southeast Asia's Second Front*, pp. 133–148, 214, 227–232, 285; Palmier, *Communists in Indonesia*, pp. 214–227; Michael Calvert, *War Since 1945* (New York: Putnam, 1981), pp. 83–98; Tony Geraghty, *Inside the SAS* (New York: Ballantine, 1982), pp. 43–60.

10. Brackman, *The Communist Collapse in Indonesia*, passim; Palmier, *Communists in Indonesia*, pp. 234–264; Van der Kroef, "The Wages of Ambiguity," pp. 543–560; John Hughes, *Indonesian Upheaval* (New York: David McKay, 1967); Mackie, *Konfrontasi*, pp. 309–322.

CHAPTER FIVE

1. For the counterinsurgency thesis, cf. Krepinevich, *The Army and Vietnam* and Cable, *Conflict of Myths*; for the opposite view, which seems to be more common among professional soldiers, cf. Harry Summers, *On Strategy* (Novato, CA: Presidio, 1982); and David Richard Palmer, *Summons of the Trumpet* (New York: Ballantine, 1983). Cf. Eric Bergerud, *The Dynamics of Defeat* (Boulder: Westview, 1991) a brilliant attempt to break out of this dichotomy.

2. *FRUS 1952–1954 Vol. XVI*, pp. 460–463, 654–664, 787, 1059, 1094, 1143. For the most complete discussion of the Geneva Agreements, see Robert F. Randle, *Geneva 1954* (Princeton: Princeton University Press, 1969). See also R. B. Smith, *An International History of the Vietnam War* vol. I (New York: St. Martin's Press, 1983), pp. 19–29, 59–60. Smith's is the only work to place the Second Indochina War within a realistic overall view of the Southeast Asia region and of Communist politics. A useful article is Robert F. Turner, "Myths of the Vietnam War," in *Southeast Asian Perspectives* 7 (September 1972), pp. 24–38.

3. Hammer, *The Struggle for Indochina*, p. 345; Turner, *Vietnamese Communism*, pp. 101–104; Turner, "Myths of the Vietnam War," pp. 35–37; *Pentagon Papers*, Vol. I, p. 127.

4. Jeffrey Race, *War Comes to Long An* (Berkeley: University of California Press, 1972), p. 34; Duiker, *The Communist Road to Power in Vietnam, p. 172; Turner, Vietnamese Communism*, p. 107; Stuart Herrington, *Silence Was a Weapon* (Novato, CA: Presidio, 1982), pp. 25–26; P. J. Honey, *Communism in North Vietnam* (Cambridge: MIT Press, 1963), p. 6; *Foreign Relations of the United States 1955–1957 Vol. I* (Washington: Government Printing Office, 1985), pp. 95–96, 103–104, 134, 208–209, 406–408, 411–412, 421–423, 641–642.

5. *FRUS 1952–1954 Vol. II*, pp. 833–834; *FRUS 1952–1954 Vol. XIII, part 2*, pp. 2419–2420; Yuen Foong Khong, *Analogies at War* (Princeton: Princeton University Press, 1992), pp. 57, 72–74.

6. *FRUS 1952–1954 Vol. XIII, part 2*, pp. 1732, 1905–1914, 2132–2135, 2215–2216, 2241–2244, 2268–2269, 2286–2301, 2419–2420; *FRUS 1955–1957 Vol. I*, pp. 15–17, 41,–45, 218–221, 229–231, 239–241, 270, 307–312, 787–792, 796; Chester Cooper, *The Lost Crusade* (New York: Fawcett, 1972), pp. 153–202; Guenter Lewy, *America in Vietnam* (New York: Oxford University Press, 1978), pp. 7–14; Charles Joiner, *The Politics of Massacre* (Philadelphia: Temple University Press, 1974), esp. pp. 13–17; Douglas Pike, *Vietcong* (Cambridge: MIT Press, 1966), pp. 57–73; Duncanson, *Government and Revolution in Vietnam*, pp. 242–285; Spector, *Advise and Support*, pp. 223, 228–229, 235–255, 263, 272–273.

7. Race, *War Comes to Long An*, pp. 32–33, 80–81; Duiker, *The Communist Road to Power in Vietnam*, pp. 174–179.

8. Race, *War Comes to Long An*, pp. xiv, 37–39, 74, 90–111, 126; Duiker, *The Communist Road to Power in Vietnam*, pp. 178–182; Smith, *An International History of the Vietnam War* vol. I, pp. 136, 156–176, 207, 226–230; Pike, *Vietcong*, pp. 62–63, 67–73, 179, 276; Bergerud, *Dynamics of Defeat*, pp. 15–18, 54–60, 98–99.

9. Race, *War Comes to Long An*, pp. 104–123; Pike, *Vietcong*, pp. 82–109, 276–279; Duiker, *The Communist Road to Power in Vietnam*, pp. 187, 196–198; Turner, *Vietnamese Communism*, p. 178–182; Michael Lee Lanning and Dan Cragg, *Inside the VC and the NVA* (New York: Ivy, 1993), pp. 84–85. An important factor in the controversy over the war was the widely accepted claim, first made by Jean Lacoutoure and Philippe Devilliers, that the war began when Diem's persecution drove the southern Communists in the south into an armed uprising despite Hanoi's orders. We know now that this story, disproven by Race and others, is a lie.

10. *FRUS 1955–1957 Vol. I*, pp. 456–458, 525–527, 756–757; Thomas C. Thayer, *War Without Fronts* (Boulder: Westview, 1985), pp. 237–238; Duiker, *The Communist Road to Power in Vietnam*, p. 181; Race, *War Comes to Long An*, pp. 56–61, 126, 129; Richard Critchfield, *The Long Charade* (New York: Harcourt, Brace, 1968), pp. 188–195; Duncanson, *Government and Revolution in Vietnam*, pp. 244–247; Sansom, *The Economics of Insurgency in the Mekong Delta of Vietnam*, pp. 56–65, 228–234; Bergerud, *Dynamics of Defeat*, pp. 16–17.

11. *Foreign Relations of the United States 1958–1960 Volume I* (Washington: Government Printing Office, 1986), pp. 446–447, 451–453, 459–462, 516–518, 536–541, 575–579, 626–627, 673, 707–711, 735–737; *Foreign Relations of the United States 1961–1963 Volume I* (Washington: Government Printing Office, 1988), pp. 25–28; Duncanson, *Government and Revolution in Vietnam*, pp. 277–279.

CHAPTER SIX

1. Blaufarb, *The Counterinsurgency Era*, pp. 128–147; Arthur Dommen, *Conflict in Laos* (New York: Praeger, 1971), pp. 79ff; Edward J. Marolda and Oscar P. Fitzgerald, *From Military Assistance to Combat* (Washington: Naval Historical Center, 1986), pp. 22–86; Paul Langer and Joseph Zasloff, *North Vietnam and the Pathet Lao* (Cambridge: Harvard University Press, 1970), pp. 58–89; Arnold Isaacs, *Without Honor* (New York: Vintage, 1984), pp. 155–180.

2. *FRUS 1961–1963 Vol. I*, pp. 1–7, 13, 201; Marolda and Fitzgerald, *From Military Assistance to Combat*, pp. 189–190; Krepinevich, *The Army and Vietnam*, pp. 27, 30–37, 47–48, 64; Blaufarb, *The Counterinsurgency Era*, pp. 82, 86–88; Fall, *The Two Vietnams*, pp. 343–348; Yuen Foong Khong, *Analogies at War*, pp. 91–93.

3. *Pentagon Papers*, vol. 2, pp. 164, 180, 200–276, 642–643, 690–716, 770–780; Cooper, *The Lost Crusade*, pp. 218–265; Lewy, *America in Vietnam*, pp. 18–28; Blaufarb, *The Counterinsurgency Era*, pp. 93–94, 101–123; Duncanson, *Government and Revolution in Vietnam*, pp. 300–359; Marolda and Fitzgerald, *From Military Assistance to Combat*, p. 20; *FRUS 1961–1963 Volume I*, pp. 32–33, 322–324; *Foreign Relations of the United States 1961–1963 Volume II* (Washington: Government Printing Office, 1990), pp. 73–90, 338–339, 448–451, 457, 478–481, 516–519, 591–601, 779; *Foreign Relations of the United States 1961–1963 Volume III* (Washington: Government Printing Office, 1991), pp. 19–22, 34–35, 38–59, 136–140, 142–143, 193, 199, 232–235, 455–465, 532–533, 551–552; *Foreign Relations of the United States 1961–1963 Volume IV* (Washington: Government Printing Office, 1992), pp. 153–160, 629, 635–636, 680, 698–700, 735–737; Bergerud, *Dynamics of Defeat*, pp. 28–38; William Conrad Gibbons, *The U.S. Government and the Vietnam War part II 1961–1964* (Princeton: Princeton University Press, 1986), pp. 108, 112, 126–127, 161, 184–186.

4. *FRUS 1961–1963 Vol. IV*, pp. 629, 635–636, 680, 698–700, 735–737; *Foreign Relations of the United States 1964–1968 Volume I* (Washington: Government Printing Office, 1992), pp. 1, 4–5, 7.

5. Pike, *Vietcong*, pp. 67–69, 116; Duiker, *The Communist Road to Power in Vietnam*, pp. 220–221; Truong Nhu Tang, *A Viet Cong Memoir* (New York: Vintage, 1986), p. 50.

6. Critchfield, *The Long Charade*, passim.

7. Gibbons, *The US Government and the Vietnam War part II 1961–1964*, pp. 112, 137, 163; Arthur Krock, *Memoirs* (New York: Popular Library, 1968), p. 333; F. M. Kail, *What Washington Said* (New York: Harper and Row, 1973), p. 37. For a more favorable view of Kennedy, see Arthur M. Schlesinger, Jr., *Robert Kennedy and His Times* (Boston: Houghton Mifflin, 1978), pp. 734–756.

CHAPTER SEVEN

1. Lewy, *America in Vietnam*, pp. 29, 38–40; Duiker, *The Communist Road to Power in Vietnam*, pp. 221, 228; R. B. Smith, *An International History of the Vietnam War vol. 2* (St. Martin's Press, 1984), pp. 107, 123, 128, 133–134, 173, 229, 233, 345–350; *Pentagon Papers*, vol. 2, pp. 270–279, 303–356; Palmer, *The Summons of the Trumpet*, pp. 59–90; Honey, *Communism in North Vietnam*, pp. 1–14; Donald J. Zagoria, *Vietnam Triangle* (New York: Pegasus, 1967).

2. *Pentagon Papers, Vol. 3*, pp. 106–107, 117–128, 149–183, 499–510, 511; *FRUS 1961–1963 Vol. II*, pp. 174–175, 231, 387–389; *FRUS 1964–1968 Vol. I*, pp. 5, 27, 71–74, 81–82, 153–167, 305–308, 450; Marolda and Fitzgerald, *From Military Assistance to Combat*, pp. 341–343, 360–369, 372, 378–387; Mark Clodfelter, *The Limits of Airpower* (New York: Free Press, 1989), pp. 40–52.

3. *FRUS 1964–1968 Vol. I*, pp. 588–598, 603, 608–631; Marolda and Fitzgerald, *From Military Assistance to Combat*, pp. 393–451; Gibbons, *The US*

Government and the Vietnam War part 2 1961–1964, pp. 282–313; William Conrad Gibbons, *The US Government and the Vietnam War part 3 1965* (Princeton: Princeton University Press, 1989), p. 10. Lewy, *America in Vietnam*, p. 30; Gelb, *The Irony of Vietnam*, pp. 100–105. The government claimed that decoded messages proved the reality of the second attack in the Gulf of Tonkin; but it is possible that the messages actually referred to the *first* attack. Cf. James Stockdale, *In Love and War* (New York: Bantam, 1985), pp. 453–461. General Philip Davidson, *Secrets of the Vietnam War* (Novato, CA: Presidio, 1990), pp. 129–132, interprets them as showing that an attack was ordered—but not carried out! The official history Marolda and Fitzgerald, *From Military Assistance to Combat*, pp. 427–436, insists that not only the messages but other evidence show that the second attack really occurred.

4. *Pentagon Papers, vol. 3*, pp. 136, 189–248; *FRUS 1964–1968 Vol. 1*, pp. 712–717, 749–754, 847–857, 861–863, 882–884.

5. *FRUS 1964–1968 Vol. I*, pp. 916–929, 932–937, 955–957, 975, 1058; *Pentagon Papers, vol. 3*, pp. 136–137, 248–254; Gibbons, *The US Government and the Vietnam War, part II 1961–1964*, pp. 363–370; Marolda and Fitzgerald, *From Military Assistance to Combat*, pp. 479–486; Brian Van DeMark, *Into the Quagmire* (New York: Oxford University Press, 1991), pp. 26–51.

6. *FRUS 1964–1968 Vol. I*, pp. 484–487, 916–929; Herbert Y. Schandler, *The Unmaking of a President* (Princeton: Princeton University Press, 1977), pp. 8–9; Johnson, *The Vantage Point*, pp. 134–137, 150–151.

7. Yuen Foong Khong, *Analogies at War*, pp. 59–61, 65, 99–104, 110–114. Cf. Larry Berman, *Planning a Tragedy* (New York: Norton, 1982), p. 143. In 1979 McGeorge Bundy still maintained that the war had not really been very different from the Korean War! Gibbons, *The US Government and the Vietnam War part III 1965*, p. 148.

8. Yuen Foong Khong, *Analogies at War*, pp. 57, 71–73; Gibbons, *The US Government and the Vietnam War part III 1965*, pp. 330, 347–348; Berman, *Planning a Tragedy*, p. 132; Gelb and Betts, *The Irony of Vietnam*, pp. 79, 181, 213, 366.

9. Such shifts seem to have been characteristic of Johnson's decision making. A similar thing occurred when he decided to intervene in the Dominican Republic. Only shortly after announcing that he was sending in a small marine force just to evacuate Americans, he abruptly decided to intervene with much larger forces for political purposes; the differing announcements, coming so close together, gave a spurious impression of deception.

10. *Pentagon Papers*, vol. 3, pp. 269–388; Lewy, *America in Vietnam*, pp. 36–38, 379–381; Berman, *Planning a Tragedy*, pp. 31, 34–51; Gelb and Betts, *The Irony of Vietnam*, pp. 106–118, 133; Van DeMark, *Into the Quagmire*, pp. 64–71; Marolda and Fitzgerald, *From Military Assistance to Combat*, pp. 496–505; Clodfelter, *The Limits of Airpower*, pp. 56–87.

11. *Pentagon Papers*, vol. 3, pp. 417, 433, 453–461, vol. 4, pp. 22–23; Lewy, *America in Vietnam*, pp. 38–51; Berman, *Planning a Tragedy*, pp. 36, 44ff.; Gelb and Betts, *The Irony of Vietnam*, pp. 118–135; Schandler, *The Unmaking of a President*, pp. 14–36; Yuen Foong Khong, *Analogies at War,* pp. 106–111, 121–132, 137, 148–159, 167–168; Van DeMark, *Into the Quagmire*, pp. 85–90, 97–196; Gibbons, *The US Government and the Vietnam War part III 1965*, pp. 166, 169–174, 179–181, 230, 330–343, 359, 387, 404, 439–440. It is difficult to convey, in a short space, the muddled thinking and often tortuous illogic among many of Johnson's civilian advisers. Some spectacular examples can be found in Gibbons, *The US Government and the Vietnam War part III 1965*, pp. 333–339; Yuen Foong Khong, *Analogies at War*, p. 168; Berman, *Planning a Tragedy*, pp. 90–91, 100–104; Van DeMark, *Into the Quagmire*, pp. 114–115, 168–170.

12. Summers, *On Strategy*, p. 17.

13. Van DeMark, *Into the Quagmire*, p. 121; David Levy, *The Debate Over Vietnam* (Baltimore: Johns Hopkins Press, 1991), pp. 34–38, 58, 65–67; Kail, *What Washington Said*, pp. 27–28, 37–38, 84–110, 115–116, 123–132, 147–153.

14. Christian G. Appy, *Working Class War* (Chapel Hill: University of North Carolina Press, 1993), p. 57; Gibbons, *The US Government and the Vietnam War part III 1965*, pp. 41–43, 72–73, 135–145; William M. Hammond, *The Military and the Media* (Washington: Center of Military History, 1988), p. 124; John E. Mueller, *War, Presidents and Public Opinion* (New York: Wiley, 1973), pp. 52–53, 58, 70–74.

15. Cf. Summers, *On Strategy*, pp. 23, 32, 107–109; Palmer, *The Summons of the Trumpet*, pp. 95–151; Lewy, *America in Vietnam*, pp. 51–53; William B. Westmoreland, *A Soldier Reports* (New York: Doubleday, 1976), pp. 98, 19–154.

CHAPTER EIGHT

1. John Tolson, *Airmobility 1961–1971* (Washington: Dept. of the Army, 1973), pp. 3–84, 88, 109; Shelby Stanton, *Anatomy of a Division* (Novato, CA: Presidio, 1987), pp. 35–39, 45–65, 219; Eric Bergerud, *Red Thunder, Tropic Lightning* (Boulder: Westview, 1993), pp. 63–65; Appy, *Working Class War*, p. 175.

2. Appy, *Working Class War*, pp. 8–12, 18–20, 30–35, 128, 132–136, 163–167, 178–182, 214–216; James Ebert, *A Life in a Year* (Novato, CA: Presidio, 1993), pp. 2–6, 17–23, 56–60, 83–88, 141–142, 156–158, 169, 186–187, 189–194, 199–206, 261–262, 277–297; Ronald Spector, *After Tet* (New York: Free Press, 1993), 26–38, 40–42, 48–49, 52; Bergerud, *Red Thunder, Tropic Lightning*, pp. 50–53, 106, 114, 122, 219–245, 266–268; Paddy Griffith, *Forward into Battle* (Novato, CA: Presidio, 1992), pp. 144–162.

3. Lanning and Cragg, *Inside the VC and the NVA*, pp. 51, 54, 149 passim.; Appy, *Working Class War*, pp. 163–166; Spector, *After Tet*, pp. 78–85, 154; Ebert, *A Life in a Year*, pp. 130, 184–185, 202–211, 255–258, 261–264; Stanton, *Anatomy of a Division*, p. 222; Bergerud, *Red Thunder, Tropic Lightning*, pp. 65,

133–139, 150–153, 252–258, 260; Bergerud, *The Dynamics of Defeat*, pp. 91–99, 132, 226–230.

4. Douglas Kinnard, *The War Managers* (Wayne, NJ: Avery, 1985), pp. 37–38, 54.

5. Lewy, *America in Vietnam*, pp. 53–86; Duiker, *The Communist Road to Power in Vietnam*, pp. 247–248; Fairbairn, *Revolutionary Guerrilla Warfare*, pp. 236–238; Bergerud, *Dynamics of Defeat*, pp. 167–169; Ebert, *A Life in a Year*, pp. 272–275; Hammond, *The Military and the Media*, p. 318; Lanning and Cragg, *Inside the VC and the NVA*, p. 149; Spector, *After Tet*, p. 14; Thayer, *War Without Fronts*, pp. 84, 90–96.

6. Krepinevich, *The Army in Vietnam*, pp. 171–172; Lewy, *America in Vietnam*, pp. 115–116; William R. Corson, *The Betrayal* (New York: Norton, 1968), esp. pp. 159–184, 275; William J. Lederer, *Our Own Worst Enemy* (Greenwich: Fawcett, 1968), pp. 148–158; Francis J. West, *The Village* (New York: Harper and Row, 1972).

7. Duiker, *The Communist Road to Power in Vietnam*, pp. 250, 257–263; Willard Pearson, *The War in the Northern Provinces* (Washington: Dept. of the Army, 1975), pp. 6–18.

8. Lewy, *America in Vietnam*, pp. 74, 113–114, 123–124, 186–187; Fairbairn, *Revolutionary Guerrilla Warfare*, pp. 240–242; Blaufarb, *The Counterinsurgency Era*, p. 240; Richard Critchfield, *The Long Charade*, pp. 333, 347–357; Joiner, *The Politics of Massacre*, esp. pp. 148, 167–168.

9. Critchfield, *The Long Charade*, p. 206; Cecil B. Currey (Cincinnatus), *Self-Destruction* (New York: Norton, 1981), pp. 68–69; Lederer, *Our Own Worst Enemy*, pp. 81–101, 107 ff.; Lewy, *America in Vietnam*, p. 90; Isaacs, *Without Honor*, p. 111.

10. *Pentagon Papers*, vol. 4, p. 18, 20, 102–118, 137; Lewy, *America in Vietnam*, pp. 374–404; Carl Berger, *The United States Air Force in Southeast Asia* (Washington: Dept. of the Air Force, 1977); *Air War Vietnam* (Indianapolis: Bobbs Merrill, 1978), pp. 4–50, 210–248; Jack Broughton, *Thud Ridge* (New York: Bantam, 1985), pp. xi–xiii, 17–18, 94; Clodfelter, *The Limits of Air Power*, pp. 85–140; Lanning and Cragg, *Inside the VC and the NVA*, pp. 84–99; Spector, *After Tet*, pp. 300–302; John B. Nicholls and Barrett Tillman, *On Yankee Station* (Annapolis: US Naval Institute, 1987), pp. 2–80, 100, 113; *Vietnam: The Naval Story* edited by Frank Uhlig, Jr. (Annapolis: Naval Institute Press, 1986), pp. 23–69; Ken Bell, *One Hundred Missions North* (New York: Brassey, 1993), pp. 154, 158–159.

11. Some decidedly anti-Communist conservatives, notably Senator Richard Russell, Phyllis Schlafly and James Burnham, had strong doubts about the wisdom of large-scale intervention on strategic grounds; but once the course was set by the administration, they rallied to it on patriotic grounds.

12. Zalin Grant, *Facing the Phoenix* (New York: Norton, 1991), pp. 221–222.

13. Schlesinger, *Robert Kennedy and His Times*, p. 860.

14. Levy, *The Debate Over Vietnam*, is the best account of a difficult subject, although it is perhaps inclined to treat opponents of the war too uncritically and portrays the atmosphere as a bit more gentlemanly than it really was. Tom Wells, *The War Within* (Berkeley: University of California Press, 1994); and Nancy Zaroulis and Gerald Sullivan, *Who Spoke Up?* (New York: Doubleday, 1984), although virtually whitewashing the antiwar movement, contain some useful information.

Insofar as American policy was subjected to rational attack, the following books give some idea of the arguments employed: Theodore Draper, *Abuse of Power* (New York: Viking 1967), although seriously flawed, is the most intelligent critique of the war and can be read with profit even today. More typical of moderate liberal attacks on the war are Arthur Schlesinger, *The Bitter Heritage* (Greenwich: Fawcett, 1968) and Richard Rovere, *Waist Deep in the Big Muddy* (Boston: Little, Brown, 1968). The extreme left's attack on the war is best exemplified by the Committee of Concerned Asian Scholars, *The Indochina Story* (New York: Bantam, 1970). The validity of the charges against American policy are examined in depth in Lewy's *America in Vietnam*, and in David Little, *American Foreign Policy and Moral Rhetoric* (New York: The Council on Religion and International Relations, 1969); and Turner, "Myths of the Vietnam War." Public opinion and media coverage are best treated in Mueller, *War, Presidents and Public Opinion*, esp. 81–103, 164–168; Melvin Small, *Johnson, Nixon and the Doves* (New Brunswick: Rutgers University Press, 1988), pp. 31–32, 36, 40–42, 46–48, 67–68; Hammond, *The Military and the Media*, pp. 227–229, 273–276, 315–318; Don Oberdorfer, *Tet* (New York: Da Capo, 1986), pp. 81–102, 339; Peter Braestrup, *Big Story* (New Haven: Yale University Press, 1978), pp. 41–48, 54.

15. Gelb and Betts, *The Irony of Vietnam*, p. 149.

16. Larry Berman, *Lyndon Johnson's War* (New York: Norton, 1989), p. 14.

17. *Pentagon Papers*, vol. 4, pp. 112–126, 335–336, 348–354; Gelb and Betts, *The Irony of Vietnam*, pp. 147–150, 168; Schandler, *The Unmaking of a President*, pp. 43–56; Krepinevich, *The Army and Vietnam*, pp. 184–185; Berman, *Lyndon Johnson's War*, pp. 12–17, 23–95; Wells, *The War Within*, pp. 107, 198–199.

18. James J. Wirtz, *The Tet Offensive* (Ithaca: Cornell University Press, 1991), pp. 1–230; Duiker, *The Communist Road to Power in Vietnam*, pp. 261–266; Oberdorfer, *Tet*, pp. 42–65, 100–102; Bergerud, *The Dynamics of Defeat*, pp. 193–199; Palmer, *Summons of the Trumpet*, pp. 207–235; Thayer, *War Without Fronts*, pp. 141–143; John Prados and Ray Stubbs, *Valley of Decision* (New York: Dell, 1993).

19. Palmer, *Summons of the Trumpet*, pp. 237–255; Duiker, *The Communist Road to Power in Vietnam*, pp. 266–275; Oberdorfer, *Tet*, pp. 120–121, 137–151; Blaufarb, *The Counterinsurgency Era*, pp. 261–267, 276–277; Lewy, *America in Vietnam*, pp. 123, 186–188; Bergerud, *The Dynamic of Defeat*, pp. 200–213, 223;

Berger, *The USAF in Southeast Asia*, pp. 259, 265–269; Tolson, *Airmobility*, pp. 185–186.

20. Lewy, *America in Vietnam*, pp. 127–132, 165; Schandler, *The Unmaking of a President*, pp. 78, 80ff; Braestrup, *Big Story*, passim.; Oberdorfer, *Tet*, pp. 174–175, 238–252, 258 passim; Palmer, *Summons of the Trumpet*, pp. 255–262; Berman, *Lyndon Johnson's War*, pp. 148–200; Hammond, *The Military and the Media*, pp. 347, 350–353, 355, 364–382.

CHAPTER NINE

1. Race, *War Comes to Long An*, pp. 268–271; Lewy, *America in Vietnam*, pp. 137–138, 153–161, 164–195; Blaufarb, *The Counterinsurgency Era*, pp. 264–277; Duiker, *The Communist Road to Power in Vietnam*, pp. 276–281, 289–290; Herrington, *Silence Was a Weapon*, pp. 94–95, 189–199; Thayer, *War Without Fronts*, pp. 131–132, 141–147, 151–152; Bergerud, *The Dynamics of Defeat*, pp. 224, 231–306; Spector, *After Tet*, pp. 98–113, 215, 223–238, 284–293; Tolson, *Airmobility 1961–1971*, p. 220.

2. Ralph Zumbro, *Tank Sergeant* (New York: Pocket Books, 1988), p. 19; *Headhunters*, edited by Matthew Brennan (New York: Pocket Books, 1988), p. 50.

3. Spector, *After Tet*, pp. 199–207; Bergerud, *The Dynamics of Defeat*, pp. 169–178; Bergerud, *Red Thunder, Tropic Lightning*, pp. 218, 223–231, 236–237, 242–243; Appy, *Working Class War*, pp. 201–209, 214–216, 273, 293–294; Ebert, *A Life in a Year*, pp. 277–315.

4. J. D. Coleman, *Incursion* (New York: St. Martin's Press, 1991), pp. 125–126, 136–137, 219–265; Keith William Nolan, *Into Cambodia* (Novato, CA: Presidio, 1990); Truong Nhu Tang, *A Viet Cong Memoir*, pp. 178–185; Duiker, *The Communist Road to Power in Vietnam*, pp. 284–286; Isaacs, *Without Honor*, pp. 183–205; Herrington, *Silence Was a Weapon*, pp. 34, 41, 86; Tolson, *Airmobility 1961–1971*, pp. 218–234; Denis Warner, *Certain Victory* (Kansas City, MO: Sheed, Andrews, McMeed, 1978), pp. 157–172.

5. Shelby Stanton, *The Rise and Fall of an American Army* (Novato, CA: Presidio, 1985), pp. 348, 357–366; Spector, *After Tet*, pp. 63–69, 244–259, 273–278; Bergerud, *Red Thunder, Tropic Lightning*, pp. 260–290; Appy, *Working Class War*, pp. 231–232, 245–247, 283–284; Richard A. Gabriel and Paul Savage, *Crisis in Command* (New York: Hill and Wang, 1978); Currey, *Self-Destruction*. Cf. C.R.M.F. Cruttwell, *A History of the Great War* (London: Granada, 1982, originally published 1934), p. 518 n1. remarks that when boys of eighteen were reluctantly sent into battle in the emergency of 1918 they "were reported to show extreme bravery and fierceness, but were quite unable to bear the prolonged strain of months in the lines of which older men were capable."

6. Duiker, *The Communist Road to Power in Vietnam*, pp. 291–297; Lewy *America in Vietnam*, pp. 194–201, 410–420; Isaacs, *Without Honor*, pp. 18–24;

Palmer, *Summons of the Trumpet*, pp. 302–326; Clodfelter, *The Limits of Air Power*, pp. 148–173, 205–207; *Air War Vietnam*, pp. 277–290.

7. Lewy, *America in Vietnam*, pp. 196–201, 412–417; Isaacs, *Without Honor*, pp. 32–79, 312; Clodfelter, *The Limits of Air Power*, pp. 177–206; *Air War Vietnam*, pp. 277–290; Duiker, *The Communist Road to Power in Vietnam*, pp. 296–297; William LeGros, *Vietnam: From Cease-Fire to Capitulation* (Washington: U.S. Army Center of Military History, 1981), pp. 2–17; Thayer, *War Without Fronts*, p. 256. According to Eastern European sources, the 1972 bombing and mining campaign was so effective that Hanoi was practically willing to agree to *any* terms. See Alan Dawson, *Fifty-five Days* (Englewood Cliffs, NJ: Prentice Hall, 1977), p. 120.

CHAPTER TEN

1. John Barron and Anthony Paul, *Murder of a Gentle Land* (New York: Crowell, 1977), pp. 2–127, 134–139, 152, 167–170, 204–206; Isaacs, *Without Honor*, pp. 205–289.

2. Lewy, *America in Vietnam*, pp. 202–209; Isaacs, *Without Honor*, pp. 310–328, 338–341; Cao Van Vien, *The Final Collapse* (Washington: U.S. Army Center of Military History, 1983), pp. 34–57; LeGros, *Vietnam: From Cease-Fire to Capitulation*, pp. 18–81, 145; Warner, *Certain Victory*, pp. 9–10, 16–17, 22; Frank Snepp, *Decent Interval* (New York: Random House, 1977), pp. 70, 74, 76–79, 131–132, 237; P. Edward Haley, *Congress and the Fall of South Vietnam* (New Brunswick, NJ: Associated University Press, 1982), p. 43, 58, 96.

3. Lewy, *America in Vietnam*, pp. 210–222; Isaacs, *Without Honor*, pp. 345–485; LeGros, *Vietnam: From Cease-Fire to Capitulation*, pp. 132–137, 145, 149–179; Snepp, *Decent Interval*, pp. 174–213, 222, 226, 245–262, 276, 280, 282–283, 288–297, 306–308, 319–331, 337, 564, 572; Stephen Hosmer, et al. *The Fall of South Vietnam* (New York: Crane Russak, 1978), p. 43, 52–61, 82–131; William Duiker, *Vietnam Since the Fall of Saigon* (Athens, Ohio: Center for International Studies, 1985).

4. Edgar O'Ballance, *The Wars in Vietnam* revised edition (New York: Hippocrene, 1980), pp. 218–225; Duiker, *Vietnam Since the Fall of Saigon*, pp. 121–123, 130–132.

5. Blaufarb, *The Counterinsurgency Era*, pp. 174–204; J.L.S. Girling, *Thailand* (Ithaca: Cornell University Press, 1981), pp. 94, 243–285.

6. Hosmer, *The Fall of South Vietnam*, pp. 30–32, 129–131. The South Vietnamese leaders interviewed for this Rand Corporation study laid the primary blame for the defeat on the lack of American aid, the blunders of Thieu and his cronies and the demoralization caused by corruption. See also Lam Quang Thi, *Autopsy* (Phoenix: Sphinx, 1986), esp. pp. 72–73, 161–163, 173–175.

7. For a strong argument that the war *was* unwinnable, see Bergerud, *The Dynamics of Defeat*, esp. pp. 5, 326–335.

8. Warner, *Certain Victory*, p. 201.

Bibliography

Adams, Sherman. *First Hand Report*. New York: Harper, 1961.

Air War Vietnam. Indianapolis: Bobbs Merrill, 1978.

Allison, John M. *Ambassador from the Prairie*. Boston: Houghton Mifflin, 1973.

Anderson, Benedict R. O'G. *Some Aspects of Indonesian Politics Under Japanese Occupation*. Ithaca: Cornell University Press, 1961.

Appy, Christian G. *Working Class War*, Chapel Hill: University of North Carolina Press, 1993.

Barnett, A. Doak. *Communist China and Asia*. New York: Vintage, 1960.

Barron, John, and Paul, Anthony. *Murder of a Gentle Land*. New York: Crowell, 1977.

Bell, Ken. *One Hundred Missions North. New York: Brassey, 1993*.

Berger, Carl. *The United States Air Force in Southeast Asia*. Washington: Dept. of the Air Force, 1977.

Bergerud, Eric. *The Dynamics of Defeat*. Boulder: Westview, 1991.

Bergerud, Eric. *Red Thunder, Tropic Lightning*, Boulder: Westview, 1993.

Berman, Larry. *Lyndon Johnson's War*. New York: Norton, 1989.

Berman, Larry. *Planning a Tragedy*. New York: Norton, 1982.

Blaufarb, Douglas. *The Counterinsurgency Era*. New York: Free Press, 1977.

Blum, Robert. *Drawing the Line*. New York: Norton, 1982.

Brackman, Arnold. *The Communist Collapse in Indonesia*. New York: Norton, 1969.

Brackman, Arnold. *Southeast Asia's Second Front*. New York: Praeger, 1966.

Braestrup, Peter. *Big Story*. New Haven: Yale University Press, 1978.

Brennan, Matthew, ed. *Headhunters*. New York: Pocket Books, 1988.

Brimmell, J. H. *Communism in Southeast Asia*. Oxford: Oxford University Press, 1959.

Broughton, Jack. *Thud Ridge*. New York: Bantam, 1985.

Cable, James. *The Geneva Conference of 1954 on Indochina.* New York: St. Martin's Press, 1986.

Cable, Larry. *Conflict of Myths.* New York: New York University Press, 1986.

Calvert, Michael. *War Since 1945.* New York: Putnam, 1981.

Calvocoressi, Peter, ed. *Survey of International Affairs 1951.* London: Oxford University Press, 1954.

Cao Van Vien. *The Final Collapse.* Washington: U.S. Army Center of Military History, 1983.

Chapman, F. Spencer. *The Jungle is Neutral.* London: Chatto and Windus, 1949.

Cheah Boon Kheng. *Red Star Over Malaya.* Singapore: Singapore University Press, 1983.

Chen, Jerome. *Mao and the Chinese Revolution.* New York: Oxford University Press, 1965.

Chen, King. *Vietnam and China.* Princeton: Princeton University Press, 1969.

Clodfelter, Mark. *The Limits of Airpower.* New York: Free Press, 1989.

Clutterbuck, Richard. *The Long, Long War.* New York: Praeger, 1966.

Clutterbuck, Richard. *Riot and Revolution in Singapore and Malaya.* London: Faber and Faber, 1973.

Cohen, Arthur A. *The Communism of Mao Tse-tung.* Chicago: University of Chicago Press, 1964.

Coleman, J. D. *Incursion.* New York: St. Martin's Press, 1991.

Committee of Concerned Asian Scholars. *The Indochina Story.* New York: Bantam, 1970.

Conquest, Robert. *Power and Policy in the USSR.* New York: St. Martin's Press, 1961.

Cooper, Chester. *The Lost Crusade.* New York: Fawcett, 1972.

Corson, William R. *The Betrayal.* New York: Norton, 1968.

Critchfield, Richard. *The Long Charade.* New York: Harcourt, Brace, 1968.

Cruickshank, Charles. *SOE in the Far East.* New York: Oxford University Press, 1985.

Cruttwell, C.R.M.F. *A History of the Great War.* London: Granada, 1982.

Currey, Cecil B. (Cincinnatus). *Self-Destruction.* New York: Norton, 1981.

Dalloz, Jacques. *The War in Indochina.* New York: Barnes and Noble, 1990.

Davidson, Philip. *Secrets of the Vietnam War.* Novato, CA: Presidio, 1990.

Dawson, Alan. *Fifty-five Days.* Englewood Cliffs, NJ: Prentice Hall, 1977.

Dennis, Peter. *Troubled Days of Peace.* New York: St. Martin's Press, 1987.

Dommen, Arthur. *Conflict in Laos.* New York: Praeger, 1971.

Donnison, F.S.V. *British Military Administration in the Far East.* London: Her Majesty's Stationery Office, 1956.

Donnison, F.S.V. *Burma.* New York: Praeger, 1970.

Draper, Theodore. *Abuse of Power.* New York: Viking, 1967.

Duiker, William, *The Communist Road to Power in Vietnam.* Boulder: Westview, 1981.

Duiker, William. *Vietnam Since the Fall of Saigon*. Athens, Ohio: Center for International Studies, 1985.

Duncanson, Dennis. *Government and Revolution in Vietnam*. New York: Oxford University Press, 1968.

Ebert, James. *A Life in a Year*. Novato, CA: Presidio, 1993.

Etzold, Thomas, and Gaddis, John Lewis. *Containment*. New York: Columbia University Press, 1978.

Fairbairn, Geoffrey. *Revolutionary Guerrilla Warfare*. New York: Penguin, 1974.

Fall, Bernard. *Hell in a Very Small Place*. New York: Vintage, 1968.

Fall, Bernard. *Street Without Joy*. New York: Schocken, 1972.

Fall, Bernard. *The Two Vietnams*. New York: Praeger, 1963.

Gabriel, Richard A., and Savage, Paul. *Crisis in Command*. New York: Hill and Wang, 1978.

Gelb, Leslie, and Betts, Richard. *The Irony of Vietnam*. Washington: Brookings Institution, 1979.

Geraghty, Tony. *Inside the SAS*. New York: Ballantine, 1982.

Gibbons, William Conrad. *The US Government and the Vietnam War part 2 1961–1964*. Princeton: Princeton University Press, 1986.

Gibbons, William Conrad. *The US Government and the Vietnam War part 3 1965*. Princeton: Princeton University Press, 1989.

Girling, J.L.S. *Thailand*. Ithaca: Cornell University Press, 1981.

Grant, Zalin. *Facing the Phoenix*. New York: Norton, 1991.

Griffith, Paddy. *Forward into Battle*. Novato, CA: Presidio, 1992.

Gruliow, Leo, ed. *Soviet Views on the Postwar World Economy*. Washington: Public Affairs Press, 1948.

Haley, P. Edward. *Congress and the Fall of South Vietnam*. New Brunswick, NJ: Associated University Press, 1982.

Hammer, Ellen. *The Struggle for Indochina*. Stanford: Stanford University Press, 1966.

Hammond, William M. *The Military and the Media*. Washington: Center of Military History, 1988.

Herrington, Stuart. *Silence Was a Weapon*. Novato, CA: Presidio, 1982.

Hess, Gary. *The United States Emergence as a Southeast Asian Power 1940–1950*. New York: Columbia University Press, 1987.

Hinton, Harold C. *China's Turbulent Quest*. Rev. edition. Bloomington: Indiana University Press, 1972.

Hinton, Harold C. *Communist China in World Politics*. Boston: Houghton Mifflin, 1966.

Honey, P. J. *Communism in North Vietnam*. Cambridge: MIT Press, 1963.

Hosmer, Stephen, et al. *The Fall of South Vietnam*. New York: Crane Russak, 1978.

Hughes, John. *Indonesian Upheaval*. New York: David McKay, 1967.

Isaacs, Arnold. *Without Honor*. New York: Vintage, 1984.

Johnson, Chalmers. *Autopsy on People's War*. Berkeley: University of California Press, 1973.

Johnson, Lyndon. *The Vantage Point*. New York: Popular Library, 1972.

Joiner, Charles. *The Politics of Massacre*. Philadelphia: Temple University Press, 1974.

Jones, F. C. *Japan's New Order in East Asia*. Oxford: Oxford University Press, 1954.

Jones, Howard P. *Indonesia: The Possible Dream*. New York: Harcourt, Brace and Jovanovich, 1971.

Kahin, George M. *Nationalism and Revolution*. Ithaca: Cornell University Press, 1952.

Kail, F. M. *What Washington Said*. New York: Harper and Row, 1973.

Khrushchev Remembers: The Last Testament. New York: Bantam, 1974.

Kinnard, Douglas. *The War Managers*. Wayne, NJ: Avery, 1985.

Krepinevich, Andrew F. *The Army and Vietnam*. Baltimore: Johns Hopkins University Press, 1986.

Krock, Arthur. *Memoirs*. New York: Popular Library, 1968.

Lachica, Eduardo. *The Huks: Philippine Agrarian Society in Revolt*. New York: Praeger, 1971.

Lam Quang Thi. *Autopsy*. Phoenix: Sphinx, 1986.

Lancaster, Donald. *The Emancipation of French Indochina*. Oxford: Oxford University Press, 1961.

Langer, Paul, and Zasloff, Joseph. *North Vietnam and the Pathet Lao*. Cambridge: Harvard University Press, 1970.

Lanning, Michael Lee, and Cragg, Dan. *Inside the VC and the NVA*. New York: Ivy, 1993.

Lansdale, Edward. *In the Midst of Wars*. New York: Harper and Row, 1972.

Larkin, Bruce D. *China and Africa 1949–1970*. Berkeley: University of California Press, 1971.

Lederer, William J. *Our Own Worst Enemy*. Greenwich: Fawcett, 1968.

LeGros, William. *Vietnam: From Cease-Fire to Capitulation*. Washington: U.S. Army Center of Military History, 1981.

Levy, David. *The Debate Over Vietnam*. Baltimore: Johns Hopkins University Press, 1991.

Lewy, Guenter. *America in Vietnam*. New York: Oxford University Press, 1978.

Little, David. *American Foreign Policy and Moral Rhetoric*. New York: The Council on Religion and International Relations, 1969.

Mackie, J.A.C. *Konfrontasi*. Kuala Lumpur: Oxford University Press, 1974.

Marolda, Edward J., and Fitzgerald, Oscar P. *From Military Assistance to Combat*. Washington: Naval Historical Center, 1986.

McCagg, William. *Stalin Embattled*. Detroit: Wayne State University Press, 1978.

McCoy, Alfred W., ed. *Southeast Asia Under Japanese Occupation*. New Haven: Yale University Southeast Asian Studies, 1980.

McLane, Charles B. *Soviet Strategies in Southeast Asia*. Princeton: Princeton University Press, 1966.

Mossman, James. *Rebels in Paradise*. London: Jonathan Cape, 1961.

Mountbatten, Earl. *Post Surrender Tasks*. London: Her Majesty's Stationery Office, 1969.

Mueller, John E. *War, Presidents and Public Opinion*. New York: Wiley, 1973.

Nicholls, John B., and Tillman, Barrett. *On Yankee Station*. Annapolis: US Naval Institute, 1987.

Nolan, Keith William. *Into Cambodia*. Novato, CA: Presidio, 1990.

O'Ballance, Edgar. *The Indochina War*. London: Faber and Faber, 1964.

O'Ballance, Edgar. *Malaya: The Communist Insurgent War 1948–1960*. London: Faber and Faber, 1966.

O'Ballance, Edgar. *The Wars in Vietnam*. Rev. edition. New York: Hippocrene, 1980.

Oberdorfer, Don. *Tet*. New York: Da Capo, 1986.

Ovendale, Ritchie. *The English-Speaking Alliance*. London: George Allen and Unwin, 1985.

Paget, Julian. *Counterinsurgency Operations*. New York: Walker, 1967.

Palmer, Dave Richard. *Summons of the Trumpet*. New York: Ballantine, 1983.

Palmier, Leslie. *Communists in Indonesia*. New York: Anchor, 1974.

Pearson, Willard. *The War in the Northern Provinces*. Washington: Dept. of the Army, 1975.

The Pentagon Papers: Senator Gravel Edition. Boston: Beacon Press, 1971.

Pike, Douglas. *History of Vietnamese Communism*. Stanford: Hoover Institution Press, 1978.

Pike, Douglas. *Vietcong*. Cambridge: MIT Press, 1966.

Prados, John. *The Sky Would Fall*. New York: Dial Press, 1983.

Prados, John, and Stubbs, Ray. *Valley of Decision*. New York: Dell, 1993.

Pye, Lucian. *Guerrilla Communism in Malaya*. Princeton: Princeton University Press, 1956.

Ra'anan, Gavriel. *International Policy Formation in the USSR*. Hamden, Conn.: Archon, 1983.

Ra'anan, Uri. *The USSR Arms the Third World*. Cambridge: MIT Press, 1969.

Race, Jeffrey. *War Comes to Long An*. Berkeley: University of California Press, 1972.

Randle, Robert F. *Geneva 1954*. Princeton: Princeton University Press, 1969.

Reid, Anthony. *The Indonesian National Revolution*. Longman: London: 1974.

Rovere, Richard. *Waist Deep in the Big Muddy*. Boston: Little, Brown, 1968.

Sansom, Robert. *The Economics of Insurgency in the Mekong Delta*. Cambridge: MIT Press, 1970.

Saulo, Alfredo. *Communism in the Philippines*. Manila, Philippines: Ateneo, 1968.

Scaff, Alvin. *The Philippine Answer to Communism*. Stanford: Stanford University Press, 1955.

Schaller, Michael. *The American Occupation of Japan*. New York: Oxford University Press, 1985.

Schandler, Herbert Y. *The Unmaking of a President*. Princeton: Princeton University Press, 1977.

Schlesinger, Arthur. *The Bitter Heritage*. Greenwich: Fawcett, 1968.

Schlesinger, Arthur. *Robert Kennedy and His Times*. Boston: Houghton Mifflin, 1978.

Schmidt, Dana Adams. *Anatomy of a Satellite*. Boston: Little, Brown, 1952.

Schnabel, James. *Policy and Direction*. Washington: Office of the Chief of Military History, 1972.

Seton-Watson, Hugh. *From Lenin to Khrushchev*. New York: Praeger, 1960.

Sharpley, Cecil. *The Great Delusion*. London: Heineman, 1952.

Short, Anthony. *The Communist Insurrection in Malaya*. New York: Crane, Russak, 1975.

Shulman, Marshall, *Stalin's Foreign Policy Reappraised*. Cambridge: Harvard University Press, 1963.

Small, Melvin. *Johnson, Nixon and the Doves*. New Brunswick, NJ: Rutgers University Press, 1988.

Smith, Joseph B. *Portrait of a Cold Warrior*. New York: Ballantine, 1981.

Smith, R. B. *An International History of the Vietnam War Volume 1*. New York: St. Martin's Press, 1983.

Smith, R. B. *An International History of the Vietnam War Volume 2*. New York: St. Martin's Press, 1984.

Snepp, Frank. *Decent Interval*. New York: Random House, 1977.

Spector, Ronald. *Advise and Support*. Washington: Office of the Chief of Military History, 1983.

Spector, Ronald. *After Tet*. New York: Free Press, 1993.

Stanton, Shelby. *Anatomy of a Division*. Novato, CA: Presidio, 1987.

Stanton, Shelby. *The Rise and Fall of An American Army*. Novato, CA: Presidio, 1985.

Stenson, M. R. *Industrial Conflict in Malaya*. London: Oxford University Press, 1970.

Stockdale, James. *In Love and War*. New York: Bantam, 1985.

Summers, Harry. *On Strategy*. Novato: Presidio, 1982.

Taruc, Luis. *He Who Rides the Tiger*. New York: Praeger, 1967.

Taylor, Jay. *China and Southeast Asia*. New York: Praeger, 1974.

Thayer, Thomas C. *War Without Fronts*. Boulder: Westview, 1985.

Thorne, Christopher. *Allies of a Kind*. New York: Oxford University Press, 1978.

Tolson, John. *Airmobility 1961–1971*. Washington: Dept. of the Army, 1973.

Trager, Frank N. *Burma: From Kingdom to Republic*. New York: Praeger, 1966.

Trager, Frank N., ed. *Marxism and Southeast Asia*. New York: Praeger, 1959.

Truong Nhu Tang. *A Viet Cong Memoir*. New York: Vintage, 1986.

Tsou, Tang. *America's Failure in China*. Chicago: University of Chicago Press, 1963.

Turner, Robert F. *Vietnamese Communism*. Stanford: Stanford University Press, 1975.

Uhlig, Jr., Frank. *Vietnam: The Naval Story*. Annapolis: Naval Institute Press, 1986.

United States Department of State. *Foreign Relations of the United States 1945 Volume VI*. Washington: Government Printing Office, 1969.

————. *Foreign Relations of the United States 1947 Volume II*. Washington: Government Printing Office, 1972.

————. *Foreign Relations of the United States 1947 Volume IV*. Washington: Government Printing Office, 1972.

————. *Foreign Relations of the United States 1947 Volume VI*. Washington: Government Printing Office, 1972.

————. *Foreign Relations of the United States 1948 Volume IV*. Washington: Government Printing Office, 1974.

————. *Foreign Relations of the United States 1949 Volume VII*. Washington: Government Printing Office, 1976.

————. *Foreign Relations of the United States 1950 Volume I*. Washington: Government Printing Office, 1977.

————. *Foreign Relations of the United States 1950 Volume VI*. Washington: Government Printing Office, 1976.

————. *Foreign Relations of the United States 1951 Volume I*. Washington: Government Printing Office, 1979.

————. *Foreign Relations of the United States 1951 Volume VI*. Washington: Government Printing Office, 1977.

————. *Foreign Relations of the United States 1952–1954 Volume I*. Washington: Government Printing Office, 1982.

————. *Foreign Relations of the United States 1952–1954 Volume XII*. Washington: Government Printing Office, 1981.

————. *Foreign Relations of the United States 1952–1954 Volume XIII*. Washington: Government Printing Office, 1982.

————. *Foreign Relations of the United States 1952–1954 Volume XVI*. Washington: Government Printing Office, 1981.

————. *Foreign Relations of the United States 1955–1957 Volume I*. Washington: Government Printing Office, 1985.

————. *Foreign Relations of the United States 1955–1957 Volume XXII*. Washington: Government Printing Office, 1989.

————. *Foreign Relations of the United States 1958–1960 Volume I*. Washington: Government Printing Office, 1986.

————. *Foreign Relations of the United States 1961–1963 Volume I*. Washington: Government Printing Office, 1988.

————. *Foreign Relations of the United States 1961–1963 Volume II*. Washington: Government Printing Office, 1990.

————. *Foreign Relations of the United States 1961–1963 Volume III*. Washington: Government Printing Office, 1991.

————. *Foreign Relations of the United States 1961–1963 Volume IV*. Washington: Government Printing Office, 1992.

————. *Foreign Relations of the United States 1964–1968 Volume I*. Washington: Government Printing Office, 1992.

Van DeMark, Brian. *Into the Quagmire*. New York: Oxford University Press, 1991.

van Mook, Hubertus. *The Stakes of Democracy in Southeast Asia*. New York: Norton, 1950.

Warner, Denis, *Certain Victory*. Kansas City, MO: Sheed, Andrews, McMeed, 1978.

Wells, Tom, *The War Within*. Berkeley: University of California Press, 1994.

West, Francis J. *The Village*. New York: Harper and Row, 1972.

Westmoreland, William B. *A Soldier Reports*. New York: Doubleday, 1976.

Wirtz, James J. *The Tet Offensive*. Ithaca: Cornell University Press, 1991.

Wolf, Charles. *The Indonesian Story*. New York: John Day, 1947.

Yuen Foong Khong. *Analogies at War*. Princeton: Princeton University Press, 1992.

Zagoria, Donald. *The Sino-Soviet Conflict 1956–1961*. Princeton: Princeton University Press, 1962.

Zagoria, Donald. *Vietnam Triangle*. New York: Pegasus, 1967.

Zaroulis, Nancy, and Sullivan, Gerald. *Who Spoke Up?* New York: Doubleday, 1984.

Zhdanov, Andrei. *The International Situation*. Moscow: Foreign Languages Publishing House, 1947.

Ziegler, Philip. *Mountbatten*. New York: Harper and Row, 1985.

Zumbro, Ralph. *Tank Sergeant*. New York: Pocket Books, 1988.

ARTICLES

Barghoorn, Frederick. "The Varga Discussion and Its Significance." *American Slavic and East European Review* (October 1948), pp. 214–236.

Barnes, Trevor. "The Secret Cold War, The CIA and American Foreign Policy in Europe 1944–1956 part I." *Historical Journal* 2 (1981) pp. 407–408.

Huynh Kim Khanh. "The Vietnamese August Revolution." *Journal of Asian Studies* (August 1971), pp. 768–769.

Jaffe, Philip. "The Varga Controversy and the American Communist Party." *Survey* (Summer 1972), pp. 138–160.

Lowenthal, Richard, and Van der Kroef, J. M. "On National Democracy." *Survey* (April 1963), pp. 119–134.

McVey, Ruth. "The Southeast Asian Revolts." In *Communism and Revolution,* ed. by Cyril E. Black and Thomas P. Thornton. Princeton: Princeton University Press, 1964, pp. 145–184.

Modelski, George. "The Viet Minh Complex." In *Communism and Revolution*, ed. by Cyril E. Black and Thomas P. Thornton. Princeton: Princeton University Press, 1964, pp. 185–214.

Shinn, William. "The 'National Democratic State'—A Communist Program for Less-Developed Areas." *World Politics* (April 1963), pp. 377–389.

Tanigawa Yoshihiko. "The Cominform and Southeast Asia." In *The Origins of the Cold War in Asia*, ed. by Akira Iriye. New York: Columbia University Press, 1977, pp. 362–377.

Turner, Robert F. "Myths of the Vietnam War." *Southeast Asian Perspectives*. (September 1972), pp. 24–38.

Van der Kroef, Justus M. "The Wages of Ambiguity." In *The Anatomy of Communist Takeovers*, ed. Thomas T. Hammond. New Haven: Yale University Press, 1975, pp. 534–562.

Index

Abangan, 69

Abrams, Gen. Creighton, 136

Acheson, Secretary of State Dean, 28, 29, 104, 133–34, 151

Adams, Sherman, 35

Aidit, D. N., 69, 71, 72, 74–76

air operations: in First Indochina War, 30, 34; in Second Indochina War, 101, 103, 104, 120–22, 128, 134, 142–43. *See also* bombing of North Vietnam

"airmobile" operations, 111–13. *See also* helicopters and helicopter warfare

Algeria, 37, 52, 112, 128

Allied forces in Vietnam, 116

Anti-Fascist People's Freedom League, 58–61, 62

anti-guerrilla doctrines, 46, 52–53, 56, 63, 92–93, 110, 117, 118, 129, 152

anti-infiltration barrier, 128, 130

"anti-war" movement, 125–26, 137–38, 153

ASEAN, 11

Aung San, Gen., 58, 59

Australia, 10, 35, 116

Australian Communist Party, 39, 49

Ball, Undersecretary of State George, 106–7

Bao Dai, Emperor, 18, 19, 26, 28, 30, 31, 84, 87

base areas, 22, 23, 24–25, 51, 57, 61, 110, 116, 129. *See also* sanctuaries

Bien Hoa, 103, 131

Binh Xuen, 83, 84

body count, 117

Bohlen, Charles, 13

bombing of North Vietnam, 101, 103, 104–5, 120–22, 128, 134, 142–43. *See also* air operations

Borkenau, Franz, 18

Borneo, 73

Bowles, Undersecretary of State Chester, 95, 99

Bradley, Gen. Omar, 133, 154

Britain: in Malaya, 4, 46–53; policy in Indochina, 19–21, 35–36; policy in post-World War II Indonesia, 40–41; relations with Southeast Asia, 1–6, 12; war with Indonesia, 73–74, 76, 77

Bundy, McGeorge, 94, 109, 166 n.7
bunkers, 114, 115
Burke, Admiral Arleigh, 91
Burma, 3, 4, 5, 12–13, 68; Communist rebellion in 1948, 39, 58–62, 68; relations with United States, 61–62
Burma, Communist Party of ("Red Flags" or national Communists), 59, 61
Burmese Communist Party ("White Flags" or orthodox Communists), 9, 39, 40, 59–62, 68
Burmese National Army, 58
Burnham, James, 168 n.11
Byrnes, Secretary of State James, 6

Calcutta conference, 9, 39, 44, 49
Cambodia, 2–3, 4; in First Indochina War, 18, 26, 29, 36; post-Geneva, 82–83; in Second Indochina War, 116, 117, 132, 136, 138–40, 145–46, 149; Vietnamese invasion of 1978, 149
Cambodian "incursion," 138–40
Can Lao, 84
Canada, 80
Cao Dai, 20, 26, 83, 84, 85, 96
Castro, Fidel, 67, 72, 89–90
Catholics in Vietnam, 26, 39, 80, 83, 84, 147
Central Intelligence Agency (CIA), 56, 61, 69, 70–71, 91–92, 93, 96, 103, 120, 152
Chin Peng, 48, 49, 52
China: and Burma, 61, 68; conflict with Soviet Union, 67–68, 72–73, 99–100, 124, 142;and Indonesia, 68, 72–77; invasion of Vietnam, 149; occupation of Indochina and First Indochina War, 19, 21–23, 26–28, 30, 33; Second Indochina War, 85, 86, 99–100, 103, 109,
120, 123, 127, 142; and Southeast Asia, 1, 2, 10, 13–14, 39
Chinese minorities in Southeast Asia, 3, 5, 46–53, 72–73, 76, 149
Chou Enlai, 49
Civil Operations and Revolutionary Development, 119
Clifford, Secretary of Defense Clark, 104, 133, 134
Cochin China, 18, 20, 23, 26
Cogny, Gen. Rene, 32, 33
Cold War and Southeast Asia, 6–15, 39–40, 62–63, 65–68, 77, 79, 81, 85, 99–100, 103, 127, 150, 153–54
Collins, Gen. J. Lawton, 12
Colombo neutral powers, 80
combined action platoons, 117
Communism, appeals of, 5, 15, 17–18, 24–25, 45, 46, 53, 54, 55, 69, 85–86, 139–40
Communism in Southeast Asia, 4–5, 9–15, 62–63, 150
Communist doctrines, 7–10, 23–29, 37, 66–67
containment, 1, 7, 14–15, 81, 104, 124
Council of Economic Advisers, 107
counterinsurgency, 89, 92–93, 110. See also anti-guerrilla doctrines
Cronkite, Walter, 133
Cuba, 67, 89–90, 93
Cyprus, 52
Czechoslovakia, 8, 12, 27, 39, 70, 71, 73

Dai Viets, 30, 97
Danang, 105, 106
de Lattre de Tassigny, Marshal Jean, 29, 30, 37
de Lattre line, 30
Decker, Gen. George, 92
defoliation, 94
Dien Bien Phu, 30, 32–36, 129, 130

Djakarta, 74–75
domino theory, 12–14, 35, 36, 81, 97, 102, 103, 106, 108, 124
Dong Minh Hoi, 21, 23
draft, 113–14
drugs, 82, 92, 140
Dulles, Secretary of State John Foster, 32, 34–36, 70, 81–82, 87
Duncanson, Dennis, 88
Durbrow, Elbridge, 88

Eden, Anthony, 35, 36
Egypt, 9, 66, 70, 72
Eisenhower, President Dwight D., and Eisenhower Administration, 30, 32, 34–36, 70–71, 80–84, 87–88, 109; and domino theory, 35, 36, 81
Ely, Paul, 34
Elysée Agreements, 26, 28, 29
Enthoven, Alain, 128

Fall, Bernard, 34, 95
Ferret Force, 49
First Indochina War: course and results, 17–37, 80–81; reasons for outcome of First War, 37
Formosa Resolution, 100
Fortas, Justice Abe, 133, 134
France: colonial rule in Indochina, 1, 3, 4, 7, 8, 17–18, 37; and First Indochina War, 23–37; negotiations with Vietminh, 19–23; relations with United States, 6, 11, 28–29, 31–32, 33–36
French Communist Party, 21–22
Fulbright, Senator William, 123

Geneva Conference on Indochina (1954) and Geneva Agreements, 33, 36, 80–82
Geneva Conference on Laos (1962), 91
Goldwater, Senator Barry, 127

Goshal, 60
Gottwald, Klement, 45
Gracey, Gen. Douglas, 20
Greece, 7, 12, 24, 39, 48, 63
Greene, Gen. Wallace, 107
Griffith, Gen. Samuel B., 63
Groups de Commando Mixte Aeroporte, 30
guerrilla warfare, 10, 24–25, 30–31, 47, 49–53, 55–58, 63, 69, 86–87, 129–30
"guided democracy," 70–71
Gulf of Tonkin incidents, 101–2, 166 n.3. *See also* Southeast Asia Resolution

Haiphong, 120, 121
Halberstam, David, 97
Halim, 75
Hanoi, 19, 23, 29, 36, 86, 120, 121
Harkins, Gen. Paul, 94
Hartini, 71
Hatta, Mohammed, 40, 44
Heilbroner, Robert, 124
helicopters and helicopter warfare, 93, 94, 111–13, 115, 129
Heng Samrin, 149
Herter, Secretary of State Christian, 88
Hilsman, Assistant Secretary of State Roger, 94
Hmong (Meo), 91–92
Ho Chi Minh, 18–19, 21–23, 27, 28, 84, 99
Ho Chi Minh trail, 86, 91–92, 112, 116, 117, 121–22, 130, 132, 134, 146
Hoa Binh, 30
Hoa Hao, 20, 26, 83, 84, 85, 96
Hovey, Joseph, 130
Hue, 82, 131, 132
Hukbalahap ("Huks"), 54–58. *See also* Philippines Communist Party

Humphrey, Vice President Hubert, 106

India, 2, 9, 80
Indochina: colonial situation, 2–4, 10, 17–18; post-World War II American policy, 5–6, 10–14
Indochina Communist Party, 18–19, 21
Indochina Wars. *See* First Indochina War; Second Indochina War. *See also* National Liberation Front; United States
Indonesia: colonial situation, 2, 3, 5, 8, 25; first attempted Communist takeover, 39–45, 58; post-independence social and political situation, 68–69; second attempted Communist takeover, 65–77; and Second Indochina War, 76–77; struggle for independence, 40–45
Indonesian Communist Party, 9, 42, 44–46, 69–75
Indonesian Socialist Party, 42–45, 69–71
Iraq, 66, 72
Isaacs, Arnold, 144

Japan: role in Indochina, 17–20; role in Indonesia, 40–41; role in Malaya, 47–48; and Southeast Asia, 1, 4–5, 10, 87–88
Java, 3, 41, 42, 43, 68–69, 75, 76
Jiang Jieshi (Chiang Kai-shek), 83, 92, 94, 151
Johnson, Gen. Harold, 105, 108
Johnson, President Lyndon, and Johnson Administration: conduct of war, 96, 97, 100–134, 135, 152, 166 n.9; decision for massive intervention, 100–9; decision not to run again, 134; and Indonesia, 68, 74, 103; and opposition to war, 124, 125–28, 133–34; policies after Tet, 132–34; unpopularity, 102, 107, 108
Joint Chiefs of Staff, 12, 34, 82, 102, 105, 106, 128, 133
Jones, Howard P., 71

Kachins, 4
Karens, 4, 59, 60, 61
Kennan, George F., 2, 29, 104, 125
Kennedy, President John F., and Kennedy Administration: and Indonesia, 71–73; policies in Laos and Vietnam, 87–88, 90–96, 97, 114, 135; policies toward "wars of national liberation," 89; support for Diem, 84, 87–88
Kennedy, Senator Robert F., 124, 126
Kenya, 52
Khe Sanh, 130, 132, 136
Khmer Loeu, 139
Khmer Rouge, 139–40, 145–46, 149
Khrushchev, Premier Nikita, 66, 67, 71–72, 76, 89
Kinnard, Gen. Douglas, 112
Kissinger, Secretary of State Henry, 135, 142–44, 148
Korea, 14, 29, 46, 80, 87, 153
Korean forces in Vietnam, 116, 137
Korean War, 14, 29, 31, 32, 46, 108, 109, 114, 118, 121, 122, 153–54
Krock, Arthur, 97

la Drang campaign, 111–13
Ladejinsky, Wolf, 87
Laird, Secretary of State Melvin, 135
land issues and land reform, 17, 50, 53, 54, 55, 58, 83, 84–86, 87–88, 93, 95, 119, 132
Lansdale, Col. Edward, 56
Lao Dong party, 29
Laos: in First Indochina War, 18, 26, 29, 32, 36, 82–83; in Second Indo-

china War, 86, 90–92, 116, 120, 132–34, 141, 149; U.S. air operations, 91, 100–101, 103, 121–22, 134
Latin America, 89–90
Le Duc Tho, 144
Lemnitzer, Gen. Lyman, 93
Lenin, Vladimir, 23, 66
Li Cheng Hu, 33
Lien Viet, 21
Linggadjati agreement, 42–43
Lippmann, Walter, 123
Liu Shaoqi, 10
Lodge, Senator Henry Cabot, 100, 102
Loi Tak, 47, 48, 49
Lon Nol, 138–39, 146
Lovett, Robert, 10, 104
Luce, Henry, 127, 128
Luzon, 53, 54

M-16 rifle, 114
Maddox, USS, 101
Madiun rebellion, 48
Magsaysay, Ramon, 56–58
Malay Democratic Union, 48
Malay Nationalist Party, 48
Malaya: colonial situation, 2, 3, 7; Communist rebellion, 39, 40, 46–53, 58; comparison with Vietnam, 52, 93; postwar social and political situation, 46–47; strategic importance, 12–13, 34, 73
Malayan Chinese Association, 50, 51
Malayan Communist Party, 9, 46–53
Malayan Peoples' Anti-British Army, 49
Malayan Peoples' Anti-Japanese Army, 47–48, 54
Malayan Races Liberation Army, 49
Malaysia, 73–74, 76, 77
Malenkov, Georgi, 9
Manila, 4, 29, 56, 57

Mao Zedong (Mao Tse-tung) and Maoism, 10, 22, 23–25, 27, 37, 39, 67, 69, 89–90, 99, 110, 129
Marcos, Ferdinand, 58
Marshall, Secretary of State George C., 12
Marshall, S.L.A., 141
Marshall Plan, 7–9, 45
Martin, Graham, 147, 148
Masjumi, 69, 70, 71
McCarthy, Senator Eugene, 126
McCloy, John, 104
McCone, John, 10, 96
McNamara, Secretary of Defense Robert, 95, 103, 105, 106, 107, 109, 111, 128
McNamara line, 128, 130
McNaughton, John, 120
Mekong Delta, 82
Mendes-France, Pierre, 36
Middle East Resolution, 100
Military Assistance Command Vietnam (MACV), 94, 105, 118, 119
Min Yuen, 49
Mindanao, 56, 58
Morgenthau, Hans, 123
Morice line, 128
Morse, Senator Wayne, 101
Morton, Senator Thruston, 127
Mountbatten, Admiral Louis, 6, 20, 40–41, 47, 58
Mozambique, 68
Murba party, 74
Musso, 44–45
My Lai massacre, 137

Nasser, Gamal, 70, 72
Nasution, Abdul, 75, 76
national Communists, 42, 59, 74
"national democracy," 57, 71
National Liberation Front ("Vietcong"), 86, 94, 96, 99, 107–8, 109, 115, 116, 117, 118, 131–32, 139

National Peasant Union, 55
National Security Council, 11, 12–13, 14, 35, 81, 103
nationalism, 4–5
Navarre, Gen. Henri, 32, 36
Netherlands: colonial rule in Indonesia, 1, 3–4, 9; postwar policy in Indonesia, 6, 8, 40–45; relations with independent Indonesia, 68, 70, 71–72
New Guinea, 70, 71–72
New Villages, 50, 51
New York Times, 97, 138
news media, 132–33, 138, 152–53
Ngo Dinh Diem and family, 83–88, 92–97, 150
Ngo Dinh Nhu, 84, 95, 96
Nguyen Cao Ky, 92, 119
Nguyen Chi Thanh, 111
Nguyen Van Thieu, 119, 143, 144, 146–47, 148, 150
Nitze, Paul, 133
Nixon, President Richard, and Nixon Administration, 135–36, 138, 141–44, 147
Nolting, Frederick, 92
Northern Ireland, 52

Oman, 52
opium traffic, 62, 92. *See also* drugs

pacification, 110, 117–18
Pakistan, 82
Paris peace agreement, 142–44
Pathet Lao, 86, 90–91, 149
People's Self-Defense Force, 136
People's Volunteer Organization (PVO), 58, 59, 60, 61
Philippines colonial, wartime and postwar situation, 3, 4, 10–11, 23; Communist rebellion, 9, 52–58, 150; social and political problems, 53–55, 58

Philippines Communist Party, 9, 54–58
Phnomh Penh, 145–46
Pleiku, 104
Pol Pot, 146, 149
Poland, 80
Popular Forces, 117

Quirino, Elpidio, 15, 55, 56, 57

race and race relations, 3, 113, 137–38, 140
Radford, Admiral Arthur, 34, 35
Rangoon, 4, 60, 61, 62
Red River delta, 25, 30, 32, 36
Reed, Charles, 28
Renville agreement, 43
Revolutionary Development, 119
Ridgway, Gen. Matthew, 34, 133
Roberts, Frank, 2
Rogers, Secretary of State William, 135
Romney, Governor George, 132
Roosevelt, President Franklin D., and Roosevelt Administration, 5–6
Rostow, Walt, 93, 133, 134
Roxas, Manuel, 55
Rusk, Secretary of State Dean, 101, 102
Russell, Senator Richard, 101, 169 n.11

Saigon, 4, 20, 82, 83, 84, 85, 119, 131–32, 141, 148, 149
Sajap Kiri, 43–44
sanctuaries, 25, 27, 51–52, 53, 61, 63, 110, 138–39, 149
Schaub, William, 14–15
Schlafly, Phyllis, 168 n.11
Seals, 92, 138
Second Indochina War: American decision to intervene on massive scale, 100–108; change from guerrilla to conventional war, 79, 132; Communist appeals and policies,

81, 84–86, consequences, 150–54; nature of, 79; origins, 80–86; peace negotiations, 134–35, 142–44; question of inevitability, 81, 104, 154; reasons for outcome, 150–54, 171 n.6; role in framework of Cold War, 65, 79, 154
Sharkey, Laurence, 44
Sihanouk, Prince Norodom, 138–40
Singapore, 4
Sjahrir, Sutan, 42–43
Sjarifuddin, Amir, 43–45
South Arabia, 52
Southeast Asia: geography and characteristics, 2–5; Japanese role, 1, 4–5; place in the Cold War, 1–2, 7–15, 39–40, 62–63, 65–68; West and, 1–5, 10–15, 19–20
Southeast Asia Command, 6, 19–20, 41, 47
Southeast Asia ("Tonkin Gulf") Resolution, 101
Southeast Asia Treaty Organization (SEATO), 82, 108
Southeast Asian revolts of 1948, 8–9, 39–63, 156 n.6, 160 n.1
Soviet Union: and Indonesia, 65–68, 69–73; and Second Indochina war, 86, 99–100, 121, 141, 146, 147; and Southeast Asia, 1, 6–10, 12–14, 21–22, 39–40, 44–45, 46, 49, 65–68, 85, 99–100, 150, 156 n.6, 160 n.1
Special Forces, 92, 138
strategic hamlets, 53, 94
strategy, 7–14, 23–25, 27, 32, 49, 50, 51, 66–67, 69, 81, 85–87, 94, 99–100, 109–10, 116–17, 128–29, 129–30, 133, 136, 141, 151–52
Suharto, 75–76
Sukarno, 40, 45, 69–76
Surabaya, 41
Syria, 8, 20, 66, 71, 72

"34-A" operations, 93–94, 100–101
Tais, 23, 30, 32, 33
Taiwan, 87, 88
Tan Malaka, 42
Tan Son Nhut, 131–32
Tanzania, 68
Taruc, Luis, 54, 57
Taylor, Gen. Maxwell, 93, 95, 102, 106, 108
Templer, Gen. Gerald, 51
Tet offensive, 123, 129–33
Thailand, 3, 4, 12–14, 27, 28, 82, 149; Communist guerrillas in, 68, 150; forces in Vietnam, 116; intervention in Laos, 90–91; and Malaya, 51–52
Than Tun, 59, 61
Thomas, Norman, 125
Tito, 7–8
Tonkin, 25, 26, 27, 30
Trotskyites, 19, 20, 125
Truman, President Harry, and Truman Administration, 6, 10–15, 28, 29, 31, 81
Truman Doctrine, 7
"two-camps" doctrine, 8–9

U Nu, 60–61
U Saw, 59
United Nations, 43, 72, 80
United States: colonial rule, 3–4; early Cold War policies in Southeast Asia, 10–15; fears of China, 10, 65, 67, 68; and First Indochina War, 28–29, 33–37; policies during Indonesian independence struggle, 40–41, 43, 45; policies toward independent Indonesia, 70–74, 76–77; policies toward Philippines, 55, 56, 57; policies in Vietnam, 1954–1960, 80–84, 87–88, 92–144, 145, 146–49; wartime planning during World War II, 5–6

United States and the Second Indochina War: Americans enter limited combat, 93; decision for massive intervention, 100–109; justifications for war, 107–8; Kennedy Administration and, 90–97; public opinion and war, 101–2, 106, 107–8, 122–28, 132–34, 137–38, 139, 140, 144, 145, 147; 168 n.11; reaction to 1972 offensive, 141–43; shift in policy, 133–36; strategy, 108–9, 116–18

United States armed forces: composition, 113–14; problems, 113–14, 137–38, 140

United States Army units: 1st Cavalry Division, 111–13

United States Marine Corps, 105, 117–18, 129, 136

United States State Department, 6, 11, 12, 28, 93, 94–96

Untung, Col., 75

Viet Bac, 23, 25, 31

Viet Minh, 18–37

Vietcong. *See* National Liberation Front

Vietnam, 2, 3, 8, 14, 46; during World War II, 17–19; independence, 19, negotiations with Allies, 19–21. *See* First Indochina War; Second Indochina War

Vietnam, North: army, 89–91, 99, 112–13, 115, 141–42; commitment of regular army units to South Vietnam, 99; conquest of South Vietnam, 146–49; intervention in Laos, 89–91; operations in Cambodia, 138–40, 149; plans and problems in 1950s, 80–81, 84–85; relations with the Soviets and Chinese, 99–100; starts Second Indochina War, 86–87; strategy, 99–100, 108–9, 118, 129–30. *See also* bombing of North Vietnam

Vietnam, South: fall of, 146–49; formation, 80–85; social and political problems, 83–87, 94–97, 118–20, 132, 136–37, 146–47, 150, 153; under Communist rule, 149

Vietnamese Communism, 17–19, 21, 23–25, 27, 31, 80–81, 84–88, 96–97, 99–100, 129–30, 132, 137, 149, 150

Vietnamese National Army, 29, 30, 31, 36

Vietnamese relations with Americans, 85, 114, 117–18, 137

Vietnamization, 136, 139, 141

VNQDD, 21, 23

Vo Nguyen Giap, 18, 29, 30, 33, 111

Voznesensky, Andrei, 9

Vulture, Operation ("Vautour"), 34, 35

"wars of national liberation," 65, 66, 89, 99

War Powers Act, 145

West Irian. *See* New Guinea

Westmoreland, Gen. William: policy recommendations in 1964–1965, 102, 106; strategy and conduct of operations in 1965–1967, 109–10, 111, 113, 116, 117–18, 126, 128; Tet and aftermath, 129, 130, 131, 132, 133, 136

Weyand, Gen. Frederick, 130

World War II, 1, 4, 6, 18–19, 40, 46–48, 54, 58, 114, 115

Xieng Khouang, 101

Zhdanov, Andrei, and Zhdanov line, 8–9, 39, 44, 49, 55, 60

About the Author

ALAN J. LEVINE is an historian specializing in Russian history, international relations, and World War II. He has published numerous articles about World War II and the Cold War and is author of *The Soviet Union, The Communist Movement, and the World: Prelude to the Cold War* (Praeger, 1990), *The Strategic Bombing of Germany, 1940–1945* (Praeger, 1992), *The Missile and Space Race* (Praeger, 1994), and *The Pacific War* (Praeger, 1995).

ISBN 0-275-95124-3

EAN

9 780275 951245

90000>

HARDCOVER BAR CODE